The QuickBooks Cookbook™ Guide to...

Simple / Smart Fixed Asset Handling In QuickBooks®

By Mark Wilsdorf

Published by

FLAGSHIP TECHNOLOGIES, INC.
MADISON, MISSOURI, USA
www.goflagship.com

The QuickBooks Cookbook™ guide to...

Simple/Smart Fixed Asset Handling in QuickBooks

For Pro, Premier, Accountant, and Enterprise Editions

ISBN-13: 978-0-9673083-4-0

PUBLISHER

Flagship Technologies, Inc.
14976 Monroe Road 1039
Madison, MO 65263

www.goflagship.com

Revised: 12/19/2018

Table of Contents

CHAPTER 1

Introduction

About this chapter	This chapter provides a basic introduction to this book and the QuickBooks Cookbook™ series.

About this Book

> *"This is not the kind of book you read cover to cover...*
> *it is the kind you read in bits and pieces,*
> *just to find out what you want to know."*

From the title, you already know that this book is about handling fixed assets in the QuickBooks desktop editions—Pro, Premier, Accountant, and Enterprise.

The main goal for the book is to provide "everything you need to know" for using the Simple/Smart (S/S) method 18 for working with fixed assets, including how to:

- ❖ Use Inventory Part Items for representing fixed assets in QuickBooks.
- ❖ Enter fixed asset purchases, sales, and trade-ins, and more, without ever having to use Journal Entries.
- ❖ Calculate depreciation with a free spreadsheet template, downloadable from the publisher's Web site.
- ❖ Automate depreciation entries by importing them into QuickBooks from the spreadsheet.

- Get quick access to all transactions for any fixed asset, by simply opening a QuickReport 211 for the Item which represents the asset.
- Prepare other reports for informational and tax purposes.

A secondary goal for the book is to provide details for handling nearly every transaction type you may face when accounting for fixed assets. For that reason, you may never need sections of this book which deal with less-common transaction types. But they are here if you should ever need them, and you can skip reading them until you do. This also means the S/S method is *simpler to use than the book's page count implies.*

Like other books in the QuickBooks Cookbook™ series, this one presents nearly every procedure as a series of detailed steps with plenty of screenshots provided along the way, to keep you from "getting lost" while following the instructions. Topics are presented in "recipe" format: each is a self-contained block of the information you need for accomplishing a particular accounting task. You won't have to skip back and forth to other parts of the book to find out what you need to know for the job you are doing. Usually, you will only need to read a few pages.

A minor downside to presenting information this way is that some of it will be repeated in several places. For example, the steps for entering a check on the Checks form are repeated frequently—because the Checks form is used for several kinds of fixed asset transactions. Again, this is done so that you can find all of the information you need in one place, but it makes for boring reading if you expect to read the book from cover to cover as if it were a novel. *(So don't!)*

You will soon learn to recognize the frequently-repeated steps and can skim over or skip the ones you are familiar with.

Written for the desktop editions of QuickBooks

All of the screenshots, examples, and procedures in this book are based on the QuickBooks desktop editions for Windows: Pro, Premier, Accountant, and Enterprise.

Most of the screenshots are from QuickBooks Pro and Premier 2018. If the QuickBooks edition you use is a few years older or newer you may notice minor differences but should have no trouble following any of the step-by-step procedures. (The layout of QuickBooks' menus, windows, and forms usually only changes in small ways from year to year.)

What about QuickBooks for Mac?

The Macintosh editions of QuickBooks essentially contain a subset of the Windows editions' features. If you use QuickBooks for Mac you should be able to follow many of the procedures in this book but probably not all of them. Accommodating all of the differences between the Windows and Mac editions would have nearly doubled the size of the book, while also making the book's organization complicated and confusing. For that reason, you won't find details specific to QuickBooks for Mac here.

What about QuickBooks Online?

QuickBooks Online is Intuit's cloud based accounting software product (accessible over an Internet connection, not installed on your local/desktop computer), and it differs from the desktop editions in a number of ways. QuickBooks Online's inventory features, for example, are significantly different from those of the desktop editions.

Products & Services are the QuickBooks Online equivalent to Items in the desktop editions. However, QuickBooks Online places significant limits on how Products & Services may be set up, and that *prevents using them for handling fixed assets* using the S/S method 18 described in this book.

You will find *very little* information here which can be applied to fixed asset handling in QuickBooks Online.

Who this book is written "to"

This book is written to "you", with the assumption that you are directly responsible for keeping the accounting records of a for-profit or nonprofit business. If that is not the case, the discussion assumes you at least have an interest in small business accounting, maybe as an educator, lender, professional accountant, or someone in a related field. The book is aimed at intermediate-level QuickBooks users. However, even if you consider yourself a beginning QuickBooks user the abundant explanations, screenshots, and examples should let you follow the step-by-step procedures without difficulties.

The discussion often refers to "you" or "your" when talking about writing checks, entering sales, and so on. This is just a handy, conversational way of referring to *the business* you are working with. You may be the owner, a partner, a bookkeeper or other employee, an advisor, or some other interested party, but think of the "you" as actually referring to the business.

About the QuickBooks Cookbook™ Series

This book is part of the QuickBooks Cookbook™ series. The series name comes from the way topics are presented: as detailed steps you can follow to complete a specific accounting task, similar to a recipe in a cookbook.

Several volumes in the series are devoted to using QuickBooks in agriculture: dealing with the unique accounting problems common to farms and ranches. Other volumes, like this one, are aimed at QuickBooks users in general.

Where to find the QuickBooks Cookbook™ series

The two main places to purchase books in the QuickBooks Cookbook™ series are:

goflagship.com. Print *and* ebook editions of all books in the series are available through the publisher's Web site. Shipping charges are combined for multi-book orders, resulting in a net cost per book which is often less than for orders placed through Amazon.com.

> **Discounts are available** for larger-quantity orders such as for a class, conference, or group activity. Email the publisher at info@goflagship.com for a price quote.

Amazon.com. Print (but not ebook) editions of all books in the series are available for purchase through Amazon.com.

Ebook editions

Most titles in the series are available as ebook editions readable on Microsoft Windows and Apple Macintosh computers, as well as Android and Apple mobile devices (Android phones and tablets, iPhone, iPad, etc.). *Currently, ebook editions are only available at* goflagship.com.

Disclaimer

This book is meant as a source of information, ideas, and techniques for using QuickBooks for managing fixed assets. It has been written with the best of intentions to provide useful, helpful, and accurate information; however, everything in this book is only the opinion of the author, not the final, authoritative word on any of the topics addressed here.

Also, keep in mind that technical books such as this one are at least somewhat out of date as soon as they are written, because accounting standards and guidelines, tax laws, IRS regulations, and QuickBooks itself are constantly changing. Consequently, do not consider anything in this book as professional advice or as a recommendation about the accounting or tax situations you may face. *Always consult a tax or accounting professional if you are unsure whether a technique described in this book is appropriate for your situation.*

Finally, this book is based on accounting and tax considerations for businesses in the United States. Much of it may be applicable in other countries; however, the information may not be a good fit in countries where accounting and tax compliance are different than in the U.S. Again, when in doubt, consult an accounting or tax professional who understands the requirements in your country.

The "Ground Rules"

The following text styles and symbols are used throughout this book to convey special meaning:

Vendors > Pay Bills	Indicates a series of menu selections needed to reach a particular command. This example means to select Vendors from the main menu, then select Pay Bills from its submenu. (The ">" character separates the individual menu selections.)
Ctrl-R	Indicates a key or keys to be pressed. This example means to press the "R" key while holding down the "Ctrl" (Control) key.

Show hints	This type style is used when describing text in a window or dialog in QuickBooks or another program.
 goflagship.com	Links to external Web pages (outside of this publication) are preceded by a small "earth" graphic. In ebook editions, clicking any of these links will open a page in your Web browser.
7	In print editions, references to other pages in the book are displayed as a small page symbol. This example is referring to page 7.
	Numbers like this identify features in screenshots. The number corresponds to a numbered item in the discussion following the screenshot.
	Informational note.
	Technical note; usually about QuickBooks settings, etc.
	Warning or cautionary note.
	General notes and comments.
	Hints, tips, and ideas.
	Discussions of accounting theory or special accounting topics.

Licensed items

Some graphic images in this publication are used under license from Shutterstock.com and IconFinder.com.

We gratefully acknowledge use of the following licensed item(s) which require specific attribution, in compliance with the authors' or owners' licenses.

Kwrite notepad icon, modified from original, (www.iconfinder.com/icons/1409/kwrite_notepad_icon). By David Vignoni (www.icon-king.com). Licensed under LGPL (www.gnu.org/licenses/lgpl-3.0.en.html).

Printing (ebook editions only)

Roughly 10% of the total page count of licensed ebook editions of this book may be printed for non-commercial personal use.

However, you ***may not*** distribute any part of the ebook or printed copies of it to ***anyone***, whether for a fee or not, without express written permission from the publisher.

This page is intentionally blank.

For information on other books in this series go to:

www.goflagship.com

CHAPTER 2

Fixed Asset in QuickBooks: What are Your Options?

About this chapter	This chapter explores your options for fixed asset record-keeping in conjunction with using QuickBooks, and explains advantages of the Simple/Smart (S/S) method.

Before we begin discussing fixed assets we probably should define them. Accountants usually divide assets into two major categories based on how long you expect to hold them:

Current assets are those which are normally used up within a year or held for a year or less. Here are a few examples:

- Your checking account balance
- Inventories of raw materials and supplies your business uses in producing/manufacturing things or in day-to-day operations
- Work-in-process inventories, and finished goods inventories

Fixed assets are things the business will likely use up, wear out, or hold over a period of more than one year. Some common fixed assets are:

- Vehicles and machinery
- Buildings
- Land

Because a fixed asset normally provides productive value or capacity to the business over several years' time, its entire purchase cost generally is not written off as an expense in the year of purchase. Instead, a portion of the cost is deducted as expense in each year of the asset's expected useful life. This annual write-off of the asset's purchase cost is known as depreciation expense[147].

What if a fixed asset's entire purchase cost was deducted as expense in the year of purchase?

That would greatly *overstate* expenses for that year—as if the fixed asset had been entirely used up or worn out during the year. And it would *understate* expenses in later years when the asset would still be providing productive capacity to the business (still helping to generate income). It would also distort the balance sheet's portrayal of the value of assets held by the business: if an asset's entire cost is deducted in the year of purchase, the asset won't have any book value to contribute to the asset value shown on the balance sheet.

This is exactly what happens with many of the accelerated depreciation write-offs allowed for income tax purposes, in which the entire cost of a fixed asset may be expensed in the year of purchase. Fixed asset accounting for income tax purposes is based on *very different goals,* compared to fixed asset accounting for evaluating business profitability and the business' equity position.

If you use QuickBooks, you have a wide range of choices for how to keep fixed asset records. The following sections provide overviews of the common ones.

Fixed Asset Accounts

Accounts for Individual Fixed Assets

The traditional accounting-textbook approach is to set up a fixed asset account plus one or two subaccounts for each fixed asset. These accounts work together to represent the asset's book value. A vehicle, for example, might be represented by these accounts:

Ford truck
- Original Basis
- Accumulated Depreciation

The truck's original purchase cost (plus the book value of any trade-in) gets posted to the Original Basis subaccount. When depreciation is entered for the truck it gets posted to the Accumulated Depreciation subaccount. The difference between the two subaccounts' balances represents the truck's book value, which appears on balance sheet reports this way:

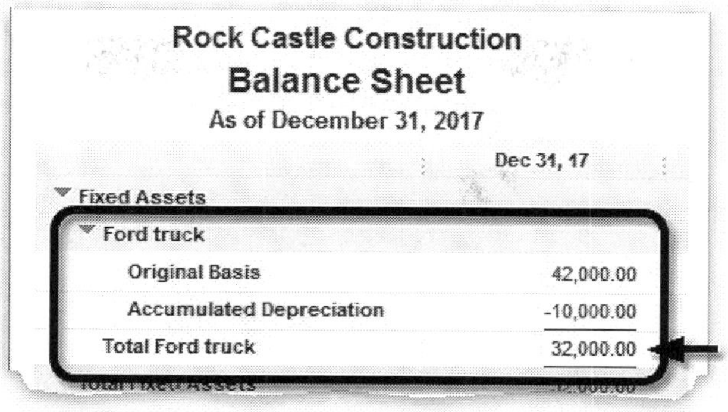

Rock Castle Construction
Balance Sheet
As of December 31, 2017

	Dec 31, 17
Fixed Assets	
Ford truck	
Original Basis	42,000.00
Accumulated Depreciation	-10,000.00
Total Ford truck	32,000.00

Most businesses have a considerable number of fixed assets, organized into categories such as:

- Machinery & Equipment
  - Ford truck
    - Original Basis
    - Accumulated Depreciation
  - Terex telehandler
    - Original Basis
    - Accumulated Depreciation
  - Ingersol-Rand air compressor/trailer
    - Original Basis
    - Accumulated Depreciation
  - .
  - .
  - .
- Buildings & Improvements
  - Shop building 2011
    - Original Basis
    - Accumulated Depreciation
  - Bulk storage shed
    - Original Basis
    - Accumulated Depreciation
  - .
  - .
  - .
- Land
  - Commercial lot, 2 acres
    - Original Basis

As you might guess, setting up individual accounts for each fixed asset eventually makes the balance sheet long, cluttered, and messy. In Quick-

Books, you can collapse some of the asset detail before printing a balance sheet report, but it's still not an ideal solution because the Chart of Accounts becomes larger and more difficult to use than it ought to be.

The accounting-textbook approach generally uses journal entries to record fixed asset transactions. Here is a journal entry (Company > Make General Journal Entries) to record the sale of the truck shown earlier, for $35,000 ($3,000 more than its $32,000 book value):

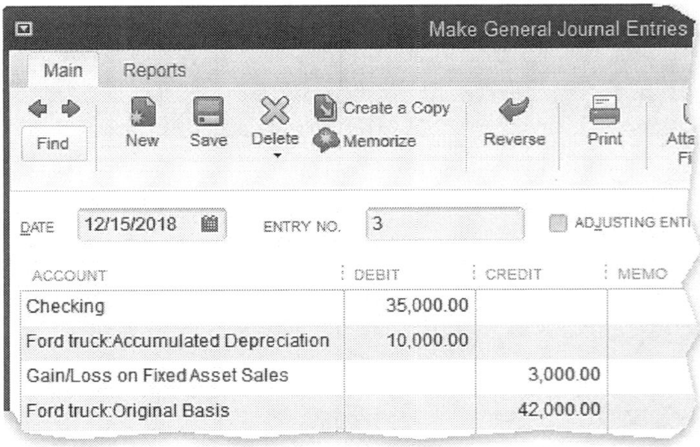

Using journal entries requires an understanding of debits and credits—which many people are uncomfortable with—and an understanding of how to record a gain or loss on the sale of a fixed asset.

One more thing to know: QuickBooks does not calculate depreciation. Unless you use the straight-line depreciation method, which is simple enough for anyone to calculate, you need some kind of external program, spreadsheet, or Internet service for doing depreciation calculations. *Calculating Depreciation with a Spreadsheet* 167, in Chapter 9, tells where you can get a free spreadsheet template for keeping a list of fixed assets and calculating depreciation for them.

The bottom line is that using separate accounts to keep track of financial details for each fixed asset is good for teaching accounting concepts but cumbersome in actual practice.

Accounts for Categories of Fixed Assets

A common alternative to using separate accounts for each fixed asset is to have only a few fixed asset accounts and letting each represent a broad category of assets:

- Machinery & Equipment
  - Original Basis
  - Accumulated Depreciation
- Buildings & Improvements
  - Original Basis
  - Accumulated Depreciation
- Land
  - Original Basis

This greatly simplifies balance sheet reports but requires keeping fixed asset details (purchase price, depreciation, trade-in value, etc.) outside of QuickBooks in a spreadsheet[14] or some other software application[13], and using journal entries to update the account balances.

Fixed Asset Software or Internet Service

You may keep fixed asset details outside of QuickBooks in a separate software application or by using an Internet-based service for fixed asset management. Here are some of the considerations involved:

- Because it is not part of QuickBooks, **you will have to spend time learning** to use the other software or service.
- **If the software integrates with QuickBooks** in some way—i.e., if you can pass fixed asset transaction information to/from QuickBooks—then **it may automate some of the necessary accounting entries.** If it does not have any integration capabilities, you may have to copy or manually enter some QuickBooks transaction data, such as for asset purchases and sales, in the other software.
- The software application or service **may calculate depreciation expense for you.** If not, you will still need some other way to get that done. (*Calculating Depreciation with a Spreadsheet*[167], in Chapter 9, describes a free spreadsheet template you can use for calculating depreciation.)

- If transactions or data from the external software application—depreciation expense, for example—need to be entered manually in QuickBooks, that **may require using journal entries,** and therefore an understanding of debits and credits.
- Using external software or a service outside of QuickBooks **lets you avoid keeping fixed asset detail in QuickBooks** while still giving you the option of printing a fixed asset list or other reports when needed, such as for supplemental documentation to accompany a balance sheet.
- The software application or service may offer **additional fixed asset management features such as location tracking,** which may help justify its additional cost.

Microsoft Excel or Other Spreadsheet

Using Microsoft Excel to keep track of fixed asset details is similar to using a stand-alone software application[13] but has the advantage of some QuickBooks support for exporting and importing data to/from Excel. And because many QuickBooks users already have Excel, this option may not require an additional financial outlay.

> **QuickBooks can only work with a *locally installed* version of Excel for data importing and exporting**; i.e., with a version installed in Microsoft Windows. It *does not* communicate with Web-based editions of Excel or other Web-based spreadsheets such as Google Sheets. However, you may be able use a third-party software application to import transactions from a Web-based spreadsheet into QuickBooks.

Some considerations:

- **Exporting fixed asset data.** QuickBooks does not support exporting "everything" to Excel. You may export some fixed asset data to Excel, such as details from a transaction report, and thus reduce the amount of typing needed to get fixed asset information into Excel. However, you will likely have to enter some information in both places (QuickBooks and Excel).
- **Importing depreciation transactions.** QuickBooks supports limited importing from Excel. If you use Excel for calculating depreciation for instance, you might or might not have to enter the depreciation expense manually in QuickBooks, depending on which QuickBooks edition you

have. Also, an understanding of journal entries, debits, and credits may be required. However, another option is to purchase a third-party software tool which can assist with importing data into QuickBooks. (Several are available.)

- **You can use Excel to calculate depreciation expense.** There's no need to create your own spreadsheet template for this purpose, because plenty of free ones are available on the Internet. One of them is discussed in *Calculating Depreciation with a Spreadsheet* 167, in Chapter 9.

- With **fixed asset list maintained in Excel,** you may print a list of fixed asset details whenever needed, such as for supplemental documentation to accompany a balance sheet report.

What about using spreadsheet programs other than Excel? You can keep a fixed asset list, calculate depreciation, etc., in any spreadsheet program. However, QuickBooks cannot export reports or data directly to any spreadsheet other than Microsoft Excel.

QuickBooks' Fixed Asset Item Type

You can use QuickBooks' Fixed Asset Item type (Lists > Fixed Asset Item List) to identify and work with fixed assets, but it really was designed to be used with Intuit's Fixed Asset Manager (FAM) software—which only comes with the Accountant and Enterprise editions of QuickBooks. If you have QuickBooks Pro or Premier the usefulness of Fixed Asset Items is *very limited.*

Fixed Asset Manager may be purchased separately if you have QuickBooks Pro or Premier. However, purchasing the full Accountant edition may be more economical.

Using Fixed Asset Items *with* Fixed Asset Manager (FAM)

- **FAM makes good use of Fixed Asset Items** because it has access to, and can update, the Items' fields directly—FAM can read and write data from/to QuickBooks, saving a lot of typing and potential errors.

- **FAM calculates depreciation,** eliminating the need for other software to do that job, and writes depreciation expense directly to the appropriate QuickBooks accounts if set up properly.

- Using **FAM requires a good understanding of accounting and depreciation concepts,** and also the tax laws if using it for calculating depreciation for income tax purposes.

Overall, using Fixed Asset Items along with the Fixed Asset Manager application is an effective and workable system for managing fixed assets in QuickBooks.

Using Fixed Asset Items *without* Fixed Asset Manager (FAM)

What's wrong with using Fixed Asset Items if you do not have Fixed Asset Manager (FAM)? Plenty. Here are some of the pros and cons:

- **Fixed Asset Items have several fields which other Item types do not have**...but surprisingly, most of those fields *are not connected to anything within QuickBooks!*

  For example, if you use a Fixed Asset Item in a purchase transaction you might assume the Item's Date and Cost fields would be automatically updated from date and price entered in the transaction. Not so. Likewise, when a Fixed Asset Item is used in a sale transaction neither its Sales Price nor Sales Date fields are updated with information about the sale. Without the FAM software, the only way to get information into these fields (and most others) is to type it in *manually*.

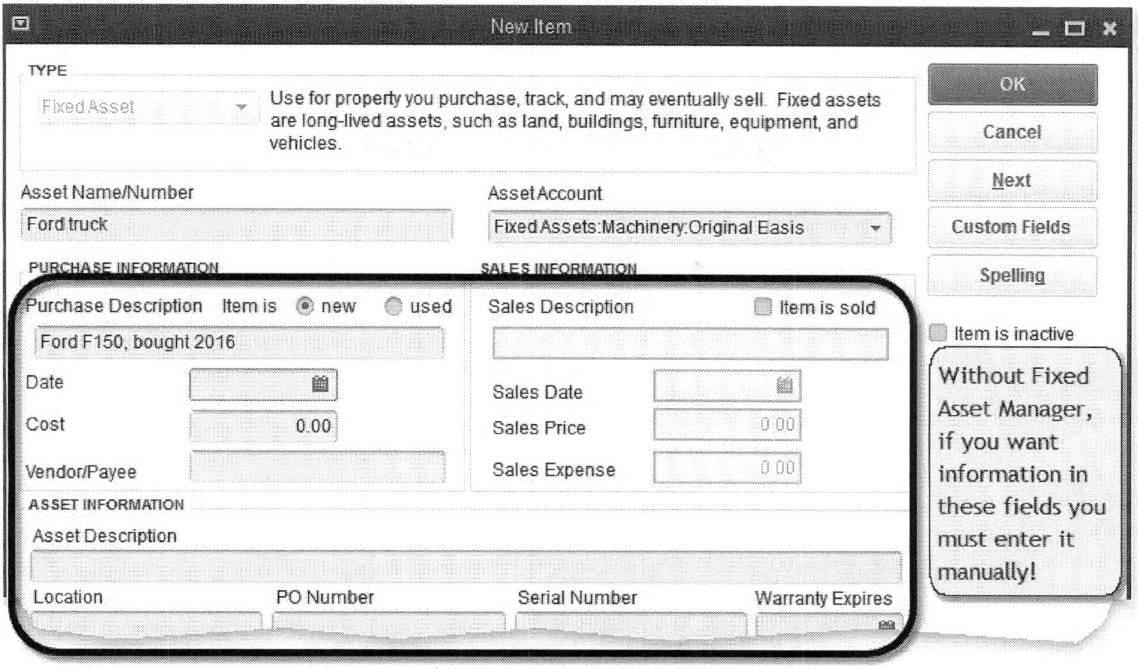

Fixed Asset Item type

- **Fixed Asset Items do not support quantities, and selling part of a Fixed Asset Item is not possible.** If you purchase a group of 5 machines of the same type and use a Fixed Asset Item to represent the group, you would have to sell all of the machines in a single transaction in order to close out the Fixed Asset Item. The only way to sell individual machines would be to set up a separate Fixed Asset Item for each one!

- **Fixed Asset Items cannot have subitems.** Without subitems, you cannot control how fixed assets are grouped on Item reports. Grouping assets into categories such as machinery, vehicles, buildings, and land is not possible.

- **Your tax preparer may *prefer* that you use Fixed Asset Items.** Do you give your tax preparer direct access to your QuickBooks company file—maybe on a flash drive, or uploaded to the preparer's Web portal, or via a QuickBooks hosting or file sharing service? If so, and if the preparer uses Fixed Asset Manager for depreciation calculations, he or she may strongly prefer that you use the Fixed Asset Item type, because it will allow the preparer to automate depreciation calculations, depreciation expense entries in QuickBooks, and so on.

Before setting up Items for fixed assets, ask your tax preparer which approach he or she prefers. That way, your QuickBooks records will be compatible with how your tax preparer wants to work with them.

The Simple/Smart (S/S) Method

Author's note...

You won't find the Simple/Smart method in any accounting textbook...or any other book about QuickBooks!

It is not an accounting method per se, but *a set of QuickBooks-specific techniques* I created to simplify working with fixed assets and make it possible to have detailed information about any fixed asset at any time. All fixed asset records kept entirely within QuickBooks, so no additional software is required, nor is any additional effort needed beyond the usual effort required for entering fixed asset transactions (purchases, sales, depreciation expense, etc.).

Why call it "Simple/Smart"?

...because I needed a short name to distinguish these techniques from other fixed asset approaches, and I wanted the name to highlight how they might benefit anyone who uses them.

What is the Simple/Smart Method?

The S/S (Simple/Smart) method—which is the main subject of this book—lets you keep fixed asset records entirely within QuickBooks using Inventory Part Items. Actually, each fixed asset is represented by a *set* of Inventory Part Items—a main Item plus two or three subitems, like the ones shown here for a pickup truck:

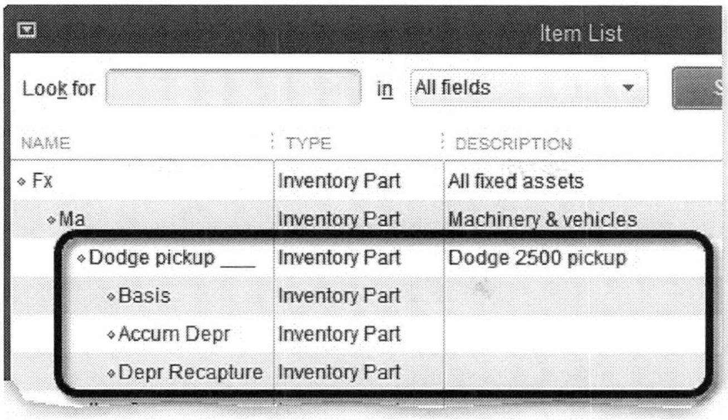

Inventory Part Items used for fixed assets *are set up very differently* from the Items you might use for tracking inventories, and this unique Item setup causes QuickBooks to automate the updating of asset book values, accumulated depreciation, and more.

Pros and cons of the Simple/Smart method

Here are some pros and cons of the regular version of the S/S method. (An even simpler method is described later in this section 23.)

- **Produces conventional accounting results** for fixed asset purchases, depreciation, sales, and disposals.
- **Fixed assets are represented as Inventory Part Items** set up in a unique way 61.
- **All fixed asset transactions are entered using Items,** on familiar QuickBooks forms (Checks, Bills, Sales Receipts, etc.).
- **No journal entries are ever needed.**
- If an asset is sold, **gain or loss on the sale 111 is calculated automatically** and appears in the Other Income section of profit and loss reports.
- Because the S/S method is based on using Inventory Part Items, **you can record quantities bought and sold** for Items which represent a group of like assets 143.

  For instance, if you purchase a fleet of five delivery vans of the same brand and model, you can use one Item to represent all five vans and can record the purchase quantity as 5. If you later sell two of the vans for some reason, the sale transaction will show that two vans were sold, and the Item List will show that you still have three vans remaining.

- **You must calculate depreciation outside of QuickBooks** and enter depreciation expense[156] for each fixed asset Item. However, there are lots of ways to automate the process. Chapter 9 - Depreciation Expense[167] shows how to use a free spreadsheet template to calculate depreciation expense and import depreciation transactions into QuickBooks—avoiding the need to enter them manually.

- You can prepare a variety of **fixed asset reports**[211], including reports for income tax preparation[222] which provide details of fixed asset purchases, sales, and trade-ins for the tax year.

- Drilling down in a report such as an Item QuickReport[211] provides **direct access to all transactions** involving any fixed asset.

  Drilling down means double-clicking a line in a report to open a window containing more detail—usually a specific transaction or list of related transactions.

- **Reports** can show things like: the asset's original basis (purchase cost), purchase date, trade-ins involved in purchasing an asset, accumulated depreciation, selling price, sale date, gain or loss on sale, and more:

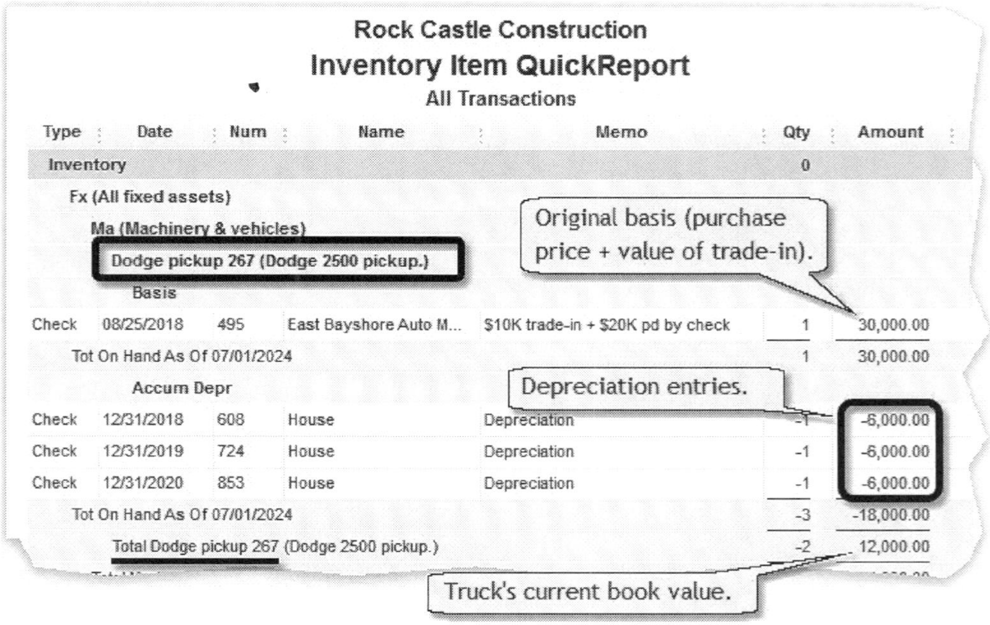

Rock Castle Construction

Inventory Item QuickReport

All Transactions

Type	Date	Num	Name	Memo	Qty	Amount
Inventory					0	
Fx (All fixed assets)						
Ma (Machinery & vehicles)						
Dodge pickup 267 (Dodge 2500 pickup.)						
Basis						
Check	08/25/2018	495	East Bayshore Auto M...	$10K trade-in + $20K pd by check	1	30,000.00
Tot On Hand As Of 07/01/2024					1	30,000.00
Accum Depr						
Check	12/31/2018	608	House	Depreciation	-1	-6,000.00
Check	12/31/2019	724	House	Depreciation	-1	-6,000.00
Check	12/31/2020	853	House	Depreciation	-1	-6,000.00
Tot On Hand As Of 07/01/2024					-3	-18,000.00
Total Dodge pickup 267 (Dodge 2500 pickup.)					-2	12,000.00

> ***Basics steps for the Simple/Smart method...***
>
> - **Set up accounts** 38 to represent fixed asset book values (original basis and accumulated depreciation), plus an Other Income account for recording gains and losses on fixed asset sales.
> - **Create Items for each fixed asset** as described in the next chapter 52.
> - **Use the Items for entering fixed asset transactions**—purchases, trade-ins, depreciation expense, and sales and disposals.
> - **Use standard QuickBooks reports** to have (1) quick, easy access to all transaction details for any fixed asset, plus (2) detailed reports for income tax preparation.

Who can use the Simple/Smart method?

- You <u>can</u> use the S/S method in any of the QuickBooks desktop editions for Microsoft Windows—Pro, Premier, Accountant, or Enterprise. (*Exception:* S/S will not work with the FIFO inventory method available for the Advanced Inventory option of QuickBooks Enterprise editions.)
- You <u>*cannot*</u> use the S/S method with QuickBooks Online (QBO).

  Why not? Because parts of QBO are designed like an overly-safe beginner's bicycle: it has "training wheels" in various places which only let you "ride it slowly on the sidewalk" for some activities. You can't take it out on the street, raise your feet up off of the pedals, and coast down Dead Man's hill (what all the neighborhood kids call it) at 30 miles an hour.

  OK, enough of that metaphor. Specifically, QBO won't let you associate Fixed Asset accounts with Inventory Products & Services—something which the desktop editions allow. That, and basic differences between the desktop edition and QBO inventory systems, prevent using Inventory type Products & Services for working with fixed assets.

If you use QuickBooks Online, your best bet is to find a third-party app for working with fixed assets.

Who should use the Simple/Smart method?

- If you keep track of fixed assets via individual fixed asset accounts in the Chart of Accounts, then you *really should* consider using the S/S method, for a variety of reasons.

- If you currently keep a fixed asset list outside of QuickBooks—maybe in a stand-alone software application which does not integrate with QuickBooks, or in a spreadsheet—then you *really should* consider the S/S method, because it lets you maintain all fixed asset information and transaction details entirely *within* QuickBooks, and gives you direct access to it for informational and tax reporting purposes.

- If you don't maintain a list of fixed assets at all (maybe you just rely on your tax preparer to do it) then you should consider using the Even Simpler method[233]. It will let you (1) have a fixed asset list in QuickBooks, (2) have a simple, organized way to get direct access to the transactions for any fixed asset, and (2) get reports of fixed asset purchases, sales, and trade-ins for income tax preparation with minimal effort.

Who *should not* use the Simple/Smart method?

- If you have QuickBooks Accountant or QuickBooks Enterprise, your QuickBooks edition includes Intuit's Fixed Asset Manager (FAM) software. Using FAM along with QuickBooks' Fixed Asset Item type provides more flexibility and automation than is possible with the S/S method. (However, some people prefer the S/S method's approach and may choose to use it instead.)

- If your tax preparer directly accesses your QuickBooks company file to gather information for tax preparation, ask which method he or she prefers that you use for handling fixed assets. If your preparer uses FAM for depreciation calculations, he or she may prefer that you use the Fixed Asset Item type for working with fixed assets.

An Even Simpler Method...

Not everyone wants to keep GAAP-compliant accounting records. Many individuals and businesses use QuickBooks mostly as an income and expense ledger—one which happens to also have easy-to-use features for customer billing, managing accounts payable and receivable, tracking customer contact information, and similar activities. If this describes how you use QuickBooks, consider using the Even Simpler method 233. Some aspects of it are:

- **Fixed assets are represented using Inventory Part Items,** but they are set up differently than in the regular S/S method.
- **Each fixed asset is represented by a single Inventory Part Item,** not a set of Items.
- **Fixed asset purchases and sales are entered on familiar QuickBooks forms** like Checks, Bills, and Sales Receipts.
- **No journal entries are ever needed.**
- The Even Simpler method assumes that you don't keep track of depreciation expense within QuickBooks, so there are **no depreciation entries to make.** (If you use QuickBooks mostly for income and expense records, it is likely that the only depreciation calculations done for your business are those done by your tax preparer.)
- **Direct access to fixed asset transactions** (purchases, sales, etc.) is available at any time, from an Item QuickReport 211 for the asset(s) you want to know about.
- This method also lets you **print reports for income tax preparation purposes,** listing fixed asset purchases, trade-ins, sales, and disposals.

This page is intentionally blank.

For information on other books in this series go to:

www.goflagship.com

CHAPTER 3

Visual Index to Examples

About this chapter	This chapter provides a visual reference to common fixed asset transaction entries in QuickBooks.

The examples in this chapter assume that you already have the necessary accounts set up as described later in Chapter 4 - *Fixed Asset Nuts & Bolts* 37.

Setting Up Items

See: *Setting Up Items for Fixed Assets* 52

With the S/S method 18, one Item represents the fixed asset itself, and subitems of that Item represent its original basis, accumulated depreciation, and—if the asset is later sold outright—depreciation recapture.

Here is an example Basis subitem for a pickup truck. *The main Item and other subitems are set up differently* (they point to other accounts), so be sure to see *Setting Up Items for Fixed Assets* 52 for details.

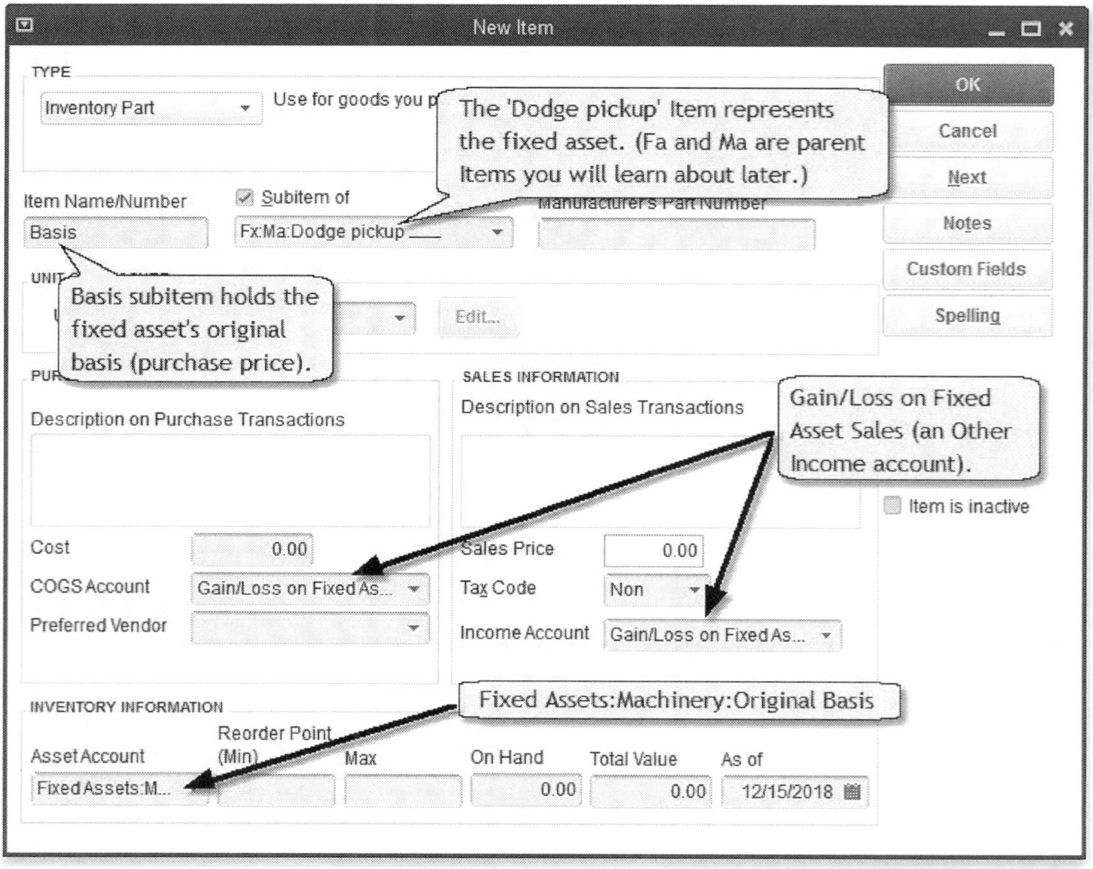

Fixed Asset Purchase

See: *Entering a Purchase* 89

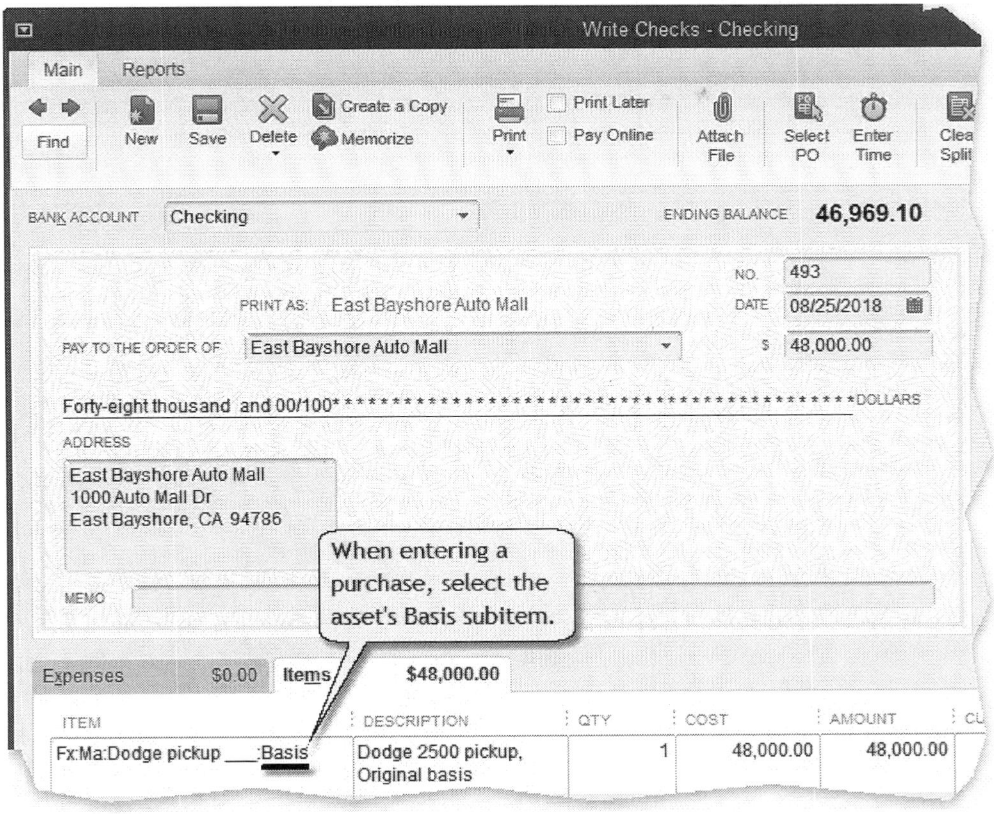

Fixed Asset Purchase with Trade-in

See: *Entering a Purchase with a Trade-In* 102

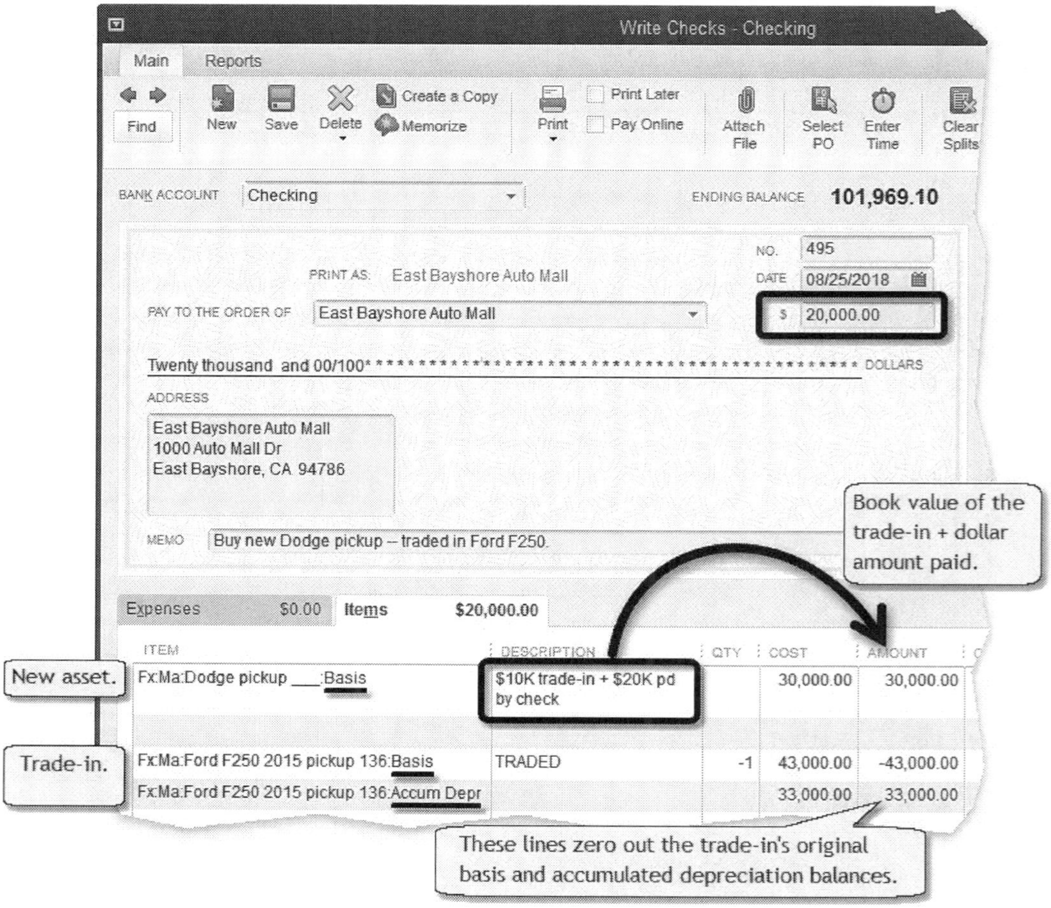

Entering a Fixed Asset Sale

See: *Entering a Sale* 110

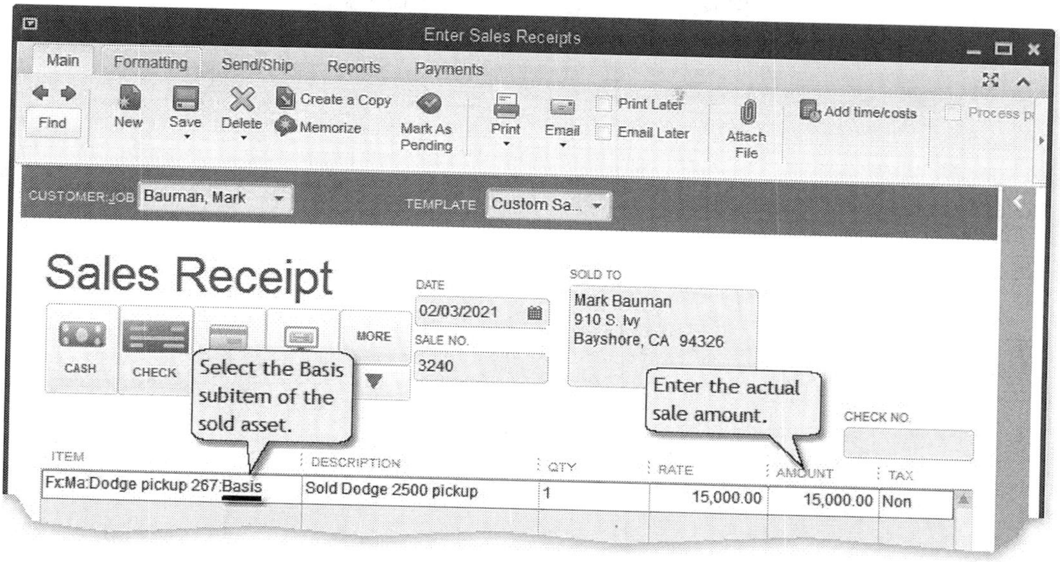

When a fixed asset is sold outright (not traded in), you also need to make a second entry to cause gain or loss on the sale to be calculated:

See: *How to Record Gain or Loss on the Sale* 111

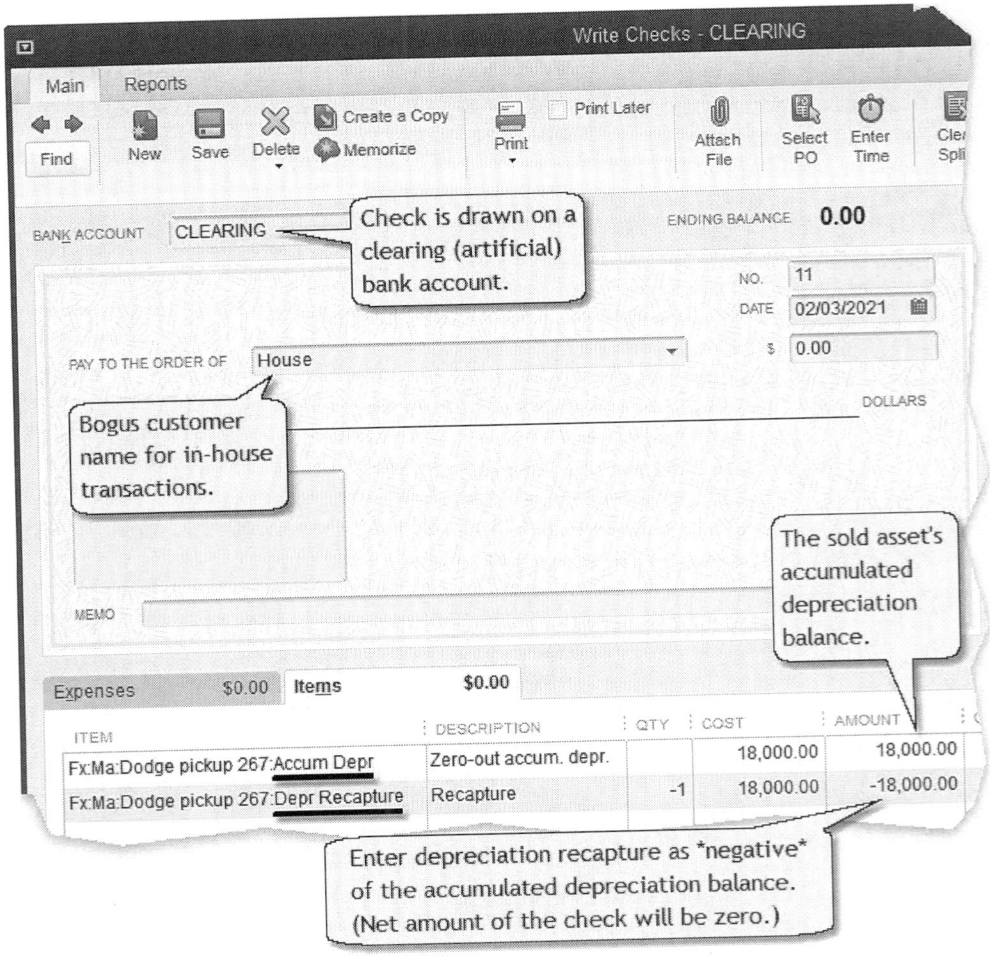

Entering Depreciation Expense

See: *Entering Depreciation Expense Manually* 156

You can record depreciation expense for any number of fixed assets using a single transaction. The example below records depreciation expense for three assets.

Yes, there is a better way! Chapter 9 - Depreciation Expense 147 shows how to calculate depreciation expense with a free spreadsheet template and import depreciation transactions from the spreadsheet into QuickBooks.

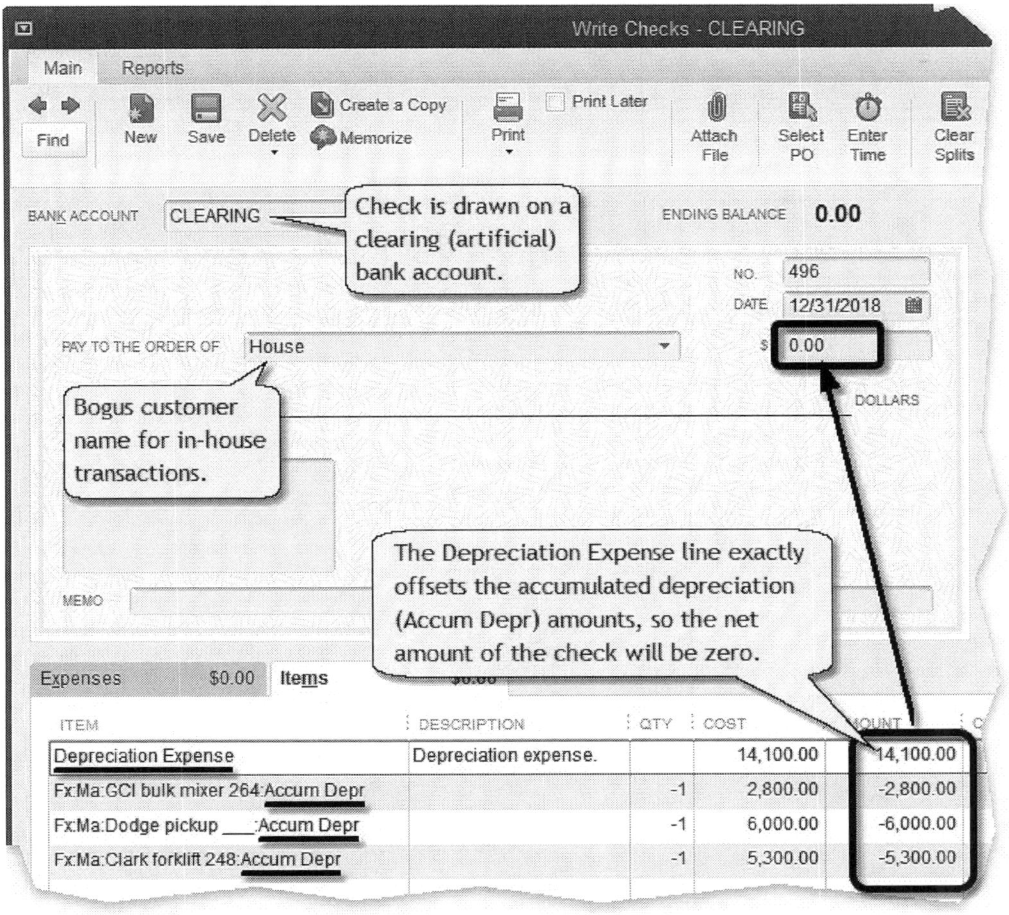

Inventory Item QuickReport

See: *Item QuickReports* 211

A QuickReport customized to include the Amount column is one of several reports you can use to quickly see the status of any fixed asset, including all of its transactions. This example shows the purchase, depreciation, and sale transactions for a pickup truck:

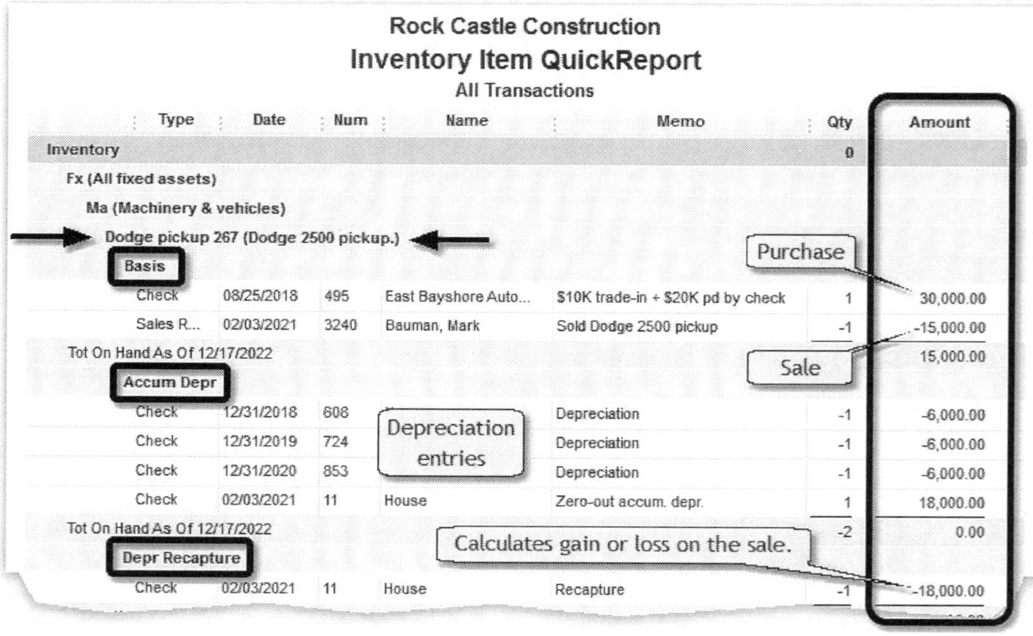

Rock Castle Construction
Inventory Item QuickReport
All Transactions

Type	Date	Num	Name	Memo	Qty	Amount
Inventory					0	
Fx (All fixed assets)						
Ma (Machinery & vehicles)						
Dodge pickup 267 (Dodge 2500 pickup.)						
Basis						
Check	08/25/2018	495	East Bayshore Auto...	$10K trade-in + $20K pd by check	1	30,000.00
Sales R...	02/03/2021	3240	Bauman, Mark	Sold Dodge 2500 pickup	-1	-15,000.00
Tot On Hand As Of 12/17/2022						15,000.00
Accum Depr						
Check	12/31/2018	608		Depreciation	-1	-6,000.00
Check	12/31/2019	724		Depreciation	-1	-6,000.00
Check	12/31/2020	853		Depreciation	-1	-6,000.00
Check	02/03/2021	11	House	Zero-out accum. depr.	1	18,000.00
Tot On Hand As Of 12/17/2022					-2	0.00
Depr Recapture						
Check	02/03/2021	11	House	Recapture	-1	-18,000.00

Fixed Asset Book Values Report

See: *Fixed Asset Book Values Report* 217

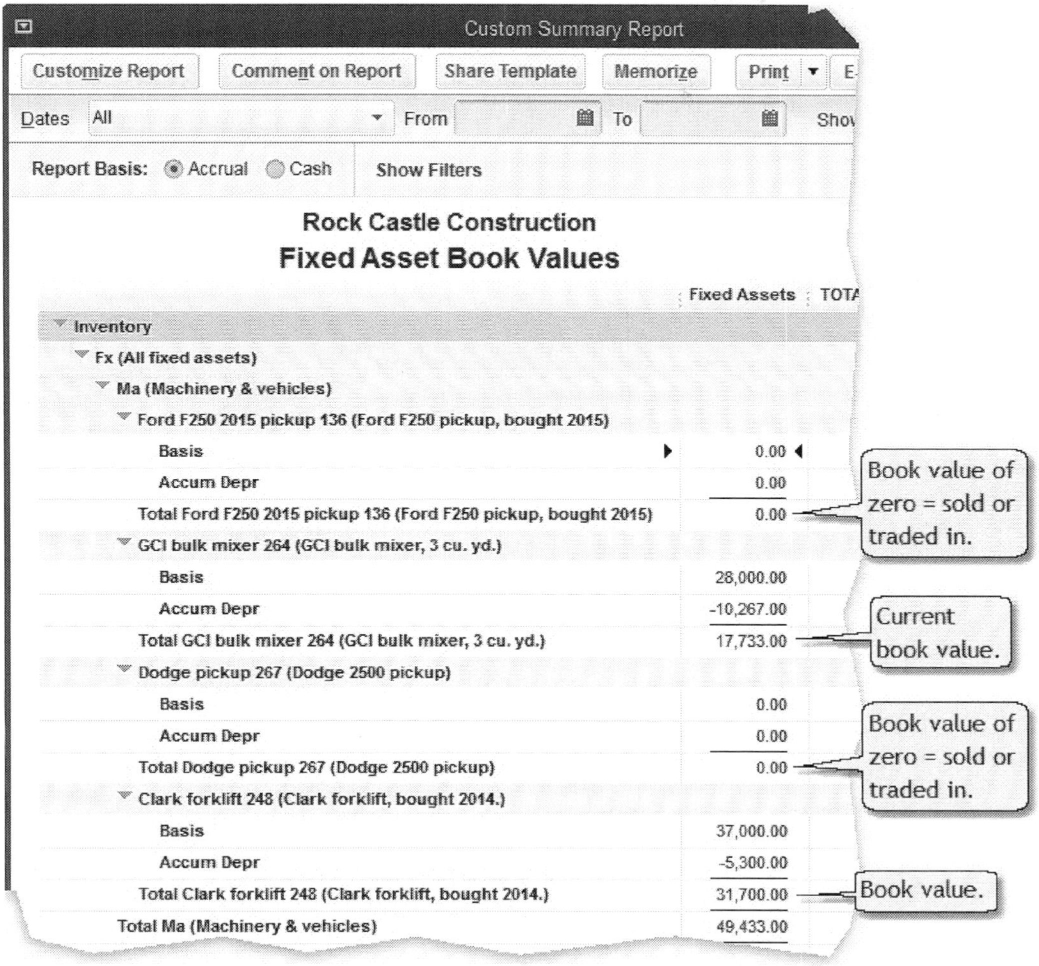

Fixed Asset Purchases & Trade-Ins Report

See: *Fixed Purchases & Trade-Ins Report* 223

This is a report you might print for your tax preparer at income tax time.

Rock Castle Construction

Fixed Asset Purchases & Trade-Ins

January through December 2018

	Jan - Dec 18 Qty	Jan - Dec 18 Amount
Inventory		
Fx (All fixed assets)		
Ma (Machinery & vehicles)		
Dodge pickup 267 (Dodge 2500 pickup.)		
Basis	1	30,000.00
Accum Depr	-1	-6,000.00
Total Dodge pickup 267 (Dodge 2500 pickup.)	0.00	24,000.00
Bobcat skidloader 141		
Basis	1	20,000.00
Accum Depr	-1	-18,000.00
Total Bobcat skidloader 141	0.00	2,000.00
Ford F250 2015 pickup 136 (Ford F250 pickup, bo...		
Basis	-1	-43,000.00
Accum Depr	1	33,000.00
Total Ford F250 2015 pickup 136 (Ford F250 pick...	0.00	-10,000.00
GCI bulk mixer 264 (GCI bulk mixer, 3 cu. yd.)		
Accum Depr	-2	-5,600.00
Total GCI bulk mixer 264 (GCI bulk mixer, 3 cu. ...	-2.00	-5,600.00

Purchased

Purchased

Negative amount = traded in

Depreciation only = neither purchased nor traded in during the year.

Fixed Asset Sales Report (with Gains and Losses)

See: *Fixed Asset Sales Report* 228

This example is for a single asset—a pickup truck—but for income tax preparation you might print it for all fixed assets bought, sold, or traded in during the year. By the way, the $3,000 gain shown on the sale of the pickup truck was calculated automatically.

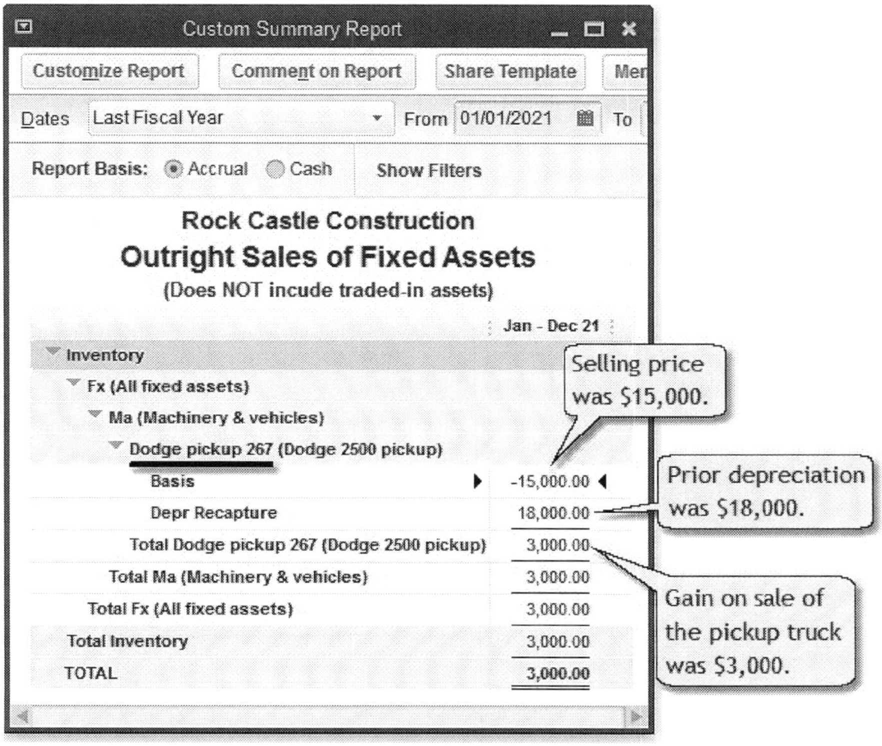

This page is intentionally blank.

For information on other books in this series go to:

www.goflagship.com

CHAPTER 4

Fixed Asset Nuts & Bolts

About this chapter

This chapter is partly informational and partly reference. It mostly focuses on setting up accounts and Items for fixed asset handling.

Do you have trouble getting to sleep at night?

If so, then be sure to read *every page* of this chapter, from beginning to end, at bedtime—a sure cure for insomnia! Why? Because this is mostly a reference chapter, chock-full of details, many of which don't amount to "fun reading".

If insomnia is not a problem for you, a better approach is to just skim this chapter for a general idea of how to set up accounts 38 and Items 52. Then later when you need more detail, come back to read just the section(s) you need.

If you want to skip this chapter for now, you can jump ahead to *Fixed Asset Purchases and Trade-Ins* 89.

Turning on QuickBooks' Inventory Features

Enabling Inventory and Purchase Orders

You must turn on QuickBooks' inventory features if you haven't done so already, so QuickBooks will allow creating Inventory Part 52 Items:

1. **Select** Edit > Preferences > Items & Inventory > Company Preferences [tab] to open the inventory settings window in Preferences.
2. **Checkmark** *Inventory and purchase orders are active.*

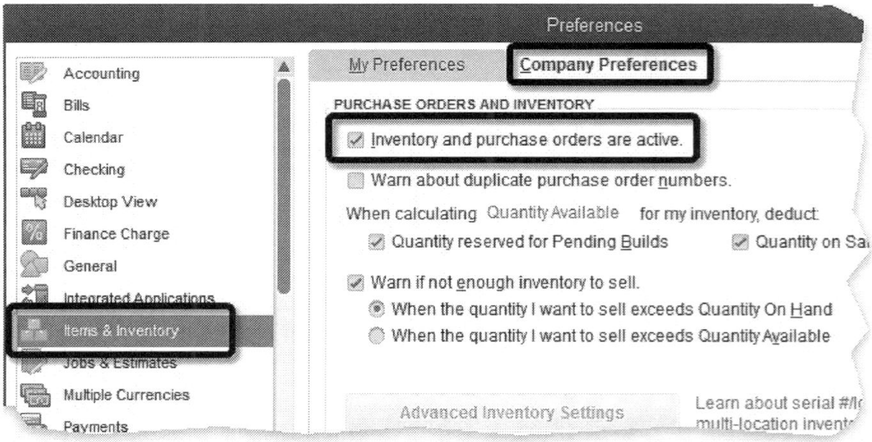

3. **Click the OK button** to save your changes and close the Preferences window.

Setting Up Accounts You Will Need

Before you begin setting up Items for fixed assets you need to have several accounts in place in the Chart of Accounts.

Clearing Bank Account

A *clearing bank account* (or simply *clearing account*) is used for moving dollar amounts around within QuickBooks—i.e., for transactions *internal to* the business. Clearing accounts are set up as Bank type accounts, but they do not represent real-world bank accounts.

> ***Do not* use a real-world bank account** for clearing transactions. If you do, reconciling the bank account will be more difficult and confusing than it ought to be. Instead, set up a separate Bank type account to use as a clearing account.

The S/S method [18] requires a clearing account so that you can enter things like depreciation expense [147] without having to use journal entries.

When is a clearing account needed?

- **$0 Checks.** Traditionally, you might use journal entries for entering some kinds of accounting transactions. However, you can avoid using journal entries—and the need to understand debits and credits—by entering those transactions on the Checks form, as positive and negative amounts which offset each other, resulting in a $0 total for the check. Depreciation expense, for example, can be entered as a $0 check. (If this sounds strange, don't worry: it will make sense later when you see a depreciation expense example 156.)

  Every check you enter in QuickBooks is linked to a bank account—that's a requirement of the Checks form. But a $0 check you enter for depreciation expense is not a "real world" check, so it should not be linked to your real-world bank account. That's where a clearing account comes in: you can use one as the source account for any $0 checks you enter.

- **Transferring funds between accounts.** QuickBooks' forms (Invoices, Sales Receipts, etc.) were designed to automate many accounting tasks, but the automation can sometimes "get in the way" of using a single transaction to accomplish what you want to do. Because of how QuickBooks forms work you may sometimes have to make two successive transaction entries to accomplish a particular accounting task. In those situations a clearing bank account may be used for temporarily holding a financial amount from the first transaction, until it can be used in the second transaction.

To set up a clearing bank account:

1. **Open the Chart of Accounts window** (Lists > Chart of Accounts) and **select** Account > New from the button menu at the bottom of the window.

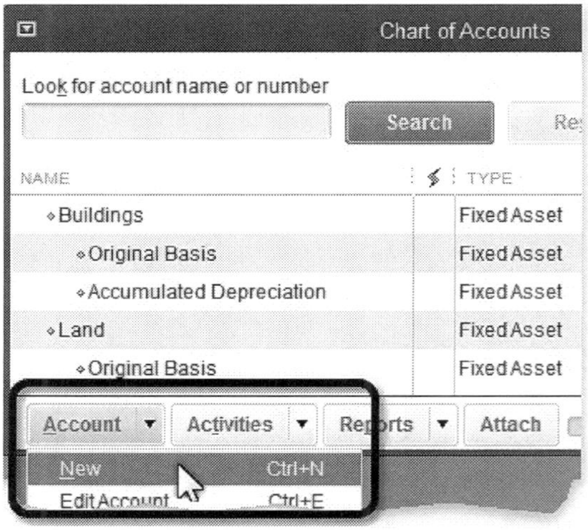

The Add New Account: Choose Account Type window will open.

2. **Select Bank** as the account type, **then click the Continue button.**

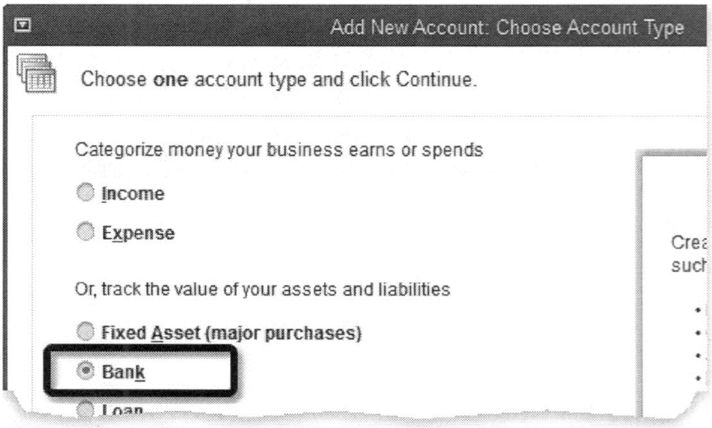

The Add New Account window will open.

3. **Fill in details for the new account,** as shown below.

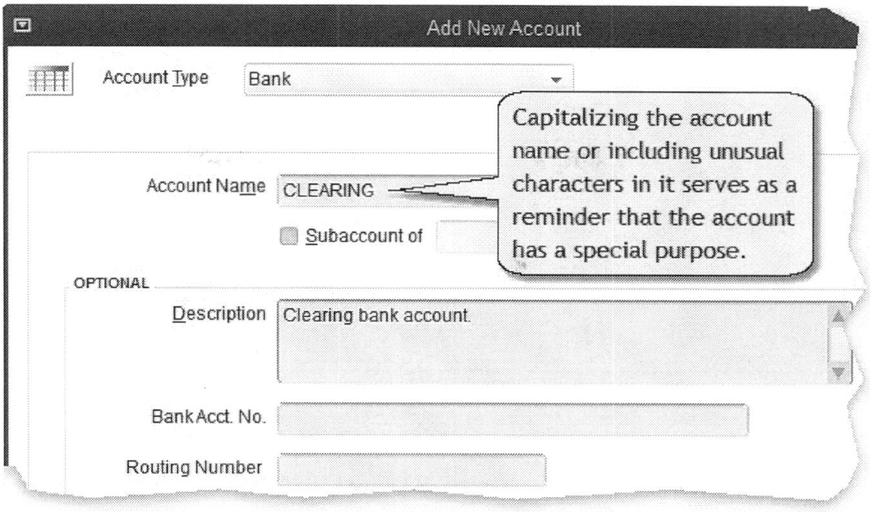

When a clearing bank account has a nonzero balance...

A clearing account's balance should normally be zero. If not, it means you may have made an error. The nonzero balance will show up on balance sheet reports the same as it would for any bank account, so if you notice a nonzero balance in a clearing account when it shouldn't have one, you need to figure out why and get the problem fixed.

A good place to begin looking for problems is in a **Register window** for the account:

1. **Open the Chart of Accounts window** (Lists > Chart of Accounts).
2. **Click on the desired account,** to select it. (Register windows are available for asset, liability, and equity accounts, but not for income or expense accounts.)
3. **Type** *Ctrl-R* to open a Register window for the account, which will list all of the account's transactions.

Fixed Asset Accounts

You need to have *at least* two fixed asset accounts to represent fixed assets on the business' balance sheets: one for the purchase cost or original value (original basis) of fixed assets owned by the business, and another for their accumulated depreciation balance—the total amount of depreciation expense which has been recorded for fixed assets. Actually, using three (or more) fixed asset accounts is more common: a parent account to represent total fixed asset value, plus subaccounts for original basis and accumulated depreciation:

Fixed Assets
  Original Basis
  Accumulated Depreciation

Balance sheet reports show accumulated depreciation as a negative amount and, when a parent account is used, will subtract the accumulated depreciation amount from the original basis amount to calculate what is known as the *adjusted basis* (remaining undepreciated book value) of the assets—what most people simply refer to as the assets' *book value.* The book value of fixed assets in this balance sheet fragment is $200,000:

Fixed Assets	
Original Basis	$300,000
Accumulated Depreciation	-$100,000
--	
Total Fixed Assets	$200,000

Many businesses use more than three fixed asset accounts, so their balance sheets can show book value detail for several fixed asset categories. For example:

Machinery
  Original Basis
  Accumulated Depreciation
Buildings
  Original Basis
  Accumulated Depreciation
Land
  Original Basis

The number of fixed asset accounts you create is up to you, and should depend on how much detail you want to see on balance sheet reports.

Accounting textbook examples often use a separate fixed asset account for *each individual fixed asset,* as described earlier [10]. That approach works well for teaching purposes but is impractical in most business situations because it clutters balance sheet reports with too much detail. Most real-world approaches keep fixed asset detail elsewhere and only post totals to the fixed asset accounts which appear on balance sheet reports. In the S/S method [18], fixed asset details are

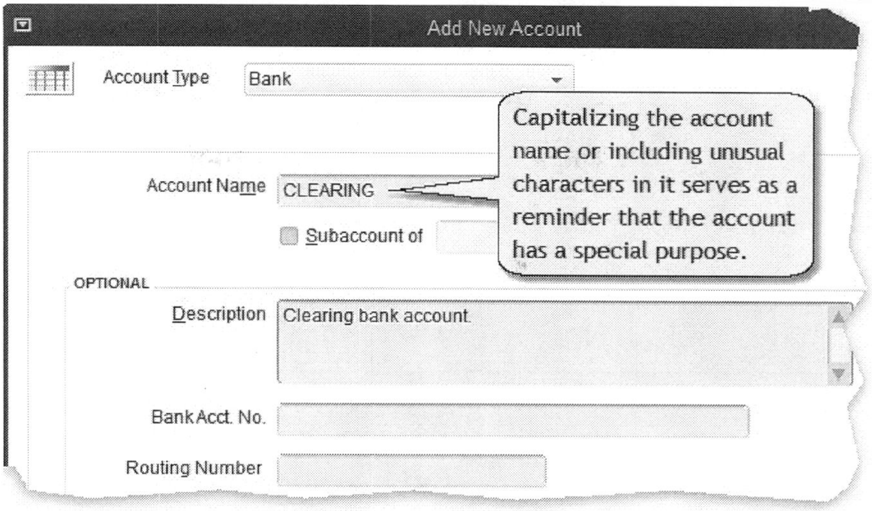

When a clearing bank account has a nonzero balance...

A clearing account's balance should normally be zero. If not, it means you may have made an error. The nonzero balance will show up on balance sheet reports the same as it would for any bank account, so if you notice a nonzero balance in a clearing account when it shouldn't have one, you need to figure out why and get the problem fixed.

A good place to begin looking for problems is in a **Register window** for the account:

1. **Open the Chart of Accounts window** (Lists > Chart of Accounts).
2. **Click on the desired account,** to select it. (Register windows are available for asset, liability, and equity accounts, but not for income or expense accounts.)
3. **Type** *Ctrl-R* to open a Register window for the account, which will list all of the account's transactions.

Fixed Asset Accounts

You need to have *at least* two fixed asset accounts to represent fixed assets on the business' balance sheets: one for the purchase cost or original value (original basis) of fixed assets owned by the business, and another for their accumulated depreciation balance—the total amount of depreciation expense which has been recorded for fixed assets. Actually, using three (or more) fixed asset accounts is more common: a parent account to represent total fixed asset value, plus subaccounts for original basis and accumulated depreciation:

Fixed Assets
  Original Basis
  Accumulated Depreciation

Balance sheet reports show accumulated depreciation as a negative amount and, when a parent account is used, will subtract the accumulated depreciation amount from the original basis amount to calculate what is known as the *adjusted basis* (remaining undepreciated book value) of the assets—what most people simply refer to as the assets' *book value*. The book value of fixed assets in this balance sheet fragment is $200,000:

Fixed Assets	
Original Basis	$300,000
Accumulated Depreciation	-$100,000
Total Fixed Assets	$200,000

Many businesses use more than three fixed asset accounts, so their balance sheets can show book value detail for several fixed asset categories. For example:

Machinery
  Original Basis
  Accumulated Depreciation
Buildings
  Original Basis
  Accumulated Depreciation
Land
  Original Basis

The number of fixed asset accounts you create is up to you, and should depend on how much detail you want to see on balance sheet reports.

Accounting textbook examples often use a separate fixed asset account for *each individual fixed asset*, as described earlier[10]. That approach works well for teaching purposes but is impractical in most business situations because it clutters balance sheet reports with too much detail. Most real-world approaches keep fixed asset detail elsewhere and only post totals to the fixed asset accounts which appear on balance sheet reports. In the S/S method[18], fixed asset details are maintained by using Items, which post amounts to a handful of fixed asset accounts.

To set up fixed asset accounts:

1. **Open the Chart of Accounts window** (Lists > Chart of Accounts) and **select** Account > New from the button menu at the bottom.

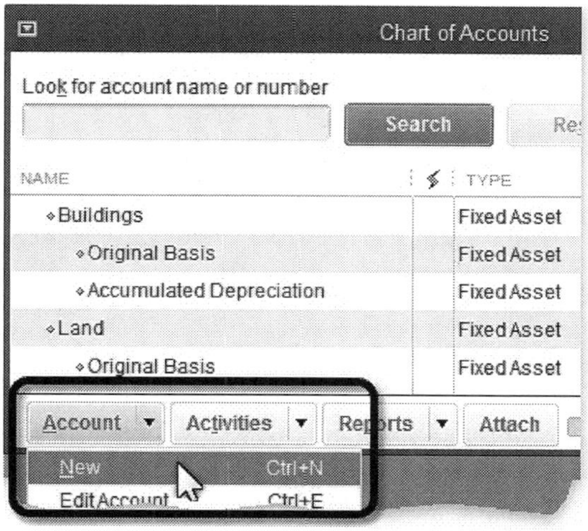

The Add New Account: Choose Account Type window will open.

2. **Select Fixed Asset** as the account type, **then click the Continue button.**

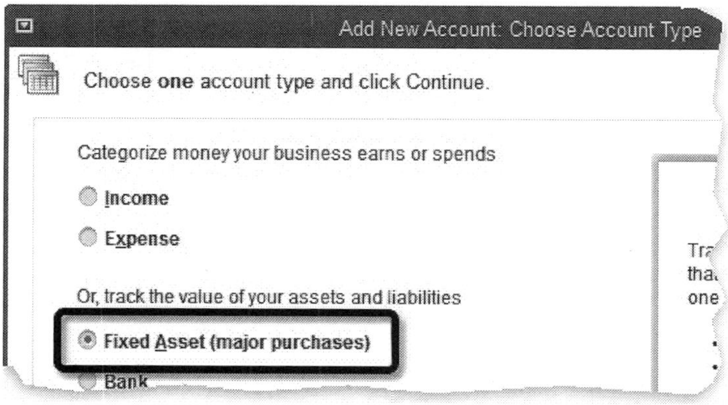

The Add New Account window will open.

3. **Fill in the account details** in the The Add New Account window.

Fixed Assets

This account defines a balance sheet category for all fixed assets, and represents the book value of all fixed assets, combined.

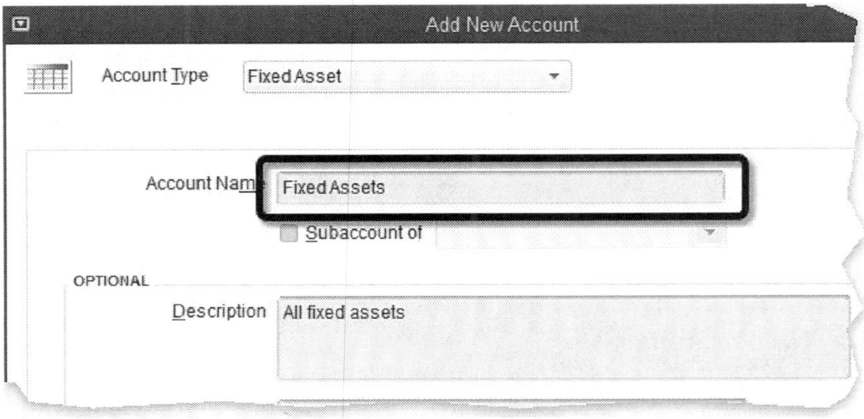

4. **Click the Save & New button** to save the account and keep the window open for adding the other accounts described below.

Fixed Assets:Machinery

This is an example of an account which defines a subcategory of fixed assets, representing machinery. Like its parent account, Fixed Assets, the Machinery subaccount's main purpose is to control how fixed assets are grouped and subtotaled on balance sheet reports.

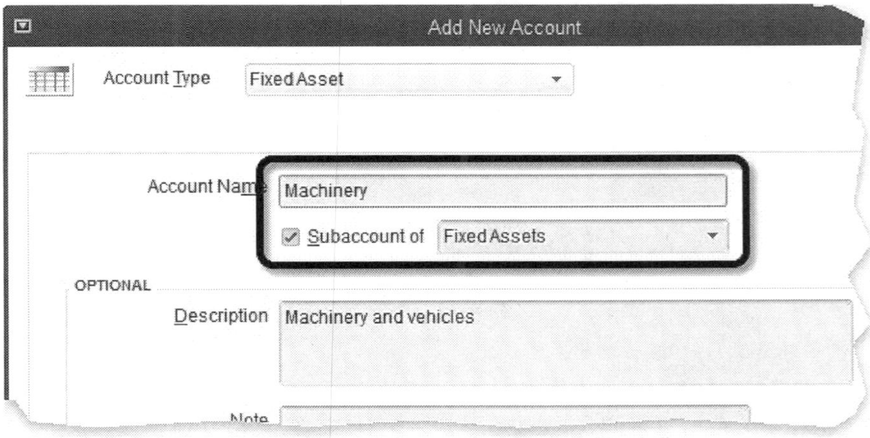

Fixed Assets:Machinery:Original Basis

As a subaccount of Machinery, this account's balance will represent the original basis (purchase cost plus the book value of any trade-ins) of all machinery assets.

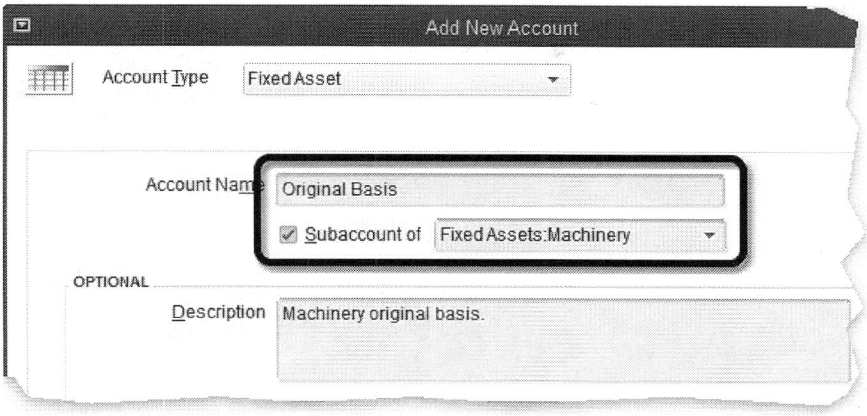

Fixed Assets:Machinery:Accumulated Depreciation

As a subaccount of Machinery, this account's balance will represent the total amount of depreciation expense recorded for machinery assets.

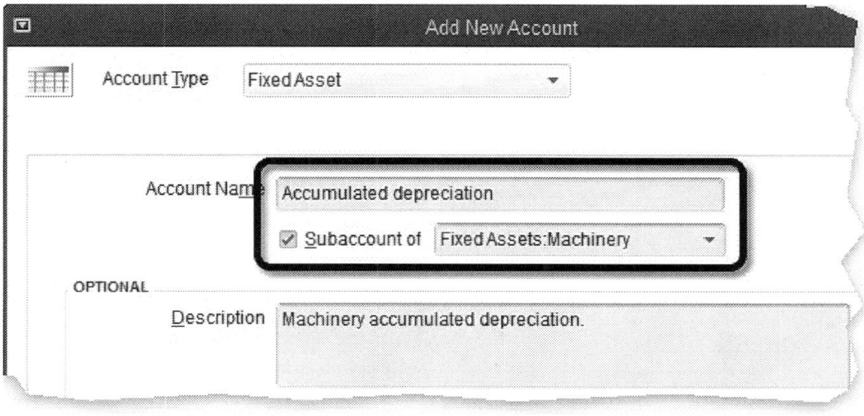

You may also want to create similar accounts for Buildings, Land, or other fixed asset categories.

Depreciation Expense Account

You need to set up an account for recording depreciation expense 147 if you don't already have one.

To set up an account for depreciation expense:

1. **Open the Chart of Accounts window** (Lists > Chart of Accounts) and **select** Account > New from the button menu at the bottom of the window.

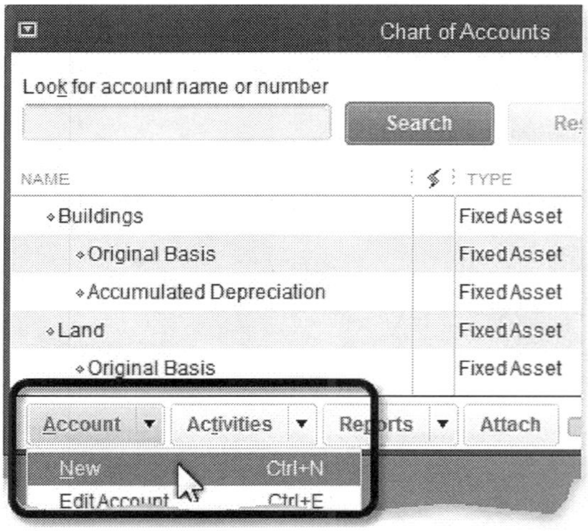

The Add New Account: Choose Account Type window will open.

2. **Select Expense** as the account type, **then click the Continue button.**

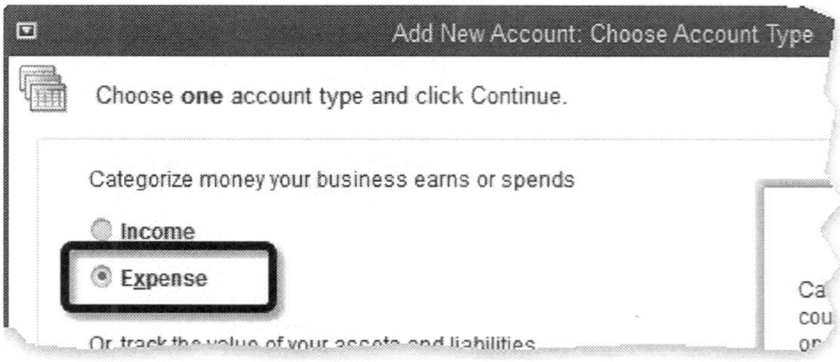

The Add New Account window will open.

3. **Fill in details for the new account.**

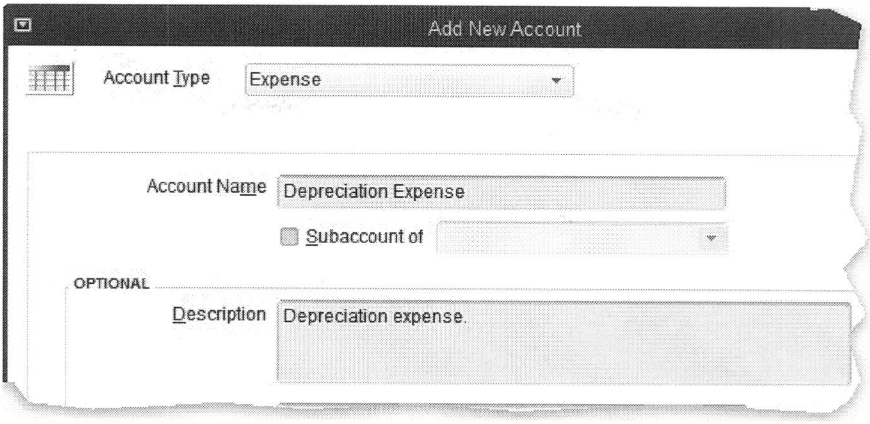

4. **Click the Save & Close button** to save the new account and close the window.

Gain or Loss on Fixed Asset Sales Account (Other Income)

When a fixed asset is sold 109 for more than its book value, the difference is considered a gain (income) on the sale of the asset. If sold for less than book value, the difference is considered a loss (expense, or negative income) on the sale of the asset. The S/S method automatically calculates the gain or loss when a fixed asset is sold, so you must have an account available for posting the gain or loss. Normally this should be an account of the Other Income type.

Other Income accounts are used for representing extraordinary income—income resulting from things outside the realm of normal business activities. They appear toward the bottom of profit and loss reports, below the Net Ordinary Income line.

The account may have *either* a positive or negative balance...

Gains and losses on all fixed asset sales are posted to the same Other Income account, so the account may have a positive or negative balance at any time. Gains are more common than losses however—especially during times of robust economic activity, and due to general inflation—so the account will more commonly have a positive balance at the end of the accounting year.

To set up an account for gains and losses on fixed asset sales:

1. **Open the Chart of Accounts window** (Lists > Chart of Accounts) and **select** Account > New from the button menu at the bottom of the window.

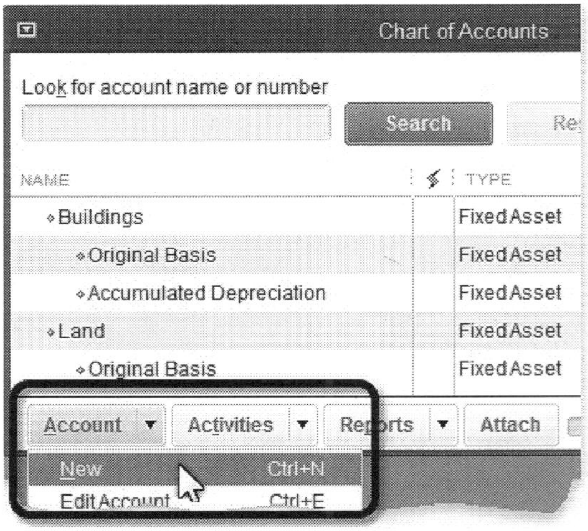

The Add New Account: Choose Account Type window will open.

2. **Select Other Account Types, then Other Income** as the account type. Finally, **click the Continue button.**

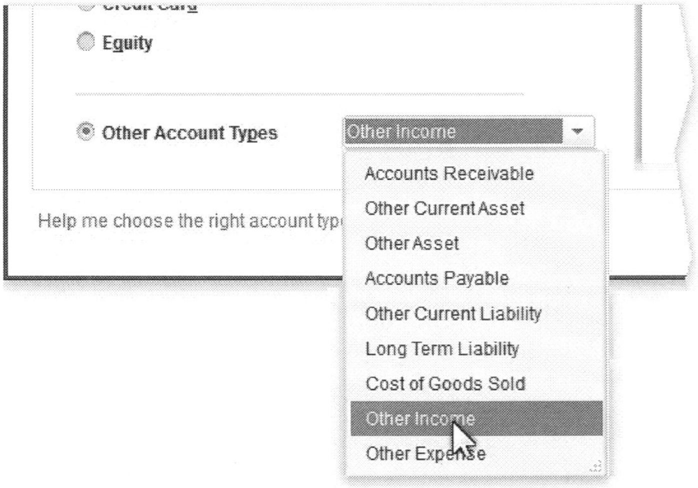

The Add New Account window will open.

3. **Fill in details for the new account.**

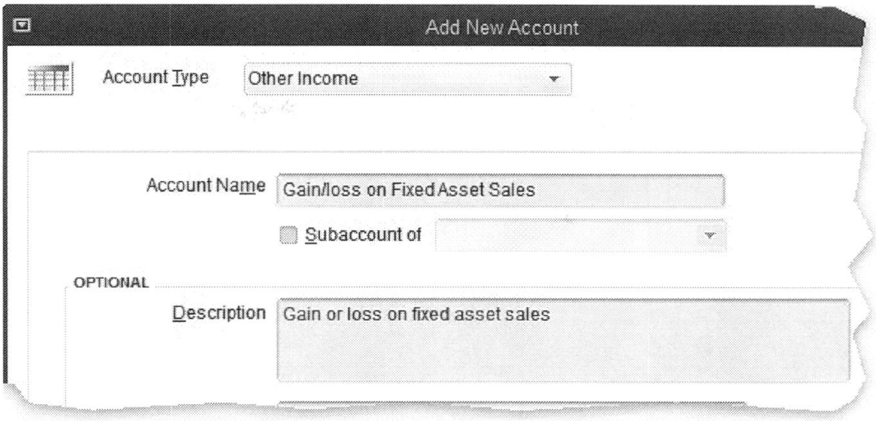

4. **Click the Save & Close button** to save the new account and close the window.

Error Indicator Account (optional but recommended)

When setting up fixed asset Items[61], some of the Items you create will be parent Items—that is, Items which have subitems (child Items).

With the S/S method[18], parent Items *should not* be used directly in transactions; *only their subitems* should be used. QuickBooks does not provide a mechanism for preventing you from using an Item in a transaction, or for providing an error message if you do. However, you can establish your own error trapping scheme by setting up an error indicator account—an account which will appear on profit and loss reports if you happen to (incorrectly) use an Item in a transaction.

To set up an error indicator account:

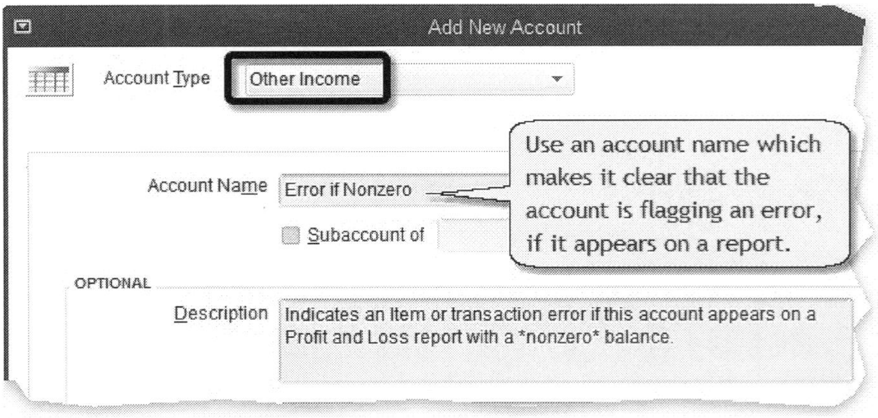

How does an error indicator account work?

When you create an Item which should not be used in transactions, assign the error indicator account to each of its account fields:

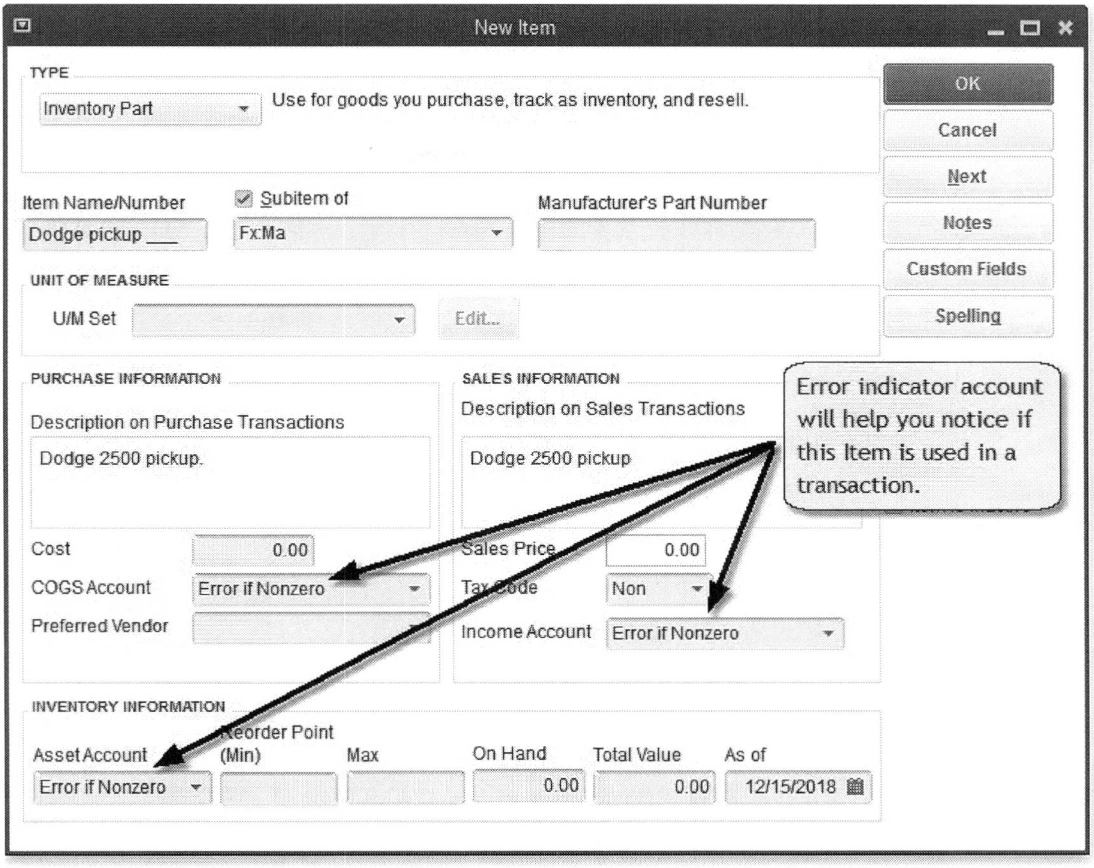

Then if the Item is ever used in a transaction, an amount will be posted to the *Error if Nonzero* account, which will show up on profit and loss reports with a nonzero balance:

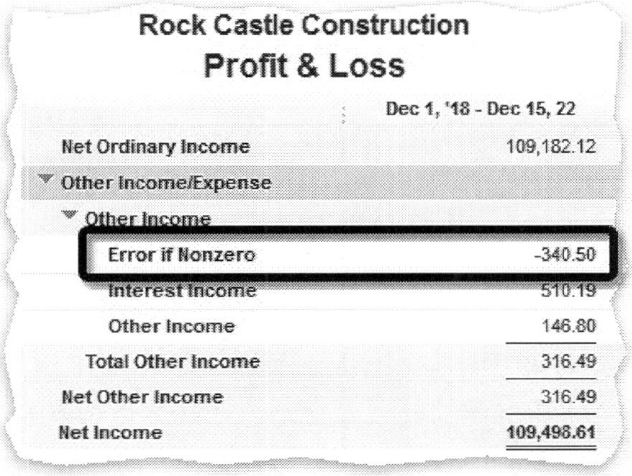

Rock Castle Construction

Profit & Loss

	Dec 1, '18 - Dec 15, 22
Net Ordinary Income	109,182.12
Other Income/Expense	
Other Income	
Error if Nonzero	-340.50
Interest Income	510.19
Other Income	146.80
Total Other Income	316.49
Net Other Income	316.49
Net Income	109,498.61

When the error indicator account appears in a report this way (with a nonzero balance) you can drill down on that line of the report to find the transaction(s) where an Item was used incorrectly, so that you may fix the problem by selecting a different Item.

Drilling down means double-clicking a line in a report to open a window containing more detail—usually a specific transaction or list of related transactions.

Other places to use an error indicator account

Error indicator accounts are not limited to being used for fixed asset Items. You may use one when setting up *any* Item which should not be used directly in transactions. Typically this will be a parent Item which represents a category of things, such as different kinds of inventory, rather than a specific inventory Item.

Setting Up Items for Fixed Assets

Basic Things to Know

What Items Do You Need, for Fixed Assets?

The S/S method 18 is based on using Inventory Part Items to represent fixed assets. Here are the Items you might need for describing a pickup truck, for example:

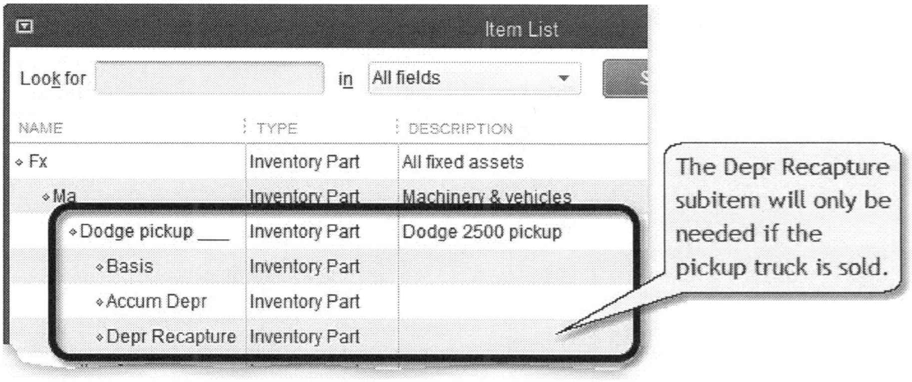

- *Dodge Pickup___* represents the fixed asset—a pickup truck in this case. This Item is not used directly in transactions; rather, its subitems (*Basis, Accum Depr,* and *Depr Recapture*) are used.

  Using underscores in Item names is optional and will be explained later in this section[56].

- *Basis* stores the truck's original basis—its purchase price plus the book value of any trade-in involved in the purchase. This subitem is used when recording the asset's purchase[89] and its sale[109], or its use as a trade-in[102] for another asset.

- *Accum Depr* (accumulated depreciation) is used for recording depreciation expense[147] for the asset, and also in recapturing depreciation[111] if the asset is later sold (sold outright; not traded in).

- *Depr Recapture* (depreciation recapture) is only used if a fixed asset is sold outright, for recapturing depreciation[111].

  Because a Depr Recapture subitem is only needed if a fixed asset is sold, you might choose not to create one unless/until the asset is sold. However, if you are adding a batch of "blank" (unused) Items[70]—a quick way to create many fixed asset Items at once—giving each of the "blank" Items a Depr Recapture subitem will avoid the need to create them manually.

Organizing the Item List

If you add a main Item and two or three subitems each time you acquire a new fixed asset, eventually your Item List may look something like this:

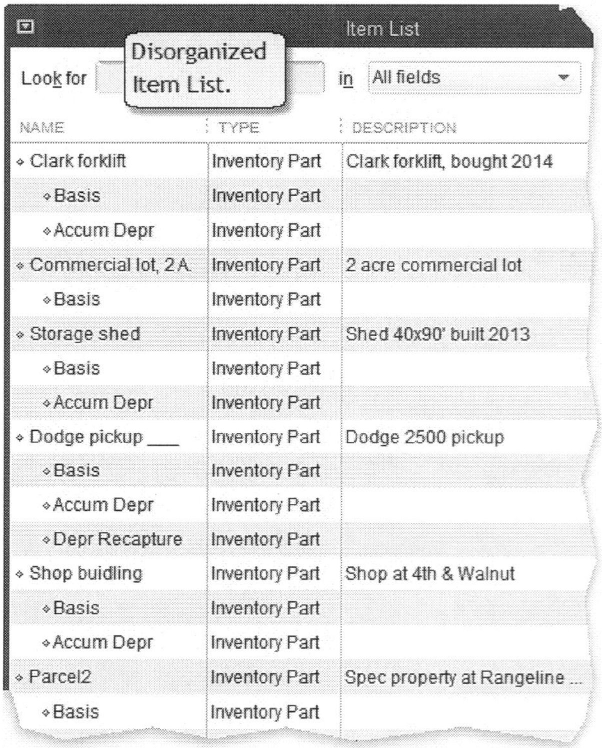

The Items in this example have been added willy-nilly, without using any higher-level (parent) Items to divide them into categories. This lack of organization makes selecting Items more difficult when entering transactions, and makes reports less useful because they don't provide subtotals for different asset categories.

Here is the same list of fixed asset Items, but with some higher-level parent Items added to group the fixed assets into categories:

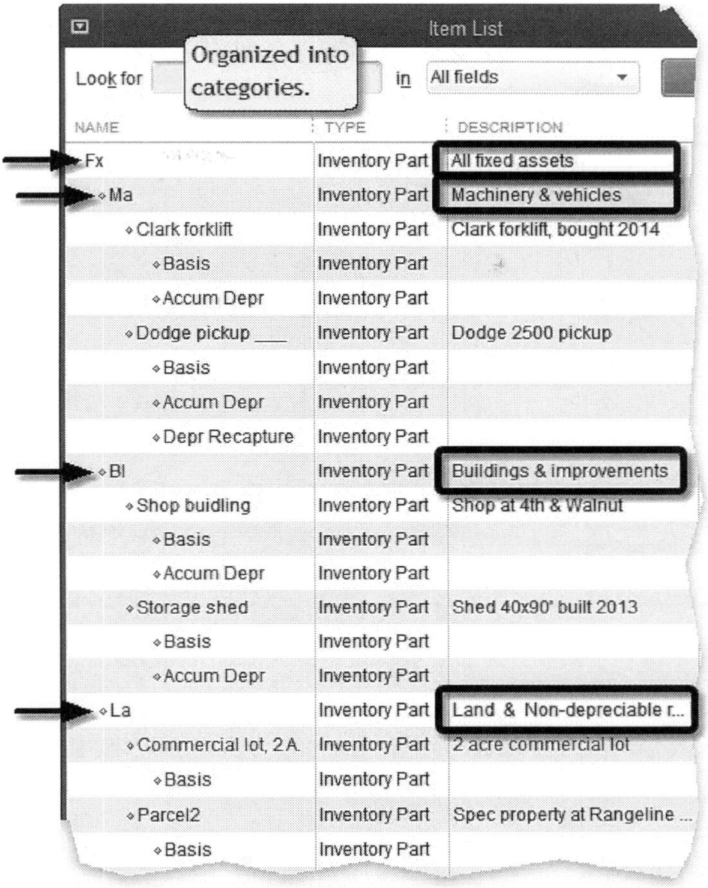

Adding parent Items to establish fixed asset categories provides these benefits:

- **Having a *master parent Item* for all fixed assets,** such as *Fx* in the list above, makes it easy to filter reports to include only fixed asset Items or transactions. (Calling *Fx* the master parent Item for all fixed assets simply means that all fixed asset Items are subitems of *Fx*.)

  Having a master parent Item is *highly recommended.* If you don't use one, filtering fixed asset reports 215 *will be very difficult.*

- **Item reports will have separate subtotals** for the categories you create, such as machinery, buildings, and land, as well as providing a grand total for all fixed assets combined—because *Fx* is the master parent Item encompassing all fixed assets.

❖ **Easier Item selection during transaction entry.** Suppose your Item List has roughly 3,000 Items in it—not just fixed assets but also inventories of retail or wholesale goods—and that you have sold the Clark forklift (*Fx:Ma:Clark forklift* in the list above), so now you need to enter the sale in QuickBooks.

How do you find the Item if you don't remember exactly how its name was spelled? You might assume you could search for an Item with "Clark" in the name, but what if the person who created the Item misspelled it as "Calrk"? Without fixed asset categories you might have to scroll through a thousand Items to find the right one. But with the list organized as shown above, finding the desired Item would be much easier:

- Typing *Fx* in the transaction's Item field would narrow the search to fixed asset Items—it would exclude Items which represent inventories.
- Typing *:M* (so that *Fx:Ma* appears in the Item field) would further narrow the search to the machinery category.
- If you then click the down arrow button at the right side of the Item field, you could scroll through just the machinery Items to more easily find the *Clark forklift* Item.

Item Names and Income Tax Preparation

Regardless of who prepares your income taxes—an employee, or a CPA or other outside professional whom you pay for tax preparation services—associating asset numbers with fixed asset Items can make working with your tax preparer simpler and easier.

A common problem for many QuickBooks users is how to accurately identify which fixed assets have been purchased, traded in, or sold. If your company has a total of five forklifts at two warehouse locations, and you sell three of them, which of the forklifts shown on your tax preparer's asset list were sold?

Answering that question becomes easy if you have associated the tax preparer's asset numbers (assigned to assets by your tax preparer) with your fixed asset Items in QuickBooks. That way, *every* transaction where a fixed asset Item is used will automatically be linked to the tax preparer's asset list via the asset number. At tax time, the reports 222 you print will clearly identify which assets were sold or traded in.

Where should you include asset numbers?

The two best places to include asset numbers are either in the Item Name, or in its Purchase and Sale Description fields:

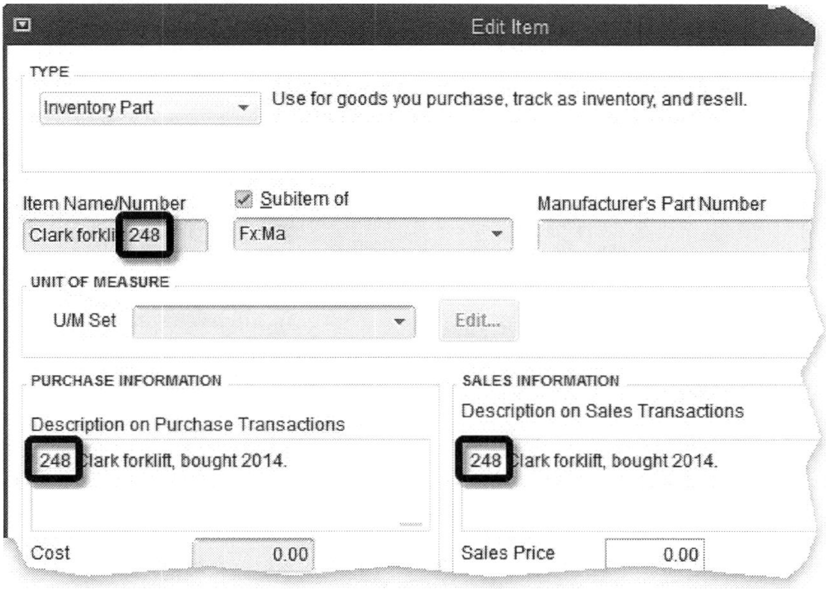

You *do not* need to put the asset number in all three locations! That was only done in this example to illustrate the possibilities. Put it in *either* the Item Name field or in both Description fields.

Comments and tips:

- QuickBooks limits the length of Item names to 31 characters, so including asset numbers there occupies part of the (somewhat limited) space available for describing the Item. The Description fields are much longer, so they don't have this limitation.
- Putting asset numbers at the end of Item names is better than putting them at the beginning, because it allows easier Item selection during transaction entry—if you are someone who selects Items by typing. For instance, you could type "cla" to quickly find an Item named "Clark forklift 248" but could not as quickly find one named "248 Clark forklift" unless you knew its asset number.
- If you add asset numbers in the Description fields, add them at the *beginning* of each field. That will keep them visible on most Item reports depending on your QuickBooks settings, and makes it possible to sort by asset number (if needed) if you export Items or reports to Microsoft Excel.
- If you put asset numbers in the Description fields, add them to *both* fields. That requires additional effort but will make the asset number visible on all Item reports, not just some reports.

Whichever location you choose, be consistent: include asset numbers in *either* the Name or Description fields but not both, and at *either* the beginning or end of those fields.

If you will be importing depreciation transactions from a spreadsheet (discussed in Chapter 9 - Depreciation Expense 147) putting asset numbers in the Description fields may be preferable. That avoids the need to update an Item's name both in QuickBooks <u>and</u> in the spreadsheet when an asset number is assigned to the Item, making it easier to keep Item names synchronized between QuickBooks and the spreadsheet.

How to manage new Items (which don't yet have asset numbers)

Fixed assets you purchase during the year won't have asset numbers assigned to them until year's end, when taxes are prepared. Here are some tips for handling the new Items you create to represent fixed asset purchases:

- When you create a new Item for a fixed asset, **include one or more special characters as a placeholder** for the asset number which will be added later, after your tax preparer has assigned one.

  You may use any character you want, but underscores work well for this:

- **Move new fixed asset Items to the beginning of their fixed asset category within the Item List.** Though not required, this groups new fixed asset Items together, making them easy to find later for adding asset numbers.

  Here, new Items for a mixer and a pickup truck have been moved to the beginning of the *Fx:Ma* (fixed assets:machinery) section of the Items List:

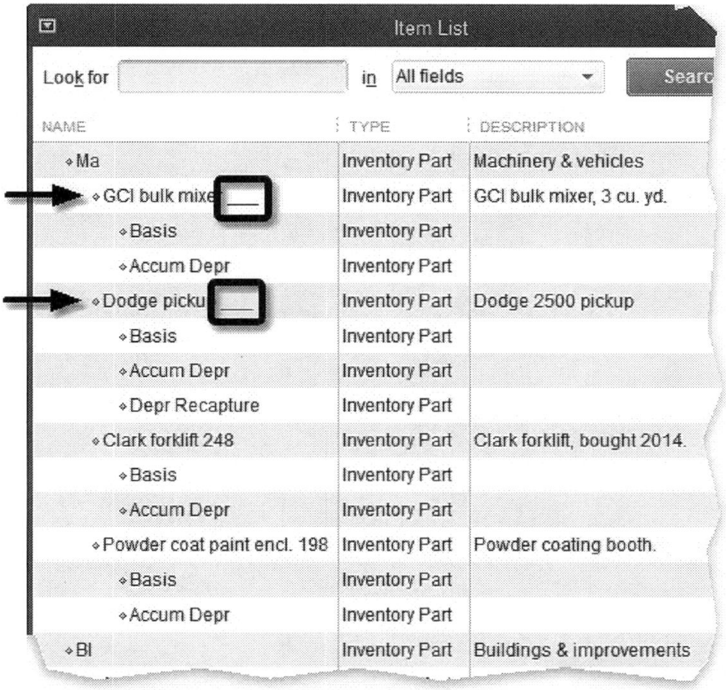

❖ After income taxes have been prepared, **edit the Item names and replace the special character(s)** with your tax preparer's asset numbers. (This assumes you receive an asset list from your preparer after taxes have been prepared, with numbers assigned to the assets acquired during the year.)

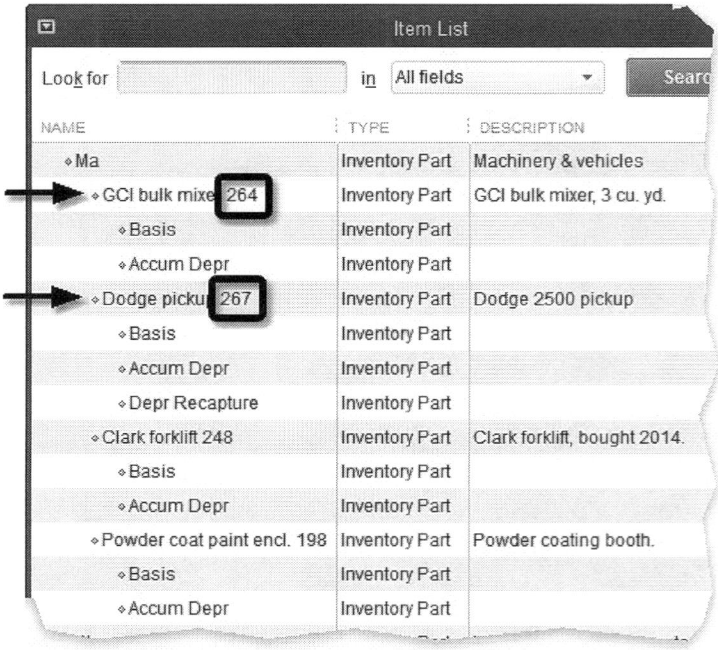

Some fixed assets might not have a number

Fixed assets not in your tax preparer's asset list won't have an asset number, nor will they need one.

Land for example, is not depreciable and may or may not be included in the preparer's asset list. Other examples would include machines or buildings which were fully depreciated before you switched to using your current tax preparer. You may have Items set up for those assets in QuickBooks, but they may not include an asset number unless your tax preparer assigns one.

Setting up Items

Parent Items for Fixed Asset Categories

The Items you set up for fixed assets should *always* be subitems of a master parent Item 55—a single top-level Item which, together with its subitems, represents all fixed assets. However, you may also want to create subitems below the master parent Item to represent categories of fixed assets such as machinery, buildings, and land.

See *Basic Things to Know* 54 for details on organizing the Item List.

These steps show how to create a master parent Item, *Fx*, and a subitem to represent machinery, *Ma*. (Subitems for buildings, land, or other categories would be created the same way.)

1. **Open the Item List window** (Lists > Item List).
2. **Select** Item > New from the button menu at the bottom of the window.

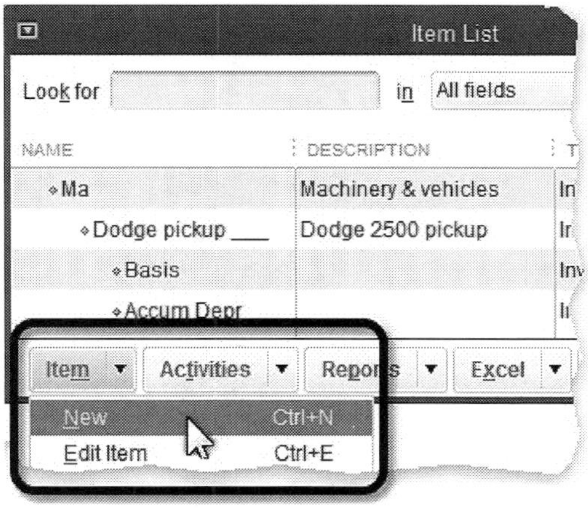

The New Item window will open.

3. **Fill in details for the new Item(s):**

You can create new Items, one after the other, by clicking the *Next* button after filling out details for an Item (see ❹ in the screenshot below).

Here is the setup window for *Fx*, an Item which will be the master parent Item [55] for all fixed assets.

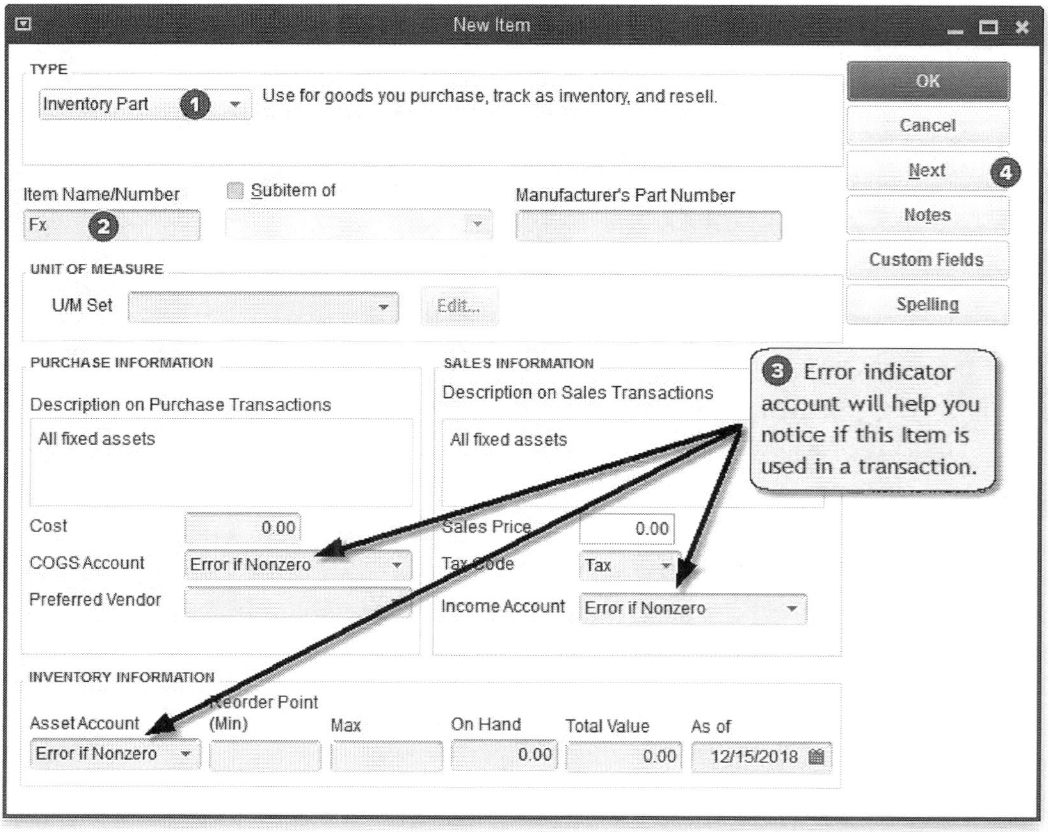

1. **Type.** Fixed asset Items you create for the S/S method [18] *must* be Inventory Part Items.

2. **Item Name/Number.** Using short names for parent Items, where possible, saves space on printed reports and allows more of an Item's name to be visible during transaction entry.

3. **Accounts.** *Error if Nonzero* [49] is selected in each of the Item's account fields because this Item should not be used directly in transactions. If that ever happens, the Error if Nonzero account will help you notice the error, by showing up on profit and loss reports with a nonzero balance.

4. ***Next* [button].** When you are finished filling out information for a new Item, you may click the *Next* button (instead of the OK button)

if you want to save the Item and keep the window open for adding another Item.

4. **Click the Next button** to add the *Ma* Item as a subitem of *Fx*, as shown below. It will represent machinery as a fixed asset category—you may create subitems for buildings, vehicles, or other categories in the same way.

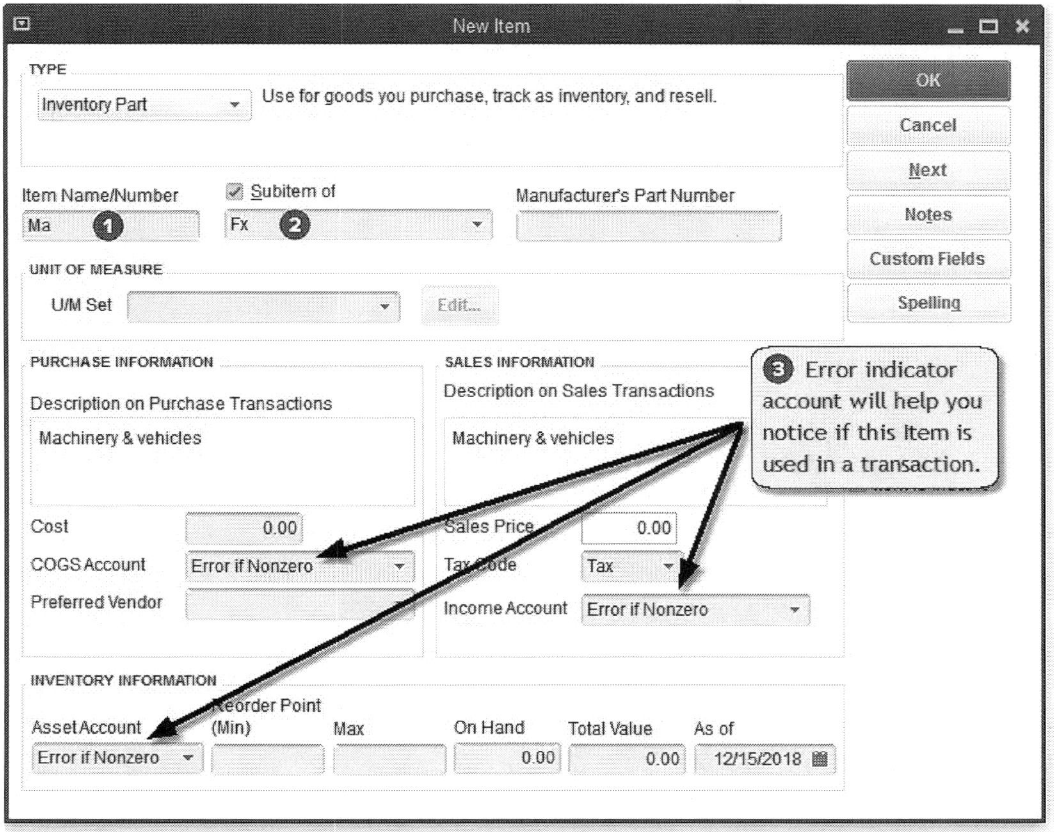

❶ **Item Name/Number.** Using short names for parent Items, where possible, saves space on printed reports and allows more of an Item's name to be visible during transaction entry.

❷ **Subitem of.** Checkmark this box, then select *Fx* as the parent Item of *Ma*, in the box immediately below it.

❸ **Accounts.** *Error if Nonzero*49 is selected in each of the Item's account fields because this Item should not be used directly in transactions. If that ever happens, the Error if Nonzero account will help you notice the error, by showing up on profit and loss reports with a nonzero balance.

5. **Click the Next button** to save the new Item and keep the window open, **or the OK button** to save the new Item and close the window.

Items for Individual Fixed Assets

In the S/S method a fixed asset is represented by a single Item which has one to three subitems. Here is a set of Items for a pickup truck as it might appear in the Item List (Lists > Item List):

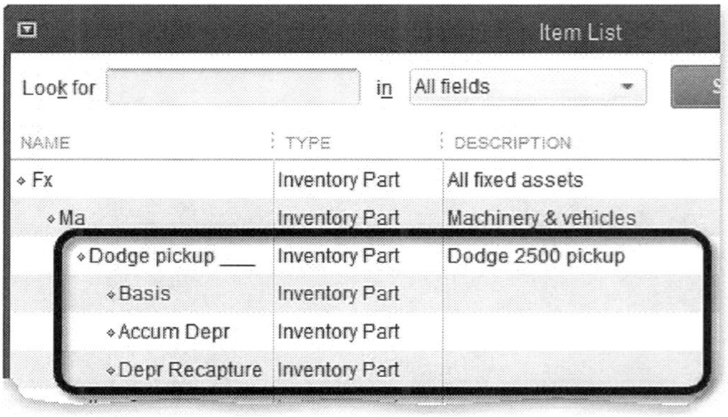

- *Fx* (Fixed Assets) is the master parent Item[55] for all fixed assets.
- *Ma* (Machinery) represents a fixed asset category, separate from other categories like buildings or land.
- *Dodge Pickup ___* represents the pickup truck. It is not used directly in transactions but is the parent Item of *Basis, Accum Depr,* and *Depr Recapture* subitems which *will* be used in transactions.
- *Basis* stores the asset's original basis—its purchase price plus the book value of any trade-in involved in the purchase. This subitem is used to record an asset's purchase[89] and its sale[109], or its use as a trade-in[102] if traded in for another asset.
- *Accum Depr* (accumulated depreciation) is used for recording depreciation expense[147] for the pickup truck, and also for recapturing depreciation[111] if the truck is sold (sold outright; not traded in).

- *Depr Recapture* (depreciation recapture) will only be used if the truck is sold outright, for recapturing depreciation 111. It is important in calculating gain or loss on the sale of the asset 111.

Here are the steps for setting up Items to represent a fixed asset.

These steps show how to set up fixed asset Items one at a time. For instructions on setting up multiple Items at a time, see *Automating Item Creation* 70.

1. **Open the Item List window** (Lists > Item List).
2. **Select** Item > New from the button menu at the bottom of the window.

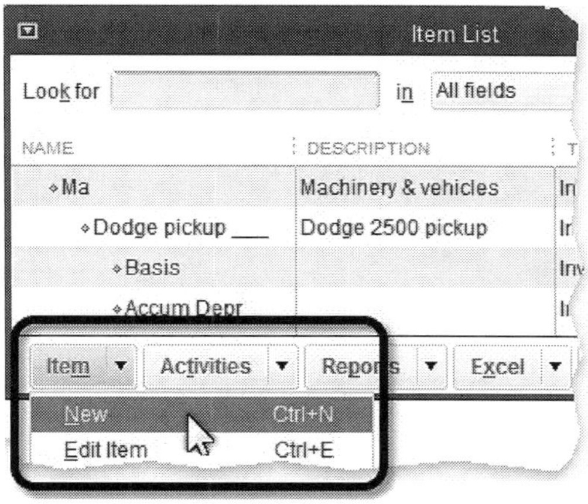

The New Item window will open.

3. **Fill in details for the new Item(s):**

Fx:Ma:Dodge pickup ___

The *Dodge pickup ___* Item identifies the pickup truck. It is a subitem of *Ma* (Machinery), which in turn is a subitem of *Fx* (all fixed assets). This Item won't itself be used in transactions, but serves as a parent Item for the *Basis*, *Accum Depr*, and *Depr Recapture* subitems to be created farther below.

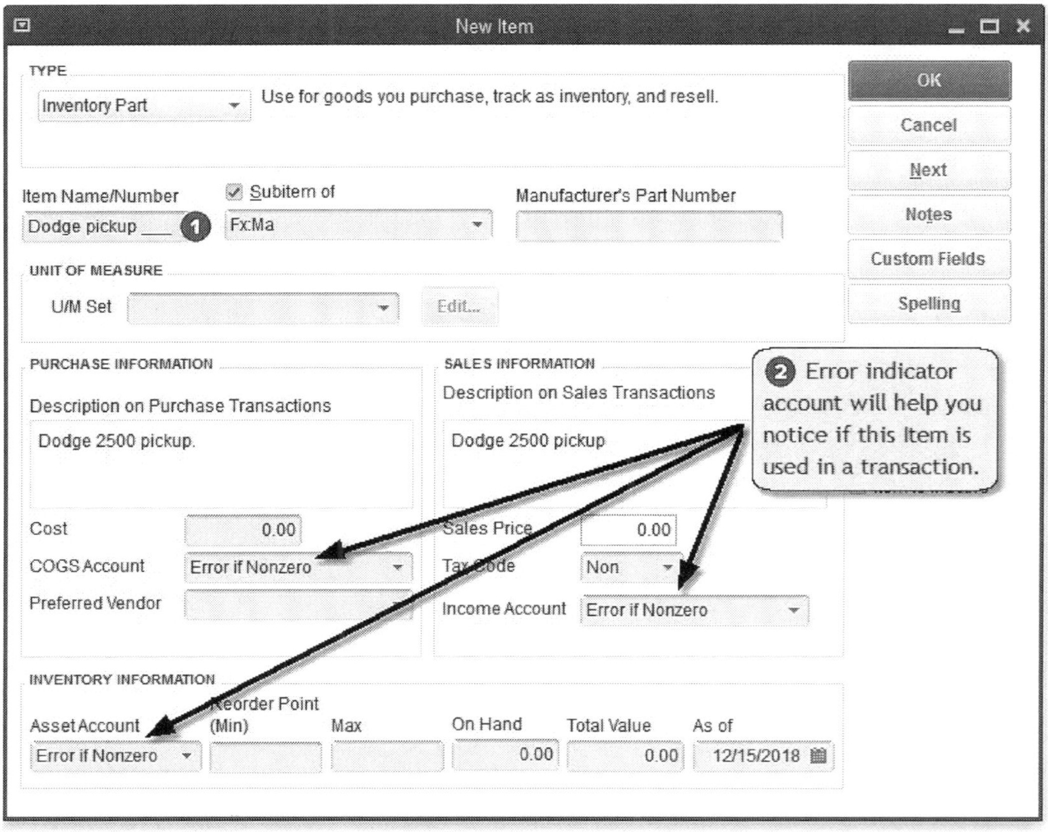

Item Name/Number. The Item name has three underscores "___" at the end to serve as a reminder to add the tax preparer's asset number there later, once it is known. As explained in *Item Names and Income Tax Preparation* 56, including the tax preparer's asset number is optional but helps connect your QuickBooks Items with the tax preparer's asset list.

Accounts. *Error if Nonzero* 49 is selected in each of the Item's account fields because this Item should not be used directly in transactions. If that ever happens, the Error if Nonzero account will help you notice the error, by showing up on profit and loss reports with a nonzero balance.

Fx:Ma:Dodge pickup ___:Basis

The *Basis* subitem is for recording the pickup truck's original basis (purchase cost), and later its selling price, if sold.

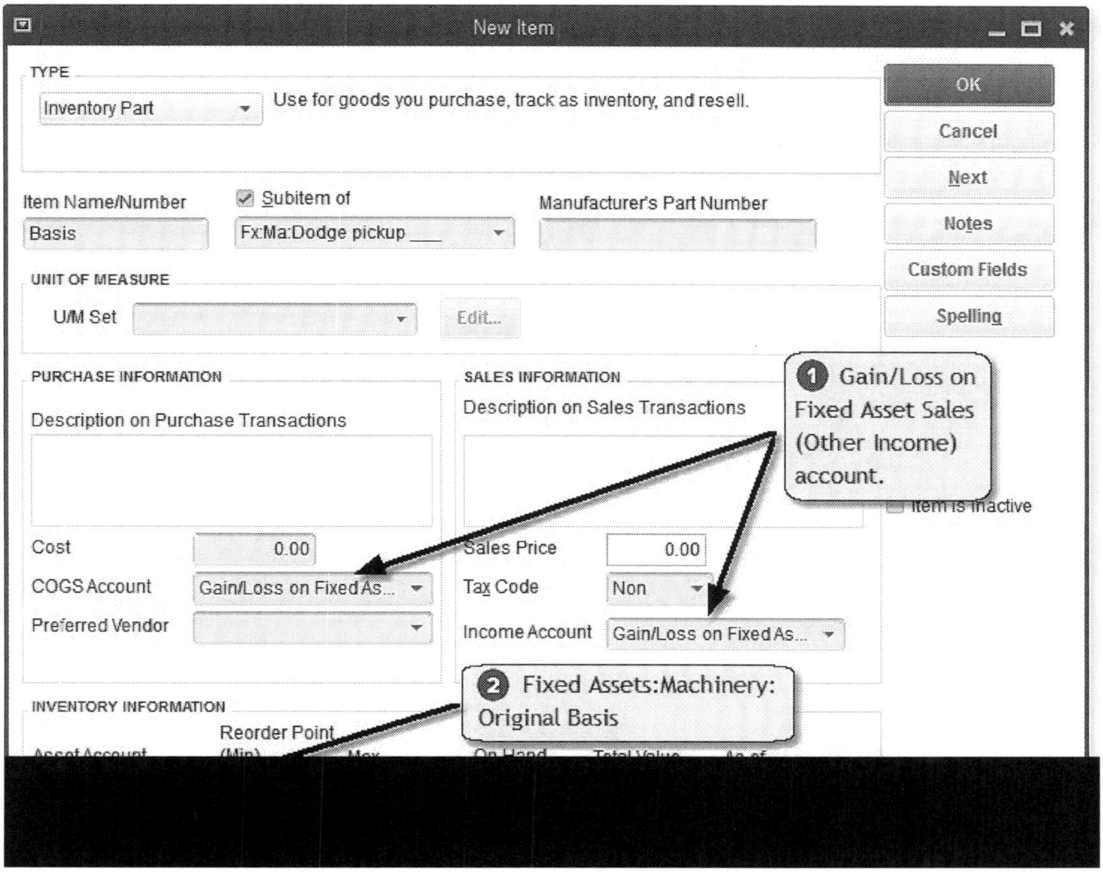

1. **COGS Account** and **Income Account.** Both point to *Gain/Loss on Fixed Asset Sales* 47, which is important for automatically calculating gain or loss if the pickup truck is later sold.
2. **Asset Account** points to *Fixed Assets:Machinery:Original Basis* 45, which stores the original basis of all machinery assets.

Fx:Ma:Dodge pickup ___:Accum Depr

Recommended: Use the <u>*same*</u> accumulated depreciation subitem name (such as Accum Depr) for all fixed assets. That facilitates automatic importing of depreciation expense transactions, as discussed in Chapter 9 - Depreciation Expense[147].

The *Accum Depr* (accumulated depreciation) subitem will be used when recording depreciation expense for the pickup truck. The balance associated with this Item will represent the total amount of depreciation expense which has been entered for the truck.

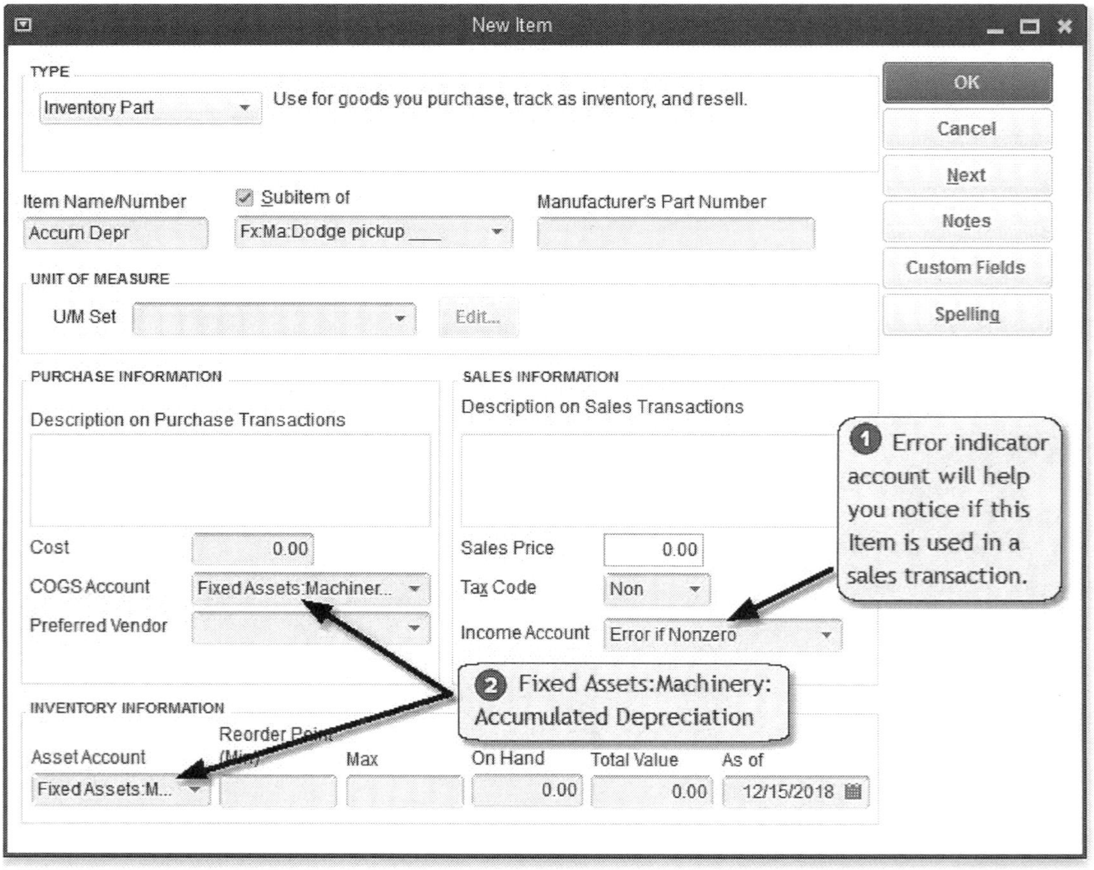

1. **Income Account** is an error indicator account[49] because Accum Depr subitems should not be used in sales transactions. Selecting

an error indicator account here will help you notice the error, if this Item should happen to be used in a sale.

2. **COGS Account** and **Asset Account** both point to *Fixed Assets:Machinery:Accumulated Depreciation* [45], which stores the accumulated depreciation total for all machinery assets.

Fx:Ma:Dodge pickup ___:Depr Recapture

The *Depr Recapture* subitem will only be used if the pickup truck is sold, for recapturing depreciation [111] on the sale. It is an important part of the S/S method's automatic calculation of gain or loss on fixed asset sales. However, because this Item is only needed if the pickup truck is sold outright, you might choose to create a Depr Recapture subitem only if needed.

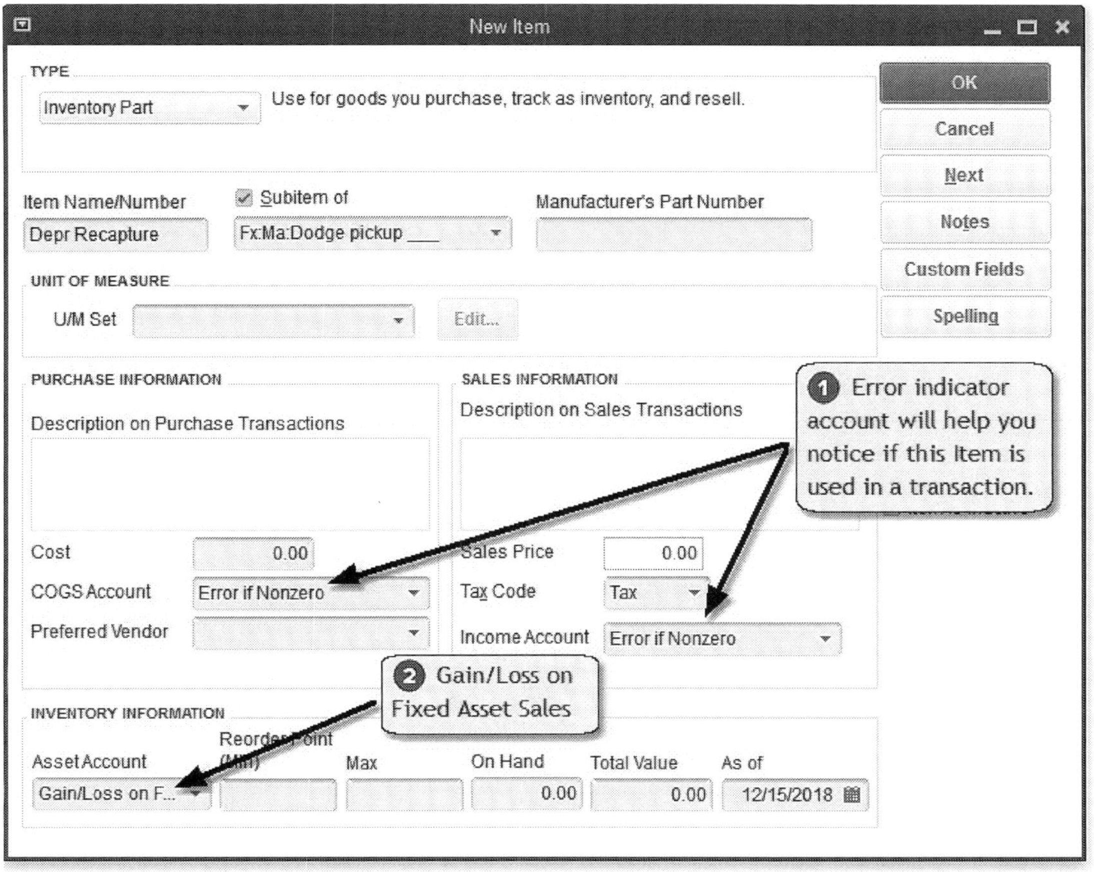

(1) **COGS Acount** and **Income Account** both point to *Error if Nonzero* [49] because QuickBooks posts to the COGS and Income accounts if the Item is used in a sales transaction—which should not happen.

(2) **Asset Account** points to *Gain/Loss on Fixed Asset Sales* [47].

Automating Item Creation

Manually setting up more than one or two fixed asset Items can take a lot of time. But there's a way to automate the process if you have a spreadsheet like Microsoft Excel, OpenOffice Calc, LibreOffice Calc, or others.

You must be using a *locally installed* version of Microsoft Excel to use the Excel procedures described below. If you are using a Web-based version of Excel, follow the more generic instructions which apply to other spreadsheets.

In QuickBooks...

1. **Open the Item List** (Lists > Item List).
2. **Select** Excel > Export All Items from the button bar menu at the bottom of the Item List window.

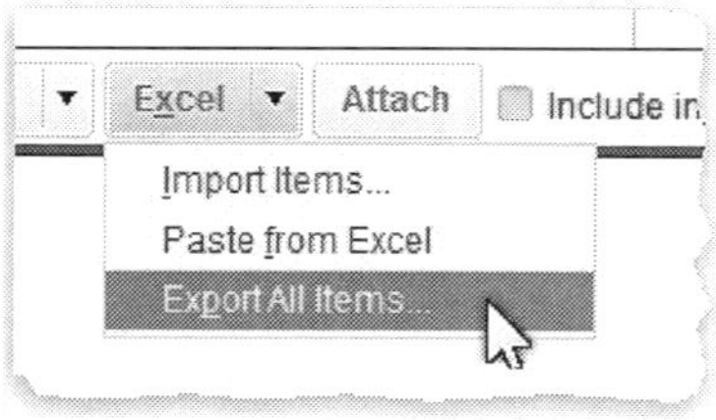

The Export window will open.

3. In the Export window, **select *Create new worksheet*** if you are using Microsoft Excel, **or *Create a comma-separated values (.csv) file*** if using some other spreadsheet.

    ❖ *If exporting to Excel,* also select the option to create a new workbook, as shown below.

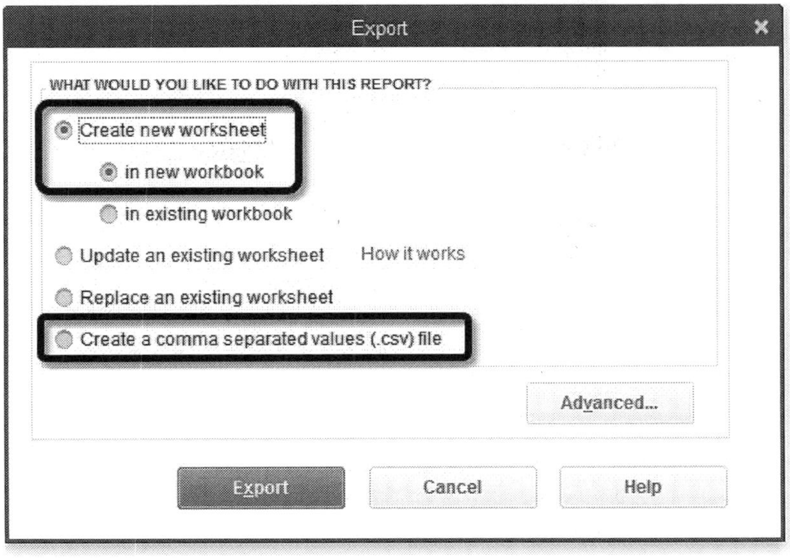

4. **Click the Export button.**

   - *If exporting to a comma-separated values (.csv) file,* you will be prompted to supply a location for the file. After QuickBooks has saved the file, import it into your spreadsheet program. (Many spreadsheet programs can open a .csv file directly, without requiring special importing procedures.)

   The spreadsheet will contain all Items from the QuickBooks Item List, including not only fixed asset Items but also Service, Non-inventory Part, and other Items:

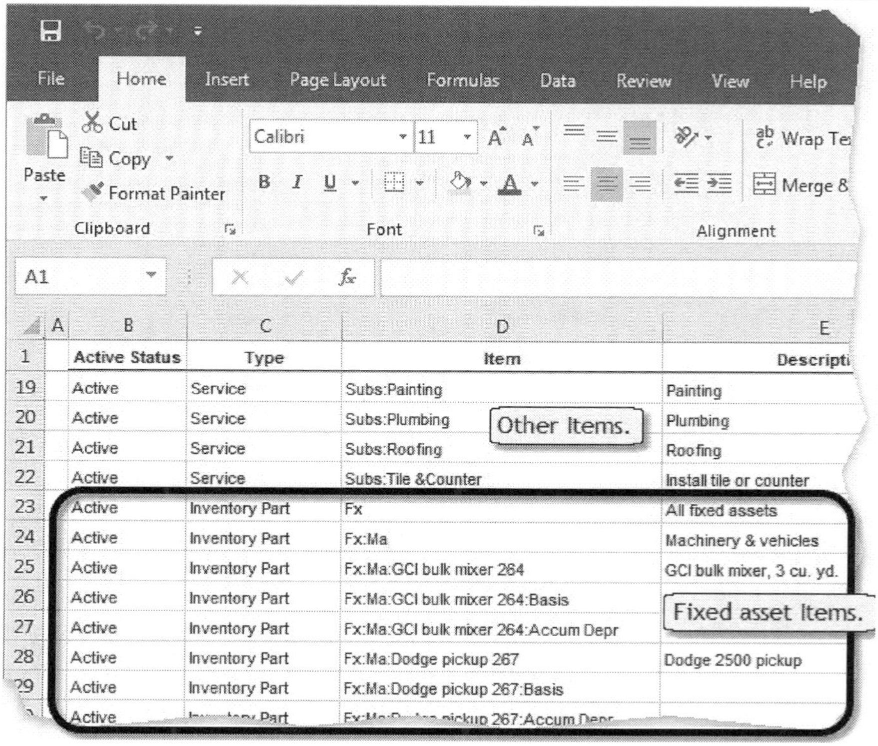

You won't do anything more with the spreadsheet until step 9 below.

5. In QuickBooks, **open the Add/Edit Multiple List Entries window** (Lists > Add/Edit Multiple List Entries).

6. **Select Inventory Parts** as the list type to view:

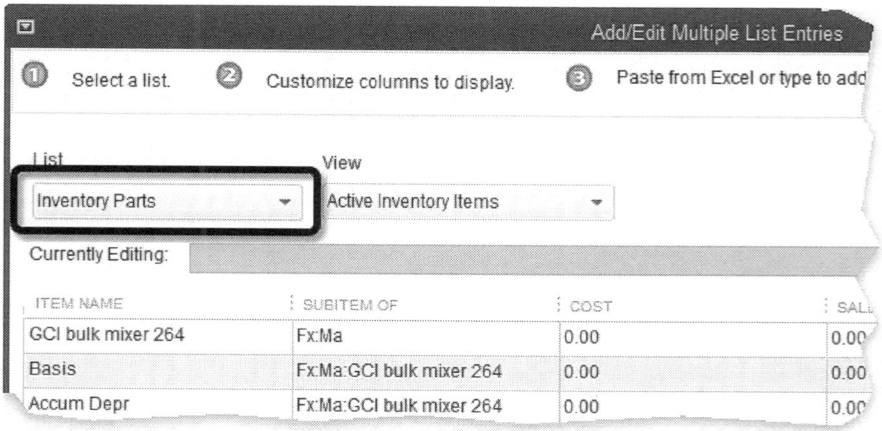

7. **Click the Customize Columns button** (in the upper right corner of the window), then use the Add and Remove buttons to **add and/or remove columns to display,** keeping only those necessary for defining new Items, such as the ones highlighted below:

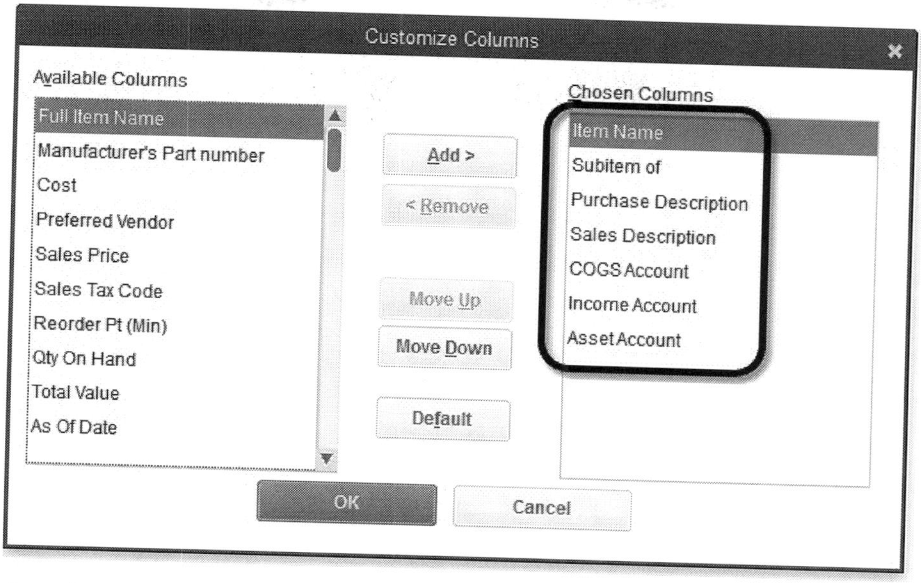

8. **Click the OK button** to close the Customize Columns window and redisplay the Add/Edit Multiple List Entries form.

In the Spreadsheet (Excel or Other)...

9. **Delete all Items rows except for a main Item and subitems for *one* fixed asset.**

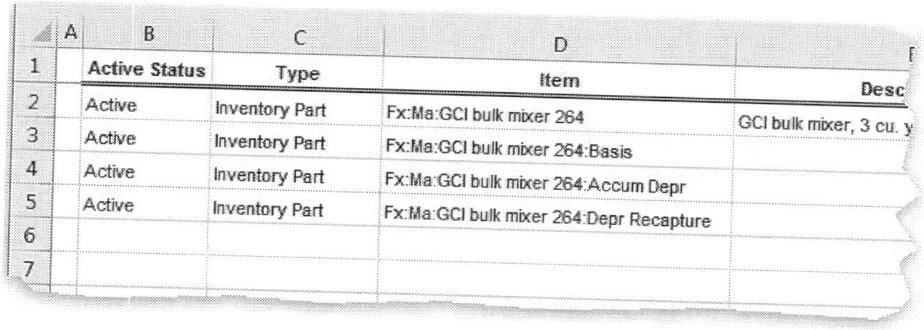

These rows will serve as a model for creating other sets of fixed asset Items.

10. **Delete worksheet columns** which are not present in the Add/Edit Multiple List Entries window in QuickBooks.

    Be careful! Some columns will have slightly different names in the worksheet, as noted here:

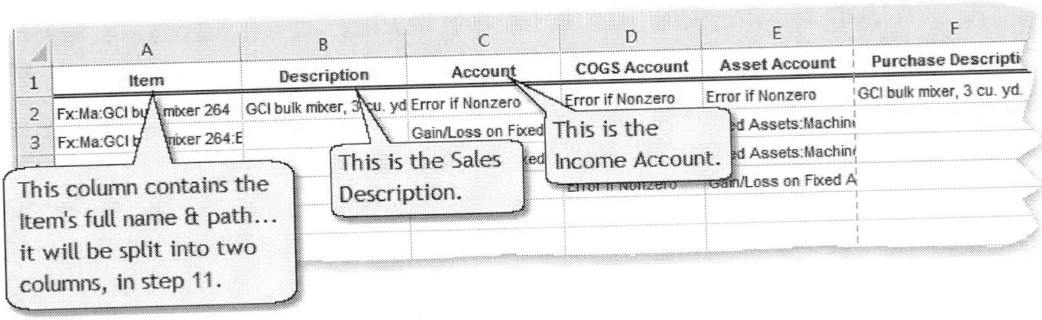

11. **Reorder and/or add columns** to match the column layout of the Add/Edit Multiple List Entries window.

    The Item column must be split into an Item Name column and a Subitem of column, as shown in the screenshot below, by inserting a blank column in the worksheet and splitting the Item column's contents appropriately. Because only a few rows are involved, you can manually split the column's contents among those two columns.

    When you are done, the worksheet's layout should match that of the Add/Edit Multiple List Entries window:

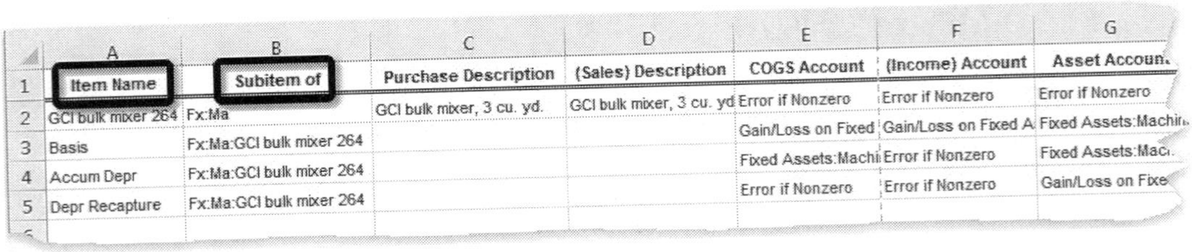

12. **Edit the rows, changing the parent Item name** to something like UNUSED, and erasing the contents of the both Description columns.

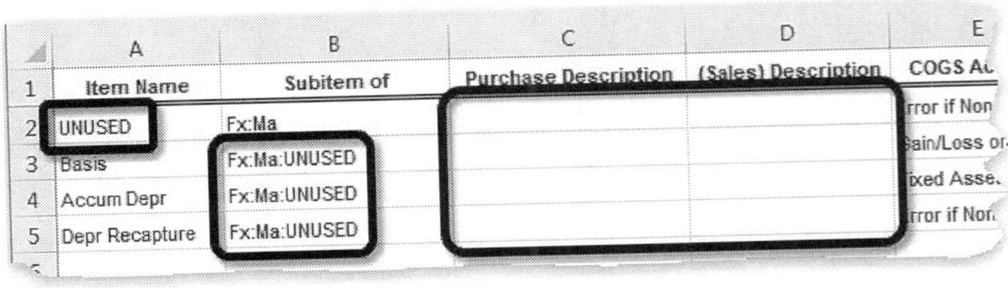

13. **Save the spreadsheet file** (File > Save), to have a permanent copy available to use again sometime in the future.

14. **Make several copies of the Item rows** (ten or more), so you will be able to adding a number of fixed asset Items to QuickBooks at one time.

   These Item definitions cannot be copied to QuickBooks just yet! They all defome *the same* parent Item name, "UNUSED", which will be changed in the steps below.

	A	B	C	D	E
1	Item Name	Subitem of	Purchase Description	(Sales) Description	COGS A
2	UNUSED	Fx:Ma			Error if No
3	Basis	Fx:Ma:UNUSED			Gain/Loss
4	Accum Depr	Fx:Ma:UNUSED			Fixed Asse
5	Depr Recapture	Fx:Ma:UNUSED			Error if Nor
6	UNUSED	Fx:Ma			Error if No
7	Basis	Fx:Ma:UNUSED			Gain/Loss
8	Accum Depr	Fx:Ma:UNUSED			Fixed Asse
9	Depr Recapture	Fx:Ma:UNUSED			Error if No
10	UNUSED	Fx:Ma			Error if No
11	Basis	Fx:Ma:UNUSED			Gain/Loss
12	Accum Depr	Fx:Ma:UNUSED			Fixed Ass
13	Depr Recapture	Fx:Ma:UNUSED			Error if No
14	UNUSED	Fx:Ma			Error if Non
15	Basis	Fx:Ma:UNUSED			Gain/Loss

15. **Edit the parent Item names to make them unique;** for instance, you might add a numeral to each one:

	A	B	C	D	
1	Item Name	Subitem of	Purchase Description	(Sales) Description	COGS
2	UNUSED	Fx:Ma			Error if
3	Basis	Fx:Ma:UNUSED			Gain/L
4	Accum Depr	Fx:Ma:UNUSED			Fixed A
5	Depr Recapture	Fx:Ma:UNUSED			Error if
6	UNUSED2	Fx:Ma			Error if
7	Basis	Fx:Ma:UNUSED2			Gain/L
8	Accum Depr	Fx:Ma:UNUSED2			Fixed As
9	Depr Recapture	Fx:Ma:UNUSED2			Error if
10	UNUSED3	Fx:Ma			Error i
11	Basis	Fx:Ma:UNUSED3			Gain/Los
12	Accum Depr	Fx:Ma:UNUSED3			Fixed A
13	Depr Recapture	Fx:Ma:UNUSED3			Error if
14	UNUSED4	Fx:Ma			Error if
15	Basis	Fx:Ma:UNUSED4			Gain/L

Experienced spreadsheet users may create formulas and macros to duplicate the rows and create unique Item names, instead of doing the job manually.

16. **Copy all of the worksheet's data cells** to the Windows clipboard (*do not* include the column headings), by highlighting the cells and then typing *Ctrl-C*.

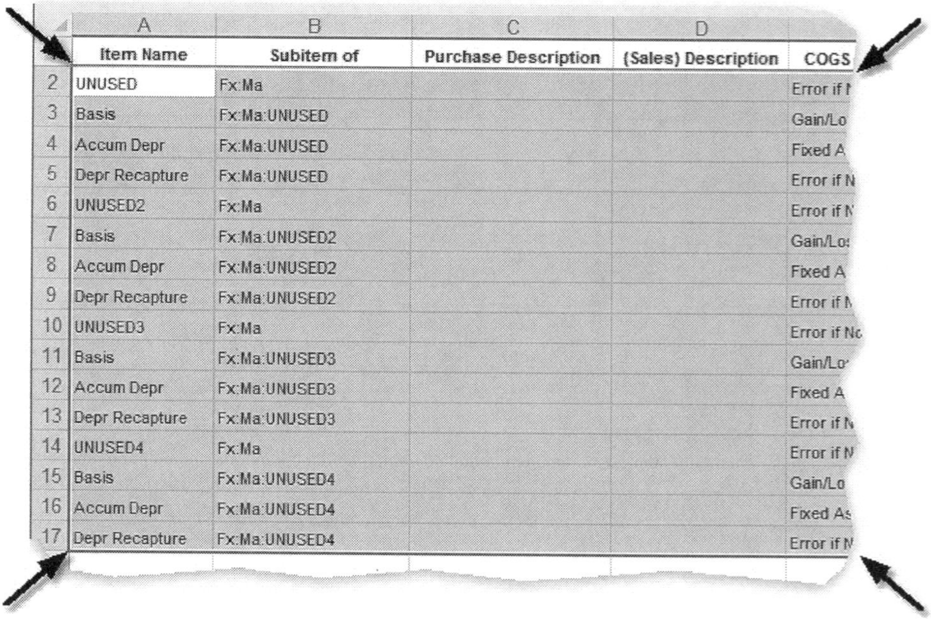

	A	B	C	D	
	Item Name	Subitem of	Purchase Description	(Sales) Description	COGS
2	UNUSED	Fx:Ma			Error if
3	Basis	Fx:Ma:UNUSED			Gain/Lo
4	Accum Depr	Fx:Ma:UNUSED			Fixed A
5	Depr Recapture	Fx:Ma:UNUSED			Error if N
6	UNUSED2	Fx:Ma			Error if N
7	Basis	Fx:Ma:UNUSED2			Gain/Los
8	Accum Depr	Fx:Ma:UNUSED2			Fixed A
9	Depr Recapture	Fx:Ma:UNUSED2			Error if N
10	UNUSED3	Fx:Ma			Error if No
11	Basis	Fx:Ma:UNUSED3			Gain/Lo
12	Accum Depr	Fx:Ma:UNUSED3			Fixed A
13	Depr Recapture	Fx:Ma:UNUSED3			Error if N
14	UNUSED4	Fx:Ma			Error if N
15	Basis	Fx:Ma:UNUSED4			Gain/Lo
16	Accum Depr	Fx:Ma:UNUSED4			Fixed As
17	Depr Recapture	Fx:Ma:UNUSED4			Error if N

In QuickBooks...

17. **Scroll down to the first blank line** at the bottom of the Add/Edit Multiple List Entries window, **and click in the first cell on that row.**

18. **Paste the clipboard contents by typing** *Ctrl-V,* to insert the Item definitions from the worksheet (which were copied to the Windows clipboard in step 16).

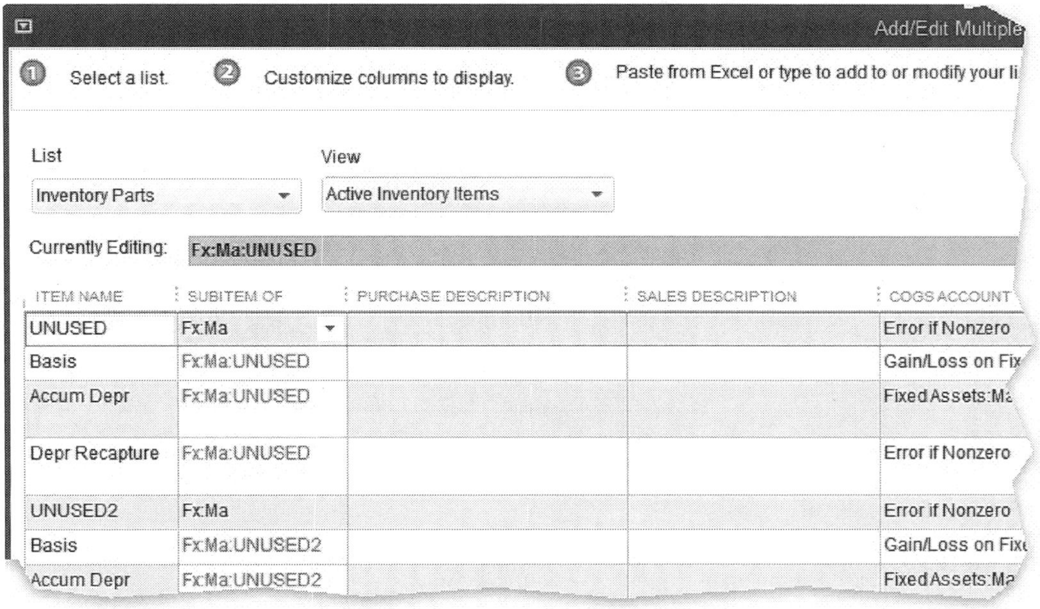

19. **Click the Save Changes button** to save the new Items.

    If QuickBooks detects any Item name conflicts or other problems it will require you to correct them before saving the new Items.

20. **Click the Close button** to close the Add/Edit Multiple List Entries window.

21. **Close the Item List window** if it was open while the new Items were being added**, then reopen it.**

The reason for this last step is that a minor bug in some QuickBooks editions keeps new Items from being immediately displayed in the Item List if they were added via Add/Edit Multiple List Entries. Closing and reopening the Item List window fixes the problem.

How to Use the New Items

When you acquire a new fixed asset and need a set of Items for it, simply edit one of the "UNUSED" parent Items, changing its Name and Descriptions to describe the new fixed asset. (The subitems do not need to be edited; only the parent Item's name needs to be changed.)

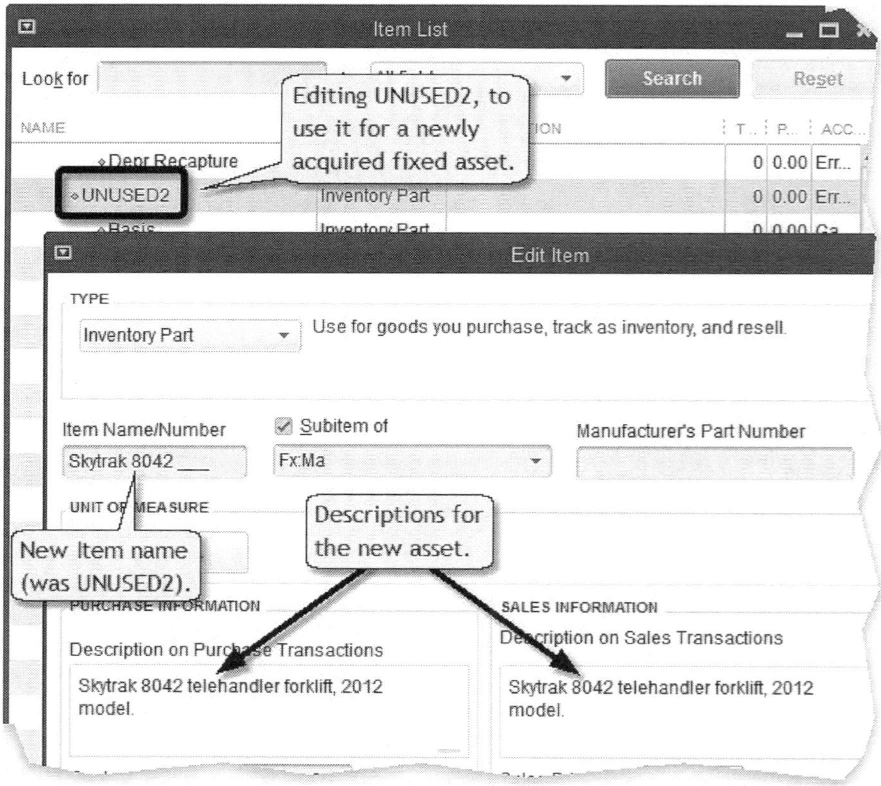

Depending on how you defined the UNUSED Items, you might also need to select a different Item in the *Subitem of* field. For example, if the UNUSED Item was created with Fx:Ma (machinery) as its parent Item but you need Item for a building, you might change the *Subitem of* to Fx:Bl (buildings).

To Add More New Items in the Future

In the above steps, the spreadsheet file containing the model set of fixed asset Items was saved [75]. So, you need only open it and repeat the subsequent steps to create more new blank/unused Items for adding to QuickBooks.

Getting Existing Fixed Assets into QuickBooks

There are several ways to get existing fixed assets established in QuickBooks. Here are two of the more straightforward approaches:

A. Only set up S/S-style Inventory Part Items [61] as you acquire new fixed assets. For existing fixed assets, continue handling depreciation expense and asset sales as you have in the past.

B. Set up S/S-style Inventory Part Items [61] for new assets as you acquire them *and* for existing assets, so that you can use the S/S method for all fixed assets. Enter transactions for the existing-asset Items to establish original basis and accumulated depreciation balances for them.

The approach you choose may depend on:

- How your assets are currently represented in QuickBooks (maybe not at all, in some cases).
- How important you feel it is to be using a single approach for all fixed asset transactions. (If you continue handling existing fixed assets as you have in the past but set up S/S-style Inventory Part Items for new assets as you acquire them, you will have to use two different methods for entering fixed asset sales, depreciation expense, etc.)

A. Only Creating S/S-style Items for Newly Acquired Fixed Assets

Assuming your existing fixed assets are represented just as asset account balances [10] in QuickBooks, you might choose to add Inventory Part Items only for new fixed assets as you acquire them. If so, here are some considerations:

- **Depreciation expense.** You will have to enter depreciation expense two different ways for a while: (1) for existing assets you will enter it as you have been (likely as an aggregate amount, in a single journal entry), and (2) for newly acquired assets, you will need to enter depreciation expense individually for each asset [156] using the S/S approach.

- **Sales** of existing assets will be entered as you have in the past, likely by using journal entries. Sales of assets you have set up using the S/S approach will be entered using Items [110].

- **Trade-ins.** Trading in an old asset for a new one will require a two-pronged approach because the new asset will be established using Items (necessary for using the S/S method), but the trade-in's book value will likely be represented as an asset account balance. This isn't difficult: in the Check (or other) transaction which records the purchase [102] of the new asset, enter the trade-in on the Expenses tab—to directly affect accounting balances—but enter the new asset on the Items tab.

What if your existing fixed assets are represented as Fixed Asset-type Items?

If so, and you have either the Accountant or Enterprise edition of QuickBooks, consider continuing to use Fixed Asset-type Items. Why? Because your QuickBooks edition includes the Fixed Asset Manager (FAM) software, which can calculate depreciation and perform other fixed asset chores, and FAM requires that you use Fixed Asset-type Items. For a discussion, see *QuickBooks' Fixed Asset Item Type* [15] in Chapter 2.

However, if you don't have the FAM software or you simply want to switch to using Inventory Part Items, you may continue entering fixed asset sales and depreciation expense as you have in the past, using Fixed Asset-type Items, and only set up Inventory Part Items for newly acquired fixed assets.

B: Creating S/S-style Items for All Fixed Assets (Existing, and Newly Acquired)

This approach requires more effort up front but may be easier in the long run, because once you have S/S-style Items set up for each of your fixed assets you will be able to handle all fixed asset transactions the same way.

Below are the three general steps for establishing S/S-style Items and asset balances for existing fixed assets. The examples assume you have been keeping track of fixed assets either outside of QuickBooks or by using Fixed Asset-type Items within QuickBooks, and that the fixed assets' book values are represented by balances in fixed asset accounts such as:

Fixed Assets
  Original Basis
  Accumulated Depreciation

(You may be using multiple accounts—more than shown here—but limiting the discussion below to these three will keep it simple.)

1. Set up Items for existing fixed assets

Set up a main Item and subitems for each fixed asset as described in *Basic Things to Know* 52 and *Item Setup Details* 61.

Because you will be setting up many Items all at once, using a spreadsheet to automate the job may save a lot of time. See *Automating Item Creation* 70 for details.

2. Establish an original basis for each fixed asset

Enter one or more checks drawn on the CLEARING account 38 to "purchase" the existing fixed assets as Items and thereby associate the assets' original basis amounts with the Items. (See *Entering a Purchase* 89 in Chapter 5 for details on entering fixed asset purchases.)

First, on the Items tab of the Checks form (Banking > Write Checks), enter an original basis amount for each fixed asset Item. (You may include any number of Items on the same check.)

Expenses $0.00 | Items $107,000.00

ITEM	DESCRIPTION	QTY	COST	AMOUNT
Fx:Ma:GCI bulk mixer 264:Basis		1	28,000.00	28,000.00
Fx:Ma:Dodge pickup 267:Basis		1	42,000.00	42,000.00
Fx:Ma:Clark forklift 248:Basis		1	37,000.00	37,000.00

Where do the original basis amounts come from? You might get them from an asset list you keep outside of QuickBooks, from the assets' purchase transaction, etc.

Next, enter the *negative* of the Items tab total on the Expenses tab, posting the amount to an asset account—usually, the same account which currently holds the assets' original basis amounts. The end result will be a check for a net amount of $0.

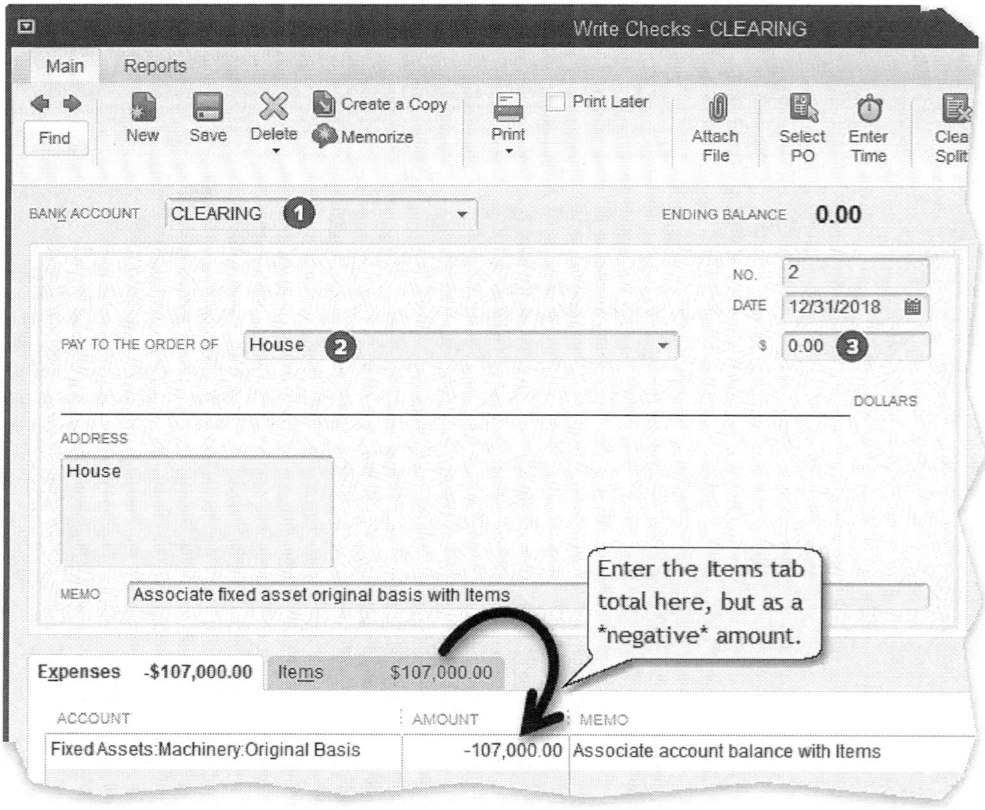

1. **Bank Account** should be a clearing bank account 38, because this is not an actual bank transaction.

2. **Payee.** *House* is a bogus customer or vendor name, set up to use for in-house transactions.

3. **$.** The net amount of the check must be $0—the Expenses tab and Items tab amounts should exactly offset each other.

If the same fixed asset account is used on the Expenses tab and also by the Items—i.e., if the Items post original basis to the same account as you were using before—then this transaction will have zero effect on the account's balance. Still, this step is necessary to get the assets' original basis amounts associated with Items.

3. Establish an accumulated depreciation balance for each fixed asset

Enter additional check(s) drawn on the CLEARING account 38 to establish accumulated depreciation balances, similar to the way checks are normally entered for depreciation expense 156.

First, on the Items tab of a Checks form (Banking > Write Checks), select fixed asset Items and enter an accumulated depreciation amount for each one. (You may include any number of Items on the same check.)

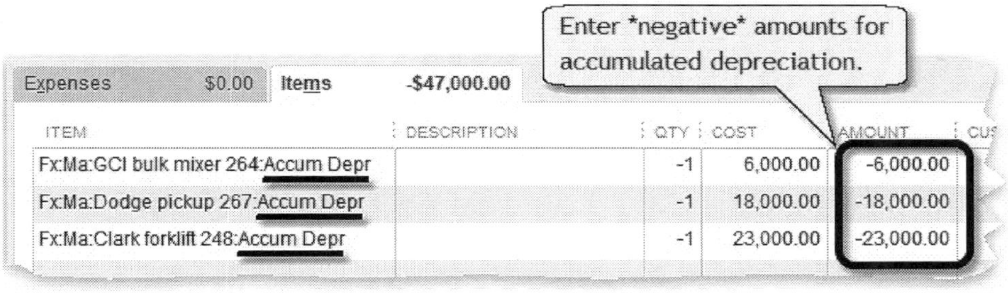

Where do the accumulated depreciation amounts come from? You might get them from an asset list you keep outside of QuickBooks, or from depreciation entries or calculations for prior accounting periods, etc.

Next, enter the *negative* of the Items tab total on the Expenses tab, posting the amount to an asset account—usually, the same account which currently holds the assets' accumulated depreciation amounts. The end result will be a check for a net amount of $0.

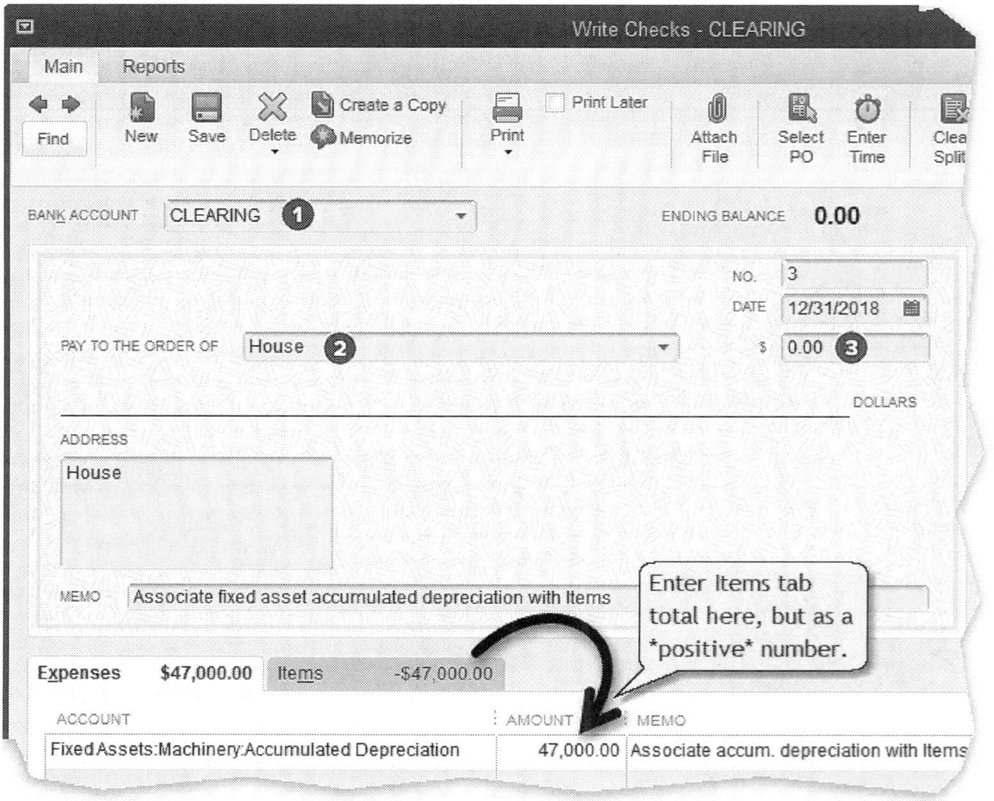

1. **Bank Account** should be a clearing bank account 38, because this is not a an actual bank transaction.

2. **Payee.** *House* is a bogus customer or vendor name, set up to use for in-house transactions.

3. **$.** The net amount of the check must be $0—the Expenses tab and Items tab amounts should exactly offset each other.

If the same accumulated depreciation account is used on the Expenses tab and also by the Items—i.e., if the Items post accumulated depreciation to the same account as you were using before—then this transaction will have zero effect on the account's balance. Still, this step is is necessary to get the assets' accumulated depreciation amounts associated with Items.

Getting Help!

When you have a question about accounting, or QuickBooks, or something related, where do you go for answers?

The first inclination of many people is to use Google, Yahoo, or another search engine and enter a search phrase related to their question. You can usually find answers this way...eventually. You might find the answers you need only after browsing through dozens of Web pages.

> **As this is written** a Google search for the word "QuickBooks" returns 15,800,000 search hits!

Here are some alternatives which are often better than doing an Internet search; places where you may ask questions and get answers specific to your question. All of these are free to use.

- **goflagship.com/forums** are forums operated by Flagship Technologies, Inc., the publisher of the QuickBooks Cookbook™ series, which includes this book. Some of the forum areas are specific to Flagship's software products but others are for general QuickBooks questions.

  > ***Author's note:*** *I monitor some of the activity in Flagship's forums. If you ask a general question there about fixed asset handling or anything else related to this book, I will try to answer.*

- **community.intuit.com** is operated by Intuit, the maker of QuickBooks. These forums have a high amount of daily traffic divided among subcategories specific to various Intuit products and services: QuickBooks desktop editions, QuickBooks Online, QuickBooks Payroll, TurboTax, and others.

  Despite a high level of message traffic, most of the informed, knowledgeable answers to questions are provided by a relatively small handful of people, especially in some subcategories. Intuit employees answer some questions, however their answers tend to be less reliable because the Intuit staffers who monitor the forums often have a limited amount of real-world experience.

- **LinkedIN.com** operates thousands of topic groups, including dozens specific to QuickBooks. (Anyone can start a LinkedIN group, on nearly any topic.) Some of the highest levels of professional accounting expertise available in any public forums can be found in some of the QuickBooks groups on LinkedIN.

You can search for "QuickBooks" to find QuickBooks-specific groups, but one of the best is called QuickBooks Tips & Tricks—a group started/owned by Ruth Perryman. (Several groups have "Tips & Tricks" in their name, which can make finding a particular group confusing if you don't know the name of the group owner.) If your question relates to income taxation, sales tax, payroll, fixed assets, or any technical QuickBooks accounting topic, this is a good place to ask it.

- **forums.QuickBooksUsers.com.** During the past few years these forums have lost part of their message traffic to Intuit's forums. However, this is still a great place to ask general QuickBooks questions. Some of the people who frequent these forums and answer questions are top notch and apparently don't spend much time on Intuit's forums.

Finding a QuickBooks Professional

The phrase "QuickBooks professional" can mean a lot of different things. It could mean someone who has extensive knowledge of QuickBooks, a good understanding of accounting, maybe some experience with software setup and with solving computer problems, or someone knowledgeable about QuickBooks and accounting in your specific type of business. Or it could just mean someone with a little QuickBooks experience who is in the business of providing QuickBooks advice.

Many CPA offices and other tax preparation firms have someone on staff with extensive QuickBooks knowledge. So a good place to seek expert QuickBooks help is often at the same firm you use for tax preparation. If they don't offer QuickBooks assistance another local firm might, or may be able to recommend someone else who has QuickBooks expertise.

Another place to find QuickBooks professionals is on Intuit's QuickBooks Pro Advisor Web site. The address of this site changes from time to time, so the best way to find it may be with an Internet search for "QuickBooks find a proadvisor". Once you've found the site, you may search by zip code for QuickBooks Pro Advisors in your area. These are QuickBooks professionals who are certified, at least to some degree, by passing an exam administered by Intuit.

Many QuickBooks professionals use remote access software to provide assistance by directly accessing your computer remotely, over an Internet connection. This allows them to make changes and corrections for you in QuickBooks, as both of you watch what is happening on the computer screen and talk by phone. The possibility of remote access gives you a broader range of QuickBooks professionals to choose from—the person you choose can literally live almost anywhere, yet still work directly with your QuickBooks data on your computer.

Maybe the most important step in choosing a QuickBooks professional is asking the right questions about their knowledge and experience. If you need help with tax or legal matters, be sure to find out whether they are knowledgeable about tax laws and regulations in your state and/or locality.

This page is intentionally blank.

For information on other books in this series go to:

www.goflagship.com

CHAPTER 5

Fixed Asset Purchases and Trade-Ins

About this chapter	This chapter show how to enter fixed asset purchases, including purchases involving trade-ins.

Entering a Purchase

Problem **We bought a new pickup truck today for $48,000—with no trade-in—and wrote a check for the purchase. How should I enter it in QuickBooks?**

Solution Because you wrote a check, enter the purchase on the Checks form.

Discussion The Checks form is for recording cash purchases, with funds withdrawn from a bank account.

In QuickBooks, the Bank account type is sometimes also used for representing accounts which are not traditional bank accounts. Examples would include a PayPal account or a prepaid MasterCard/VISA account—any financial account which normally carries a positive (asset) balance. If you use PayPal to pay for a fixed asset purchase, for example, the purchase would also be entered on the Checks form, but with your PayPal account selected in the Bank Account field.

- A ***cash purchase*** means making payment when you receive (or take delivery) of something. (The "cash" in cash purchase does not mean currency; it means any form of immediate payment, including checks, currency, money orders, etc.)

- A ***credit purchase*** means receiving or taking delivery of something but not making payment until later, with credit provided by a dealer, a bank, or another third party. The QuickBooks form you use for entering a credit purchase will depend on the kind of credit or financing involved. For details, see *Entering a Purchase with Financing* 93.

How to Enter a Fixed Asset Purchase, Paid by Check

1. **Open the Checks form** (Banking > Write Checks).

2. **Fill in the form** as shown below.

   The Items used is example are described in *Setting Up Items* 65 in Chapter 4.

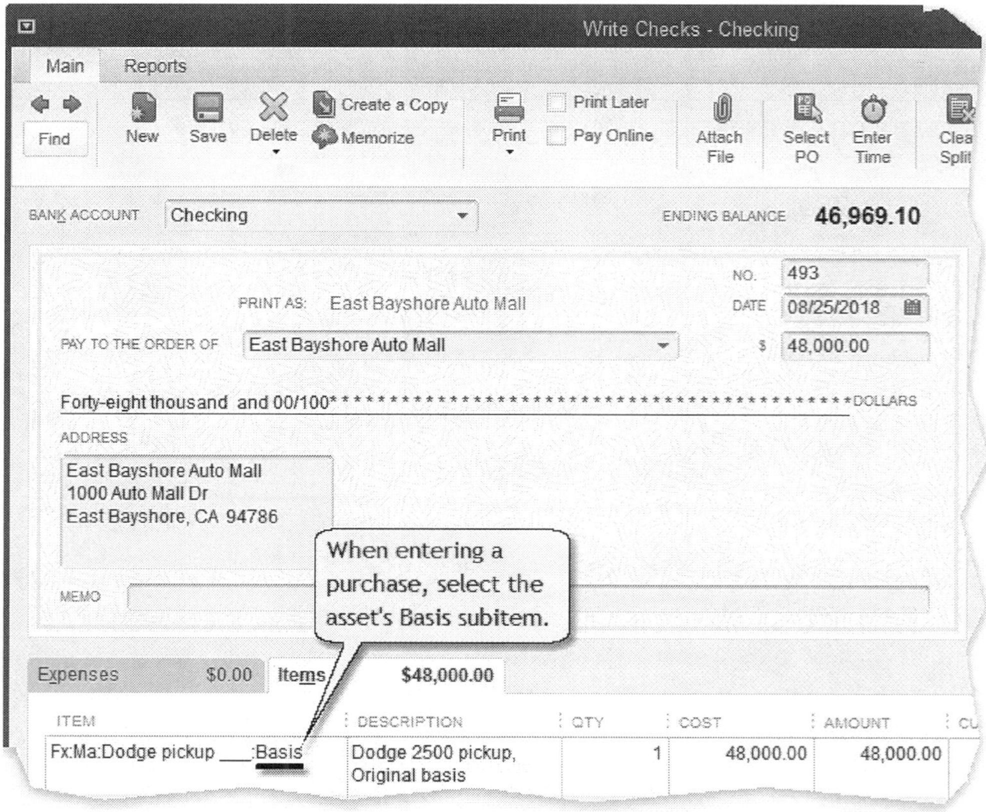

This is pretty much a "plain vanilla" check entry with no special requirements. Just be sure to select the asset's *Basis* subitem, not its main Item (which is *Fx:Ma:Dodge pickup ___* in this case).

3. **Click the Save & Close button** to save the check and close the form, **or Save & New** to save the check but keep the form open for entering another check.

Where to keep detailed notes for an asset

If you want to keep track of details about a fixed asset such as a serial number, machine hours at the time of purchase, model number, location code for property taxation, etc., you may (1) edit the asset's main Item (*Fx:Ma:Dodge pickup ___* in the example above) and add notes in the Purchase Description or Sales Description fields, or (2) click the *Notes* button when editing the Item, to add free-form notes:

However, including notes in fixed asset transactions—purchase and sale transactions, usually—may be quicker and easier, and makes the notes more accessible: you can find all of the notes entered for a fixed asset by opening a QuickReport 211 for its main Item, then drilling down to any transactions in the report to see the notes they contain. Here is an example of a note added in a purchase transaction:

To *drill down* in a report double-click any line in the report window, to open the source transaction for that line.

Seeing the Status of a Fixed Asset

At any time, you may want to see what transactions have been entered for a fixed asset. A good way to do that is to open an Item QuickReport 211 (customized to include the Amount column) for the asset's main Item. For the purchase example shown above, the main Item is *Fx:Ma:Dodge pickup ___*, and here is how its QuickReport might look after entering the purchase:

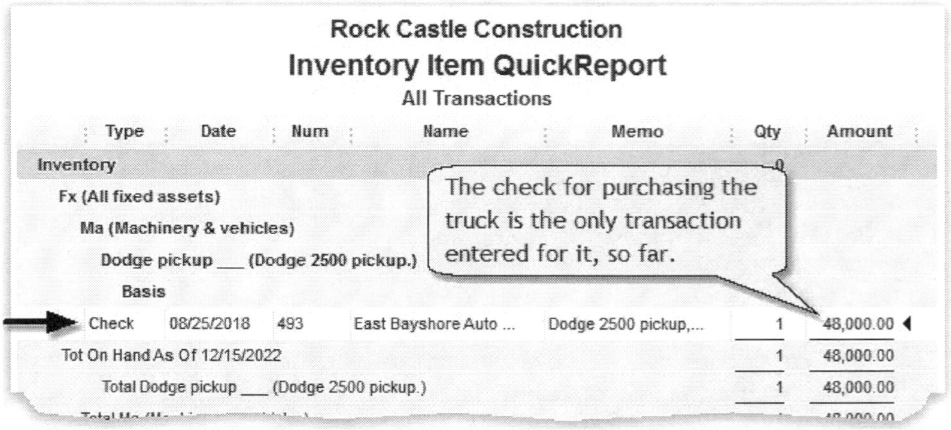

Entering a Purchase plus Financing

This section discusses common ways to finance a fixed asset purchase, and how to enter a financed purchase in QuickBooks.

Dealer Financing

Problem

We bought a new pickup truck today for $48,000, with no trade-in. We financed $40,000 of that amount through Chrysler Capital and wrote an $8,000 check for the difference. How should I enter this in QuickBooks?

Solution

You wrote a check, so record the purchase on the Checks form. Enter the pickup truck at its full cost, $48,000, on the Items tab, and enter the loan on the Expenses tab as a *negative* amount: -$40,000. This will leave the net amount of the check at $8,000—the amount you paid.

Discussion

Dealer financing means a loan obtained through a dealer in conjunction with an asset purchase. Like a bank loan, dealer financing agreements specify both an interest rate and a repayment schedule. The loan funds, however, are usually provided by a non-bank third party. For example, Chrysler Capital, GM Financial, and Ford Credit provide funds for dealer financing of vehicles purchased through Fiat Chrysler, General Motors, and Ford dealers.

Dealer financing is different from purchasing on an open account. With an open account 100 (dealer credit, trade account, etc.) the dealer (not a third party) provides the credit, and you normally must pay the balance you owe within a shorter period of time—typically 30 to 90 days.

When dealer financing is involved, it is usually an integral part of the fixed asset purchase, and all parts if the transaction—financing, plus any cash payment or trade-in—can be entered together on the Checks form. (Trade-ins will be discussed in the next section 102 of this chapter.)

Setting up a loan account

Before entering the purchase it's a good idea to set up an account in QuickBooks to represent the dealer financing loan. Here are the steps for setting up the account.

1. **Open the Chart of Accounts window** (Lists > Chart of Accounts) and **select** Account > New from the button menu at the bottom.

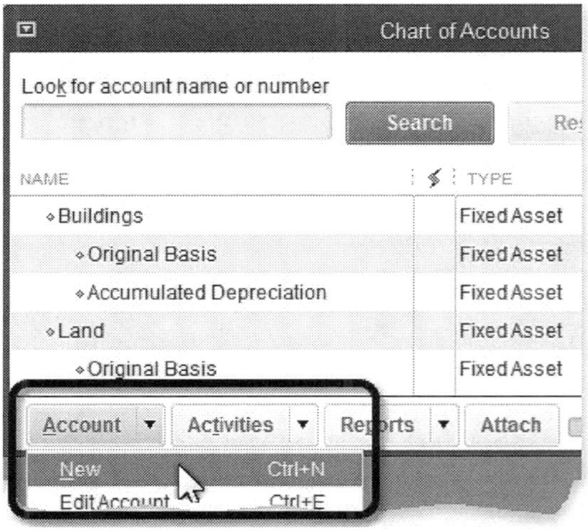

The Add New Account: Choose Account Type window will open.

2. **Select Long Term Liability** as the account type, **then click the Continue button.**

   Loans you expect to pay off over more than one year's time are long term liabilities.

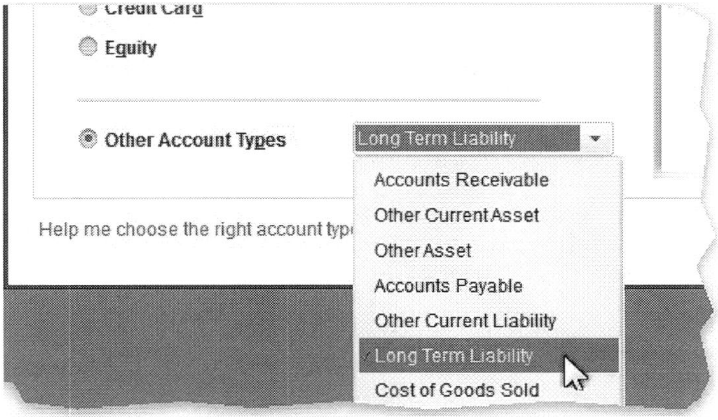

   The Add New Account window will open.

3. **Fill in the account details** in the The Add New Account window.

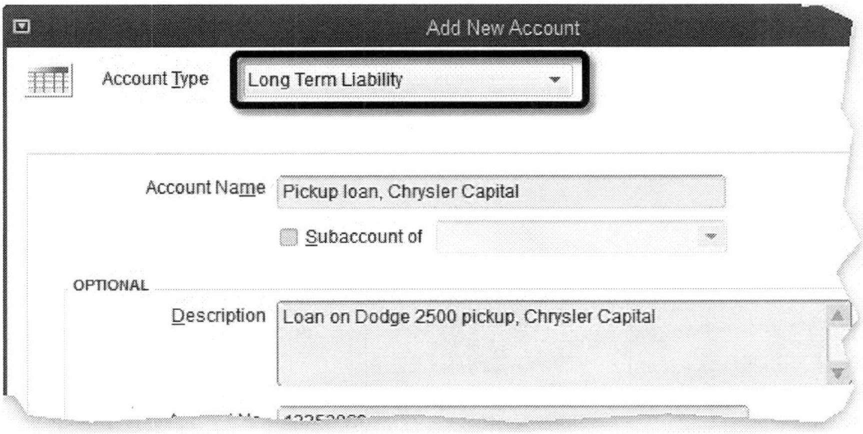

4. **Click the Save & Close button** to save the new account and close the window.

Entering a check for the asset purchase (plus dealer financing and a down payment)

The Items used in this example are described in *Setting Up Items* 65 in Chapter 4.

1. **Open the Checks form** (Banking > Write Checks).

2. **Fill in the Items tab of the Check** as shown below.

   Use the asset's *Basis* subitem for recording the purchase.

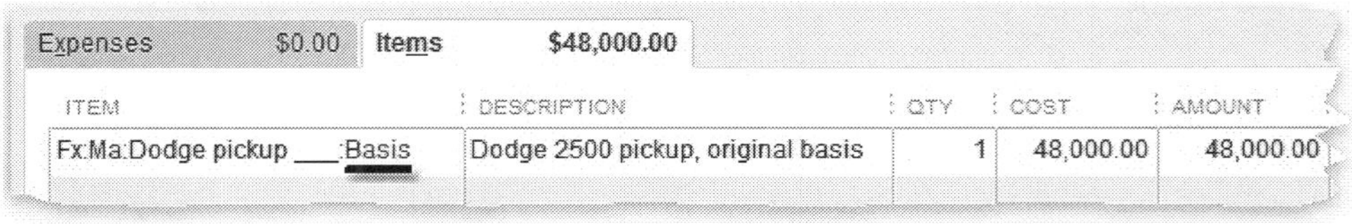

3. **Fill in the Expenses tab of the check** as shown below.

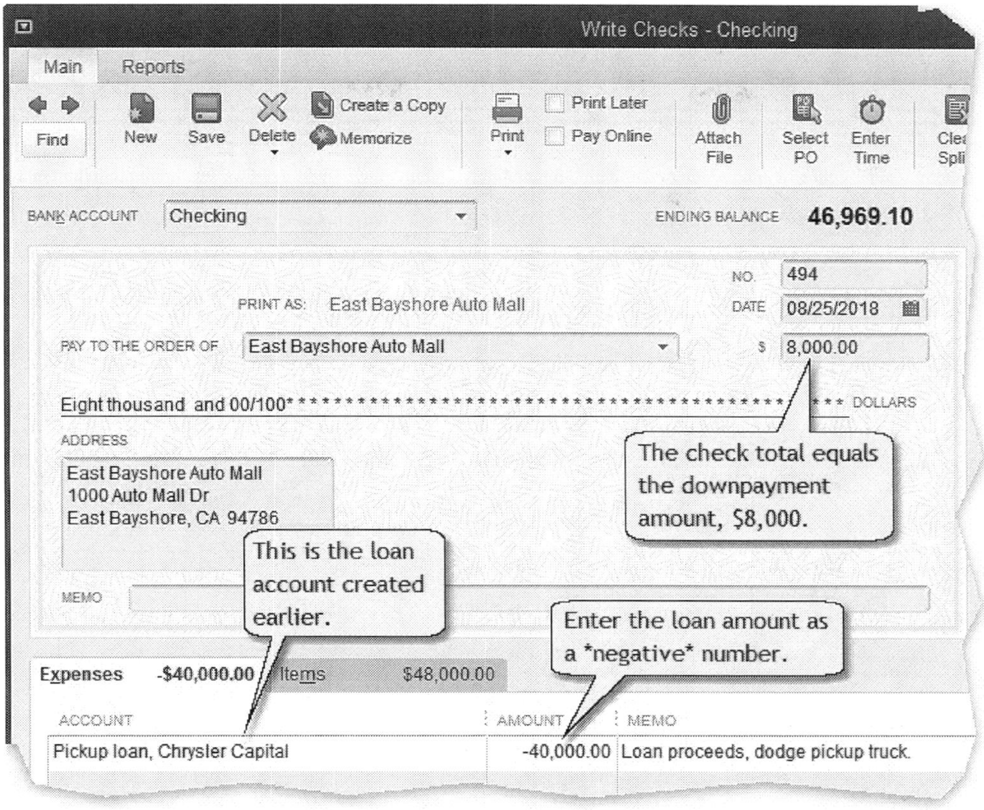

The difference between the truck's purchase price, $48,000, and the loan amount, $40,000, results in a net amount of $8,000 for the check.

Why is the loan amount a negative number? Think of it this way: normally you would enter loan proceeds as a *deposit* to your checking account. But here the loan proceeds are being entered on a check, which is the opposite of a deposit. So the loan is entered as a *negative* amount here—the equivalent of entering it as a *positive* amount on the Deposits form.

4. **Click the Save & Close button** to save the transaction and close the window, or **Save & New** to save the transaction and keep the window open for entering another check.

What if no down payment was involved?

Asked differently, what if you were allowed to finance the entire purchase and therefore did not make a down payment? In that situation, how should the fixed asset purchase and the loan be entered in QuickBooks?

Though you would not be writing a check to the dealer you would still enter the purchase on the Checks form—but for a net amount of $0 (known as a *zero-dollar check*). And the check would be drawn on a clearing bank account 38—a bogus bank account set up for such transactions. A clearing account lets you enter transactions on the Checks form without involving a real-world bank account.

Zero-dollar checks are a popular QuickBooks technique. They let you enter transactions on the Checks form which otherwise would typically have to be made as journal entries.

Here is the same pickup truck purchase shown earlier except that this time the entire purchase was financed, resulting in a $0 net amount for the check (which is drawn on the CLEARING bank account 38).

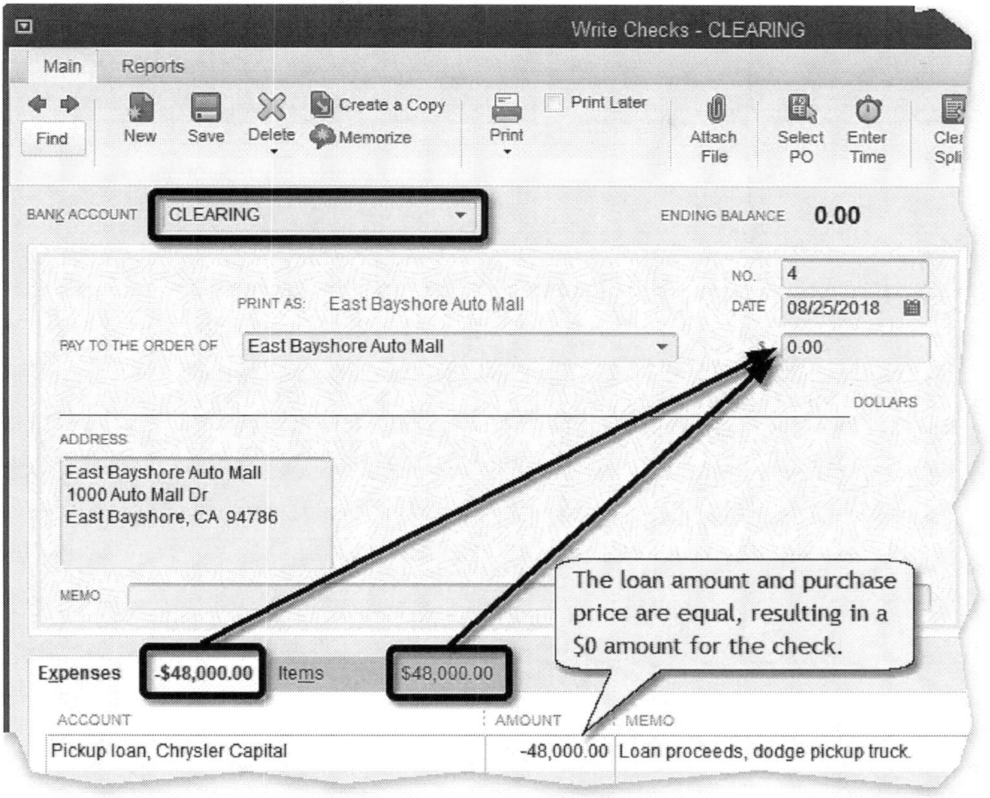

Bank Loans

When you take out a bank loan to buy a fixed asset, the loan transaction is usually separate from the fixed asset purchase, and both are entered in QuickBooks as separate transactions. Assuming the bank deposits the loan proceeds into your checking account you would:

1. **Set up a liability account** in the Chart of Accounts to represent the loan, as shown earlier 94 for dealer financing.

2. **Enter a Deposit** (Banking > Make Deposits) to record receipt of the loan proceeds into your checking account:

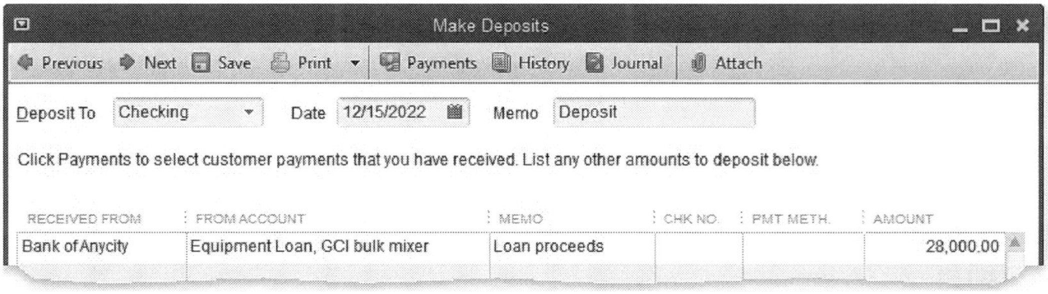

The fixed asset would then be paid for by check, and entered as shown earlier in *Entering a Purchase* [89].

Open Account (Dealer Credit, Trade Account, etc.)

When you make a purchase on an open account, also known as dealer credit or a trade account, the credit is provided by a dealer—no third party lender is involved. Also, the credit terms tend to be less formal than for a loan: the interest rate on unpaid balances you owe may not be specified in a formal lending agreement but set by company policy (limited by your state's lending laws). Often, no set repayment schedule is involved.

> **If you read the fine print on the dealer's invoice,** in many cases you may see that by signing the invoice—or simply by making the purchase—you have agreed to make payment within 30 days or some other specified time period. However, some dealers allow customers to carry significant open account balances for much longer.

Amounts you owe on open accounts are *accounts payable*, a category of current liabilities managed using QuickBooks' Bills features (Enter Bills, Pay Bills). If you purchase a fixed asset on an open account, enter the purchase using the same approach as in the Check example [90] shown earlier in the chapter, but on the Bills form (Vendors > Enter Bills).

Credit Cards

Credit cards are another category of current liabilities, with credit provided by credit card-issuing banks. If you purchase a fixed asset using a credit card, enter the purchase on the Credit Card Charges form (Banking > Enter Credit Card Charges), using the same approach as shown in the Check example 90 earlier in the chapter.

Whose credit card is it?

Before entering a business purchase made by credit card, the first question to ask is "Whose credit card is it?" Is the card owned by the business, or is it a personal card?

❖ **Sole proprietorships.** The best approach is to sign up for two or more credit cards, then reserve one of them for business purchases and the other(s) for personal use. This simplifies bookkeeping for business purchases because only those made using the business' card will need to be entered in QuickBooks.

  Another approach—especially appropriate if you have only one checking account and use it for both business and personal funds—is to consider all of your credit cards to be "owned" by the business. Then you can enter business purchases made by credit card as business expenses, and enter personal spending as owner's draws (withdrawals of capital) from the business. You can do that by posting personal expenses to Equity type accounts when you enter the credit card charges (Banking > Enter Credit Card Charges).

❖ **Partnerships.** Credit card purchases made by partners (using their own personal cards) should be reimbursed by the partnership or treated as capital additions to the partnership. Having a credit card account owned by the partnership is ideal, but qualifying for a credit card account in the partnership name is not always easy. Often, one of the partners applies for a card that will be used by the partnership, with the partnership paying the monthly bill.

❖ **LLCs and Corporations.** Having a credit card account owned by the LLC or corporation is best. If that is not possible, individuals (partners, shareholders, employees) may use their own credit cards to make company purchases, so long as:

  - The purchases are fully reimbursed by the company, based on a receipt provided by the individual. A receipt is necessary as documentation of the purchase, so the company can verify that the reimbursement was for a business purchase and was not a payment to the individual.

- Reimbursements are made in a timely manner. If reimbursements are delayed for several months, the credit card purchases may appear to have actually been a casual "loan" to the LLC or corporation by its partners or shareholders—which increases the risk of piercing the veil of corporate liability protection.

Entering a Purchase with a Trade-In

Problem **We bought a new pickup truck today, trading in an old pickup plus writing the dealer a check for $20,000. How should I enter the purchase in QuickBooks?**

Solution You wrote a check so record the purchase on the Checks form, and record the trade-in as part of the same transaction. Follow the steps in the example below to determine your basis in the new pickup, which consists of the $20,000 cash amount you paid plus the remaining basis (undepreciated book value) of the pickup which was traded in.

Discussion If you create the Check entry in the proper order—by following the steps in the example below—*QuickBooks will calculate the trade-in's remaining basis for you,* making the entry much easier.

Including the new asset purchase and the trade-in on the same Check provides several benefits:

- Having the trade-in's details on the Check **allows QuickBooks to calculate the trade-in's remaining basis,** which you will need for determining the original basis (beginning book value) of the new asset.
- It **eliminates the need to enter a separate transaction** to zero out the trade-in's book value (basis and accumulated depreciation).
- It **creates a two-way linkage between the trade-in and the newly acquired asset.** From an Item QuickReport 211 for the new asset, you can drill down to the purchase transaction to find out what was traded in for it. And from an Item QuickReport 211 for the traded-in asset, you can drill

down to the transaction which closed out the Item's book value, to find out what new asset was acquired with the trade-in.

How to Enter a Purchase with a Trade-In

What about entering partial-year depreciation for the trade-in?

To properly account for a trade-in, depreciation expense[147] should be entered for the part of the year you owned the asset before it was traded in (if it has any remaining depreciable value). Enter the partial year of depreciation expense first, so the trade-in's accumulated depreciation balance will be up-to-date when you record its use as a trade-in.

The *Calculate partial-year depreciation*[177] topic in Chapter 9 shows a simple way to figure the partial-year amount.

Do I really have to enter partial-year depreciation?

Whether or not to enter partial-year depreciation is an accounting choice—something to discuss with your accountant. It may be important to do if the business' financial statements are viewed by others outside of the business and are assumed to have been prepared using standard accounting practices, but many small businesses—especially sole proprietorships and partnerships whose financial statements are mostly for internal purposes—forgo entering partial-year depreciation to avoid the extra effort it requires.

Advanced user tip:

You can enter partial-year depreciation on the same Check where you record the trade-in. To do that, enter the partial year of depreciation expense on the Check *first*, then *save the Check* to update the trade-in's accumulated depreciation balance. After that, you can add the trade-in and the purchased Item to the same Check (see detailed steps below). The Check will have a $0 amount when first saved but will have a positive amount after you have added the trade-in and purchase amounts.

The Items used in this example are described in *Setting Up Items*[65] in Chapter 4.

1. **Open the Checks form** (Banking > Write Checks).

2. **Select the trade-in's Org Basis and Accum Depr subitems,** on the Items tab.

   Recommended: leave a couple blank rows at the top for adding the new Item you are purchasing, which will happen in step 5.

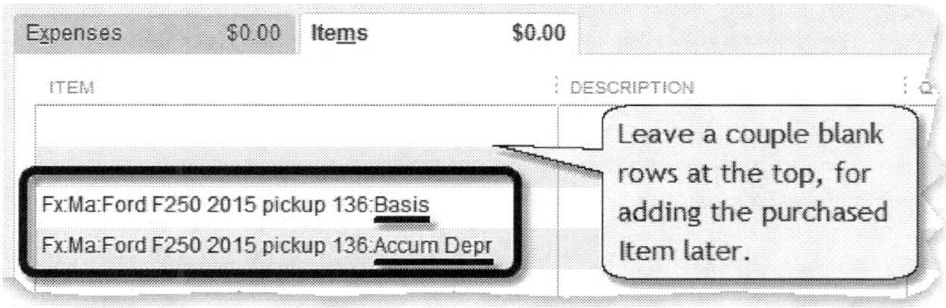

3. **Look up the trade-in's Org Basis and Accum Depr balances.**

   You must *look up* the current balance for both Items. *Do not rely on the Cost which QuickBooks has calculated for them.* The S/S method manipulates Items in a nonstandard way, which can cause QuickBooks' calculated Cost for a fixed asset Item to be *incorrect*.

One place to look up each Item's balance is in a Fixed Asset Book Values report[217], like the one shown below. (Another would be in an Item QuickReport[89] customized to include the Amount column.)

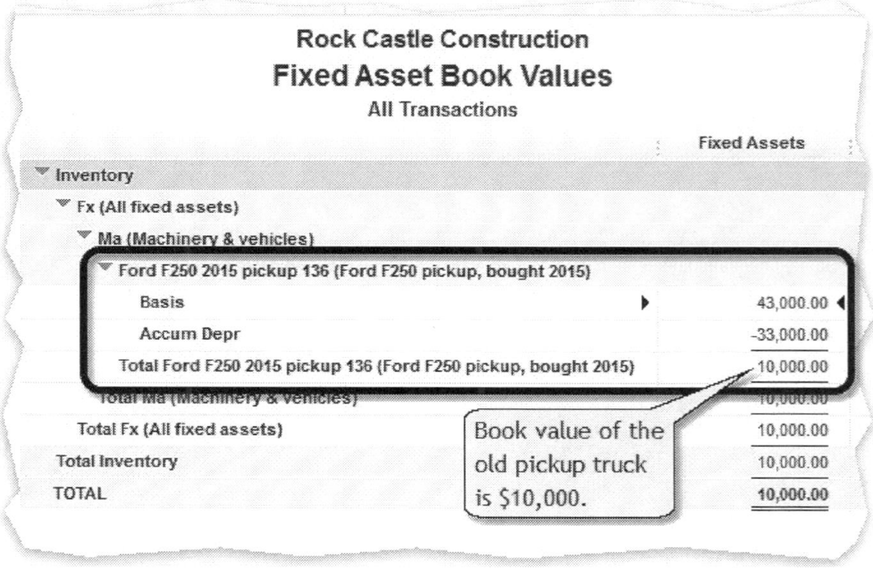

4. **Enter the Org Basis and Accum Depr balances,** on their respective lines of the Items tab.

   A major reason for including the trade-in's Items on the Check is to zero out their balances. To do that, enter the Basis amount as a *negative* number and the Accum Depr amount as a *positive* number:

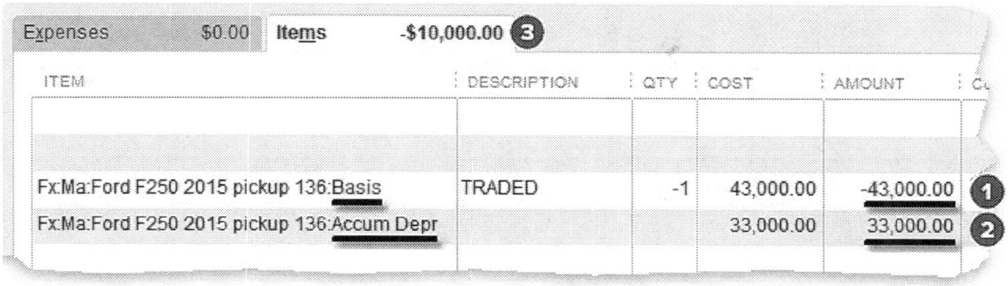

   ❶ **Basis.** Enter the *negative* of the balance for the Basis subitem, from the report in step 3.

   ❷ **Accum Depr.** Enter the the Accum Depr subitem's balance from the report as a *positive* number. The balance shown in the report is -$33,000, but it must be entered here as $33,000 (a *positive* number).

   ❸ **Items tab [total].** This tells us that the Ford F250 pickup's remaining undepreciated book value is $10,000. (Note that this matches the book value in the report shown farther above.)

   Is the trade-in part of an asset group? An Item can represent a group of like assets [143] which were all purchased at the same time. If only part of the group is being traded in, the Qty (quantity) on the Basis line should be the number of group members being traded in. Also, the Basis and Accum Depr amounts must be *proportional to the number of group members begin traded in*. For details, see *Working with Group Assets* [143].

5. **Select the new asset's Basis subitem** on the first line of the Items tab, **and enter its original basis** in the Amount column.

   This example assumes you have created an Item for the new asset [65]. If not, you will need to do that first.

Let's think about this...in step 4 we saw that the old pickup's remaining book value was $10,000. If the additional cash to be paid is $20,000, together they make the new pickup's original basis (beginning book value) $30,000. As you can see below, entering an original basis amount of $30,000 leaves $20,000 as the net amount of the check—which is exactly the amount paid by check.

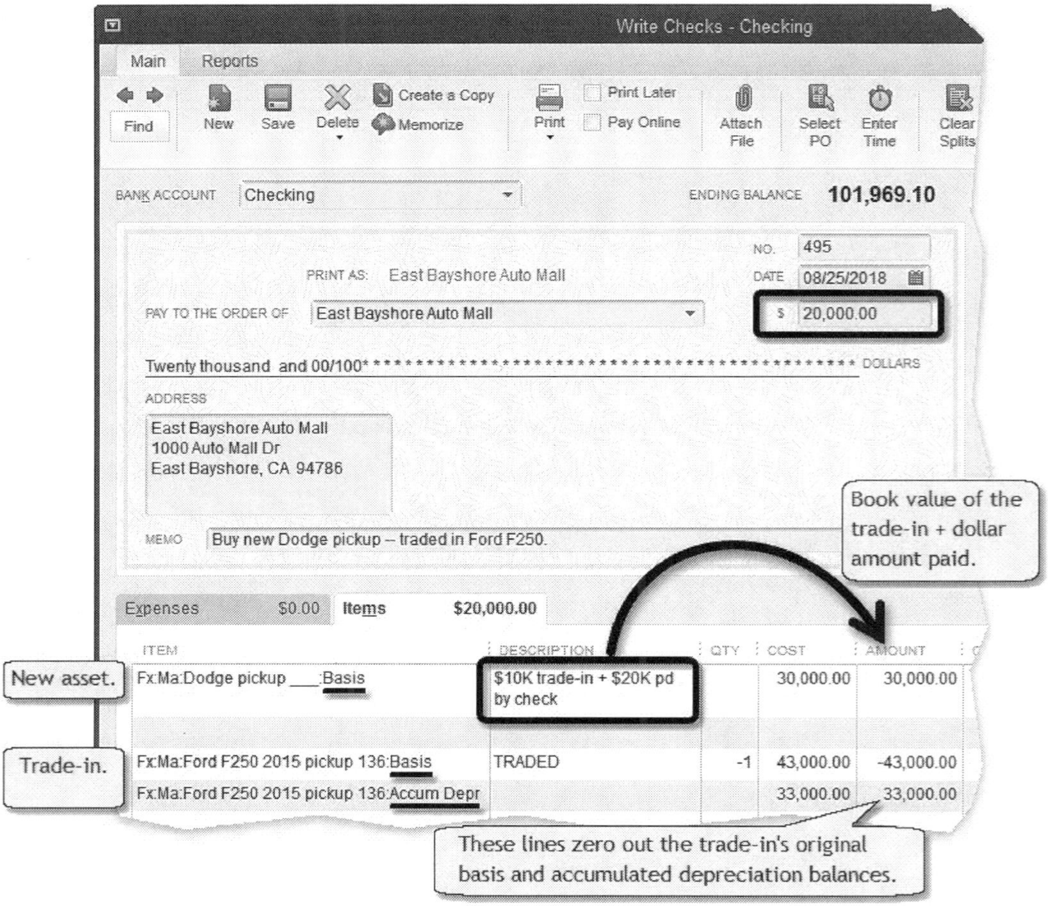

Putting the new asset's Item on the first line is optional, but because it is the asset being purchased, that seems like the most sensible location for it. (Use Edit > Insert Line if you need to insert blank lines at the top of the Items tab.)

6. **Click the Save & Close button** to save the check and close the form, **or Save & New** to save the check and keep the form open for entering another check.

Seeing the Trade-In's Status

If you want to see the status of a fixed asset after trading it in on another, you can use an Item QuickReport 211 customized to include the Amount column. The trade-in's book value should be zero, because the entire book value has been transferred to the new asset as part of its original basis (beginning book value).

This report example was prepared by filtering it by *Fx* (the master parent Item 55 for all fixed assets) so it includes both the old pickup which was traded-in, and the new pickup. (In a real-world report other assets would likely be included also.)

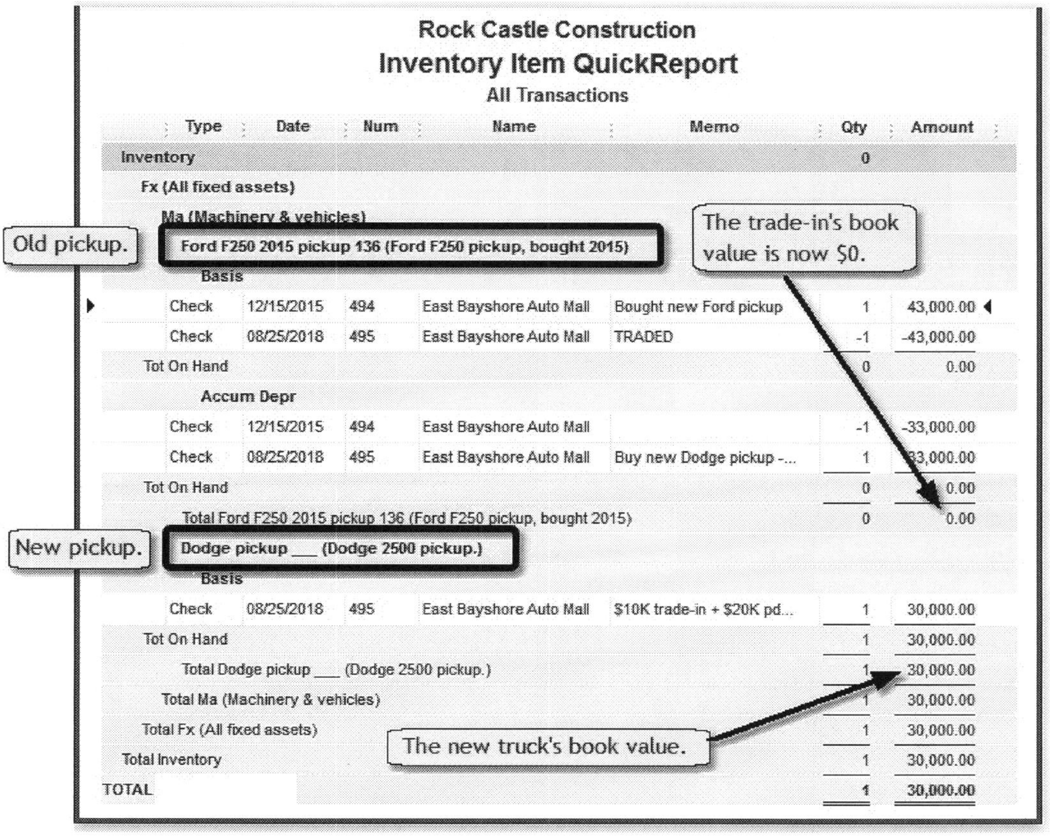

Rock Castle Construction
Inventory Item QuickReport
All Transactions

	Type	Date	Num	Name	Memo	Qty	Amount
Inventory						0	
Fx (All fixed assets)							
Ma (Machinery & vehicles)							
Ford F250 2015 pickup 136 (Ford F250 pickup, bought 2015)							
Basis							
	Check	12/15/2015	494	East Bayshore Auto Mall	Bought new Ford pickup	1	43,000.00
	Check	08/25/2018	495	East Bayshore Auto Mall	TRADED	-1	-43,000.00
Tot On Hand						0	0.00
Accum Depr							
	Check	12/15/2015	494	East Bayshore Auto Mall		-1	-33,000.00
	Check	08/25/2018	495	East Bayshore Auto Mall	Buy new Dodge pickup -...	1	33,000.00
Tot On Hand						0	0.00
Total Ford F250 2015 pickup 136 (Ford F250 pickup, bought 2015)						0	0.00
Dodge pickup ___ (Dodge 2500 pickup.)							
Basis							
	Check	08/25/2018	495	East Bayshore Auto Mall	$10K trade-in + $20K pd...	1	30,000.00
Tot On Hand						1	30,000.00
Total Dodge pickup ___ (Dodge 2500 pickup.)						1	30,000.00
Total Ma (Machinery & vehicles)						1	30,000.00
Total Fx (All fixed assets)						1	30,000.00
Total Inventory						1	30,000.00
TOTAL						1	30,000.00

This page is intentionally blank.

For information on other books in this series go to:

www.goflagship.com

CHAPTER 6

Fixed Asset Sales & Disposals

About this chapter	This chapter shows how to enter transactions when a fixed asset leaves the business—is sold, destroyed, or salvaged.

Entering a Sale

Problem **We sold an old pickup truck today—the buyer wrote us a check for $15,000, and no trade-in was involved. How should I enter the sale in QuickBooks?**

Solution This is a cash sale, so enter it on the Sales Receipts form. Because the truck was sold outright, also make a second entry to record gain or loss on the sale.

Discussion Purely from an accounting standpoint, a *cash sale* means selling or delivering something and being paid immediately, and a *credit sale* means selling or delivering something but not expecting to receive payment until later—even if "later" is only a few days later.

Cash sales are normally entered on the Sales Receipts form (Customers > Create Sales Receipts).

Some people also enter sales on the Deposits form (Banking > Make Deposits). However, it does not support using Items, which are required for the S/S method 18.

Credit sales are entered in two steps: (1) you enter the sale on an Invoice (Customers > Create Invoices) when you deliver whatever was sold, or when it is picked up by the buyer, then (2) when the buyer pays, you receive payment on the invoice (Customers > Receive Payments) to "close" it—to cancel out the amount the buyer owes on the invoice.

From a practical standpoint, things sometimes work a bit differently. If the buyer in this example had offered to write you a check next Tuesday, and you agreed to those terms, *technically* the sale of the pickup truck would be a credit sale. But especially in small businesses where avoiding paperwork is often an important goal, you might just wait until payment is received to record the sale—in which case you would enter it as a cash sale, on the Sales Receipts form.

How to Enter a Fixed Asset Sale

With the S/S method [18], two steps are involved in recording the sale of a fixed asset: (1) enter the sale, then (2) enter a second transaction to record gain or loss on the sale [109] and zero out the asset's accumulated depreciation balance.

Here are the steps for entering the sale:

1. **Open the Sales Receipts form** (Customers > Enter Sales Receipts).

   (If the pickup truck were being sold on credit, you would enter the sale on an Invoice.)

2. **Fill in the form** as shown below.

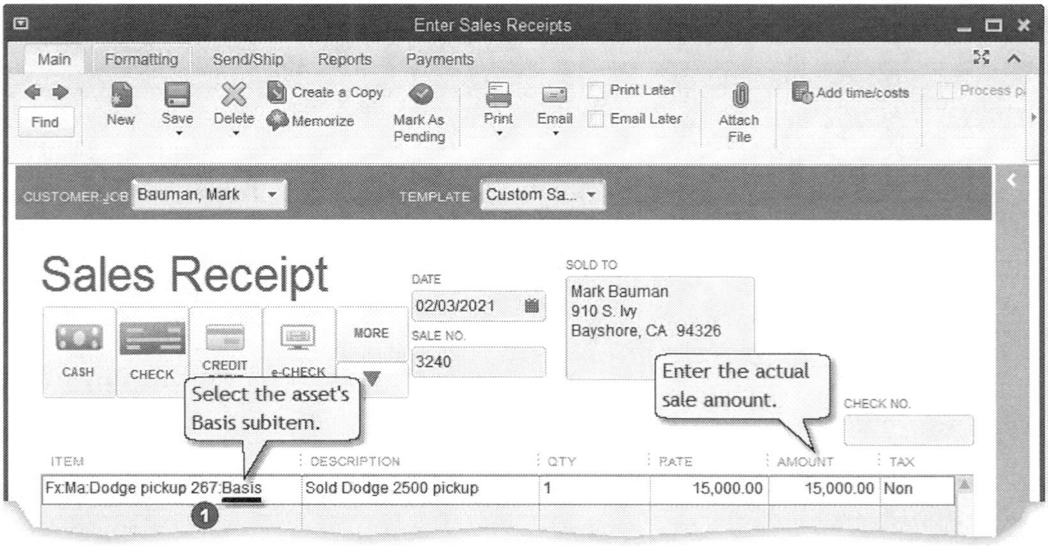

1 **Item.** This pickup truck is the same asset as shown in the Fixed Asset Purchases 89 chapter, but here the Item name has a number (267) at the end, while in the Purchases chapter it had underscores (___). Why? The number is an asset number assigned by the business' tax preparer 56 when income taxes were prepared for the year in which the truck was purchased. The Item name has been edited to include this number.

3. **Click the Save & Close button** to save the transaction and close the form, **or Save & New** to save the transaction and keep the Sales Receipts form open for entering another sale.

How to Record Gain or Loss on the Sale (and Zero Out Accumulated Depreciation)

When a fixed asset is sold outright, in addition to the sale you need to make a second entry to (1) calculate gain or loss on the sale (the calculation happens automatically), and (2) zero out the asset's accumulated depreciation balance, to remove it from the balance sheet.

Making this entry requires two steps: first you need to look up the sold asset's accumulated depreciation balance, then enter the transaction on the Checks form.

Accounting 101: What does "gain or loss on sale of an asset" mean?

Depreciation 147 involves writing off the purchase cost of a fixed asset as an expense over the years of its expected useful life. Let's suppose you purchase a machine for $50,000, and that you will depreciate it at the rate of $10,000 per year over an expected lifetime of five years. Let's further suppose that after the second year you sell the machine.

The machine's book value is its original purchase cost minus the total amount of depreciation expense which has been written off so far, known as accumulated depreciation. The original purchase cost was $50,000 and the total depreciation amount, or accumulated depreciation, is $20,000 (2 years * $10,000 per year), so the machine's book value is $50,000 - $20,000 = $30,000.

But what if you sell the machine for $35,000? That's $5,000 more than its book value, which means that owning the machine actually cost you only $15,000 instead of the $20,000 which has been written off as depreciation expense. The $5,000 then, is a *gain on the sale* of the machine. It is treated as income on profit and loss statements to offset the "excess" amount of depreciation expense you have deducted during the prior two years.

What if instead of $35,000 you sold the machine for $25,000—or $5,000 *less* than the machine's $30,000 book value? That would amount to a $5,000 *loss on the sale* of the machine. The loss would be reported as an expense on profit and loss statements, to reflect the fact that not enough depreciation expense was written off during the two years of owning the machine—the machine's actual value declined faster than its book value implied.

This explanation is a bit simplistic but should give you a general idea of what "gain or loss on the sale of a fixed asset" means.

Gain or loss is only involved when an asset is sold, not when it is traded in for another asset [102]: the remaining book value of a trade-in simply becomes part of the book value of the newly acquired asset.

What about partial-year depreciation?

To properly account for the sale of a fixed asset, depreciation expense [147] should be entered for the part of the year you owned the asset before it was sold—if the asset had any remaining depreciable value, that is. Enter the partial year of depreciation expense *before* entering the depreciation recapture transaction shown below [115], so the asset's accumulated depreciation balance will be correct ahead of entering that transaction.

The *Calculate partial-year depreciation* [177] topic in Chapter 9 shows a simple way to figure the partial-year amount.

The reason for entering partial-year depreciation is to meet the accounting goal of matching fixed asset costs with the revenue those assets helped to produce. However, entering partial-year depreciation is an accounting choice —something to discuss with your accountant. It may be important to do if the business' financial statements are viewed by others outside of the business and are assumed to have been prepared using standard accounting practices, but many small businesses—especially sole proprietorships and partnerships whose financial statements are mostly viewed internally—forgo entering partial-year depreciation to avoid the extra effort it requires.

(1) Look up the sold asset's accumulated depreciation total

To zero out an asset's accumulated depreciation balance you have to know what that balance is. You can find it in a couple different ways. One is in a Fixed Asset Book Values report [217]—a custom report described in Chapter 10 [211]. Another is an Item QuickReport [211] customized to include the Amount column, which is described in Chapter 10 [211].

Here are the steps for using the QuickReport to look up an asset's accumulated depreciation balance. The steps assume you have memorized the report [215] to allow recreating it quickly and easily.

1. **Select** Reports > Memorized Reports to see the list of memorized reports.

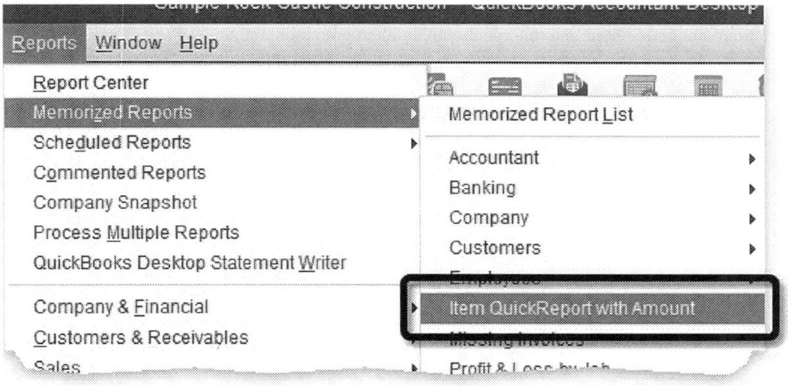

2. **Click on *Item QuickReport with Amount*** (or whatever other name you may have used when you memorized the report).

   The report window will open.

3. **Click the Customize Report button** at the top of the report window.

   The Modify Report window will open.

4. **Set an Item filter** for the report, by selecting the Item you want to know about—the Dodge pickup truck in this case.

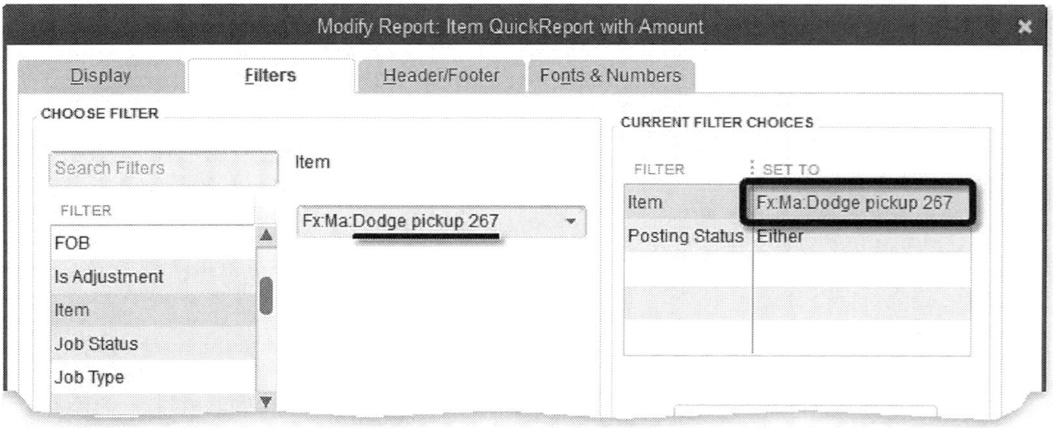

5. **Click the OK button** to close the Modify Report window and update the report:

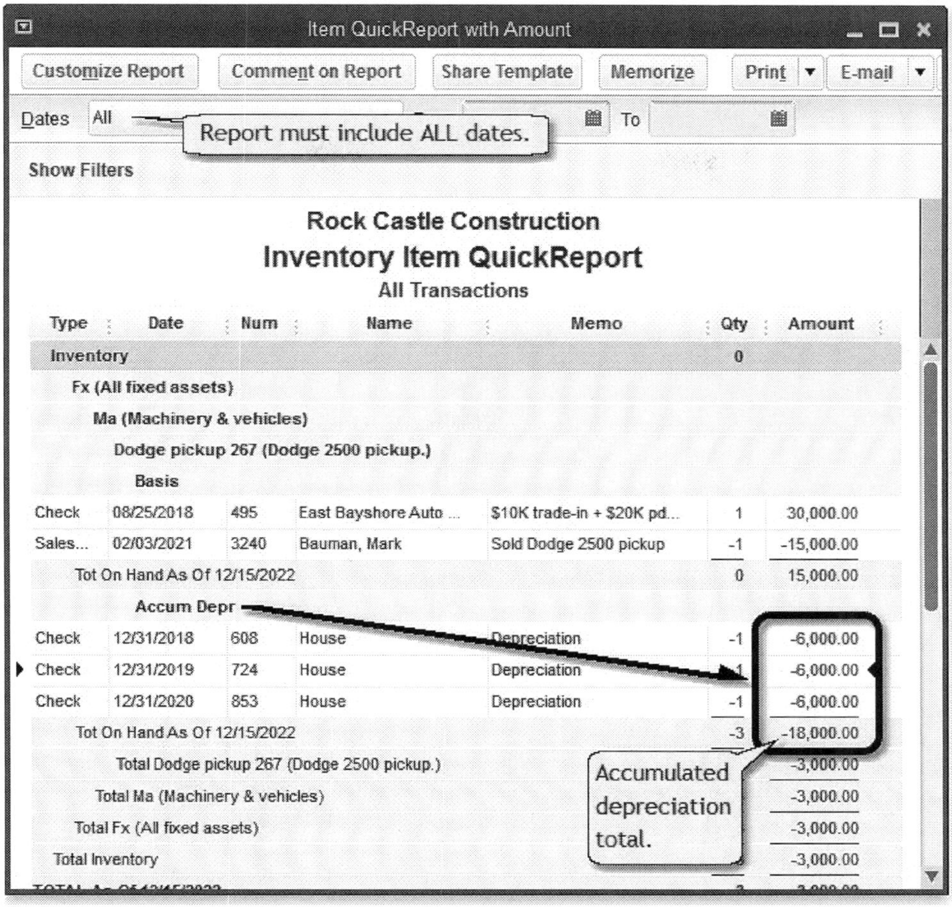

6. **Write down or remember the accumulated depreciation total** to use in the Check entry, described next.

(2) Enter a zero-dollar Check to record depreciation recapture

A *zero-dollar check* is a check entered for a net amount of $0, usually drawn on a clearing bank account 38 to avoid confusion with transactions in your real bank account.

1. **Open the Checks form** (Banking > Write Checks).
2. **Fill in the form** as shown below.

> **You might think that you could avoid making this entry** by simply adding the depreciation recapture details to the Sales Receipt or Invoice

which recorded the sale of the asset. *But that is not so!* Different accounts are affected when an Inventory Part Item is used on a sales form vs. a purchases form, so depreciation recapture _must_ be entered on the Checks form.

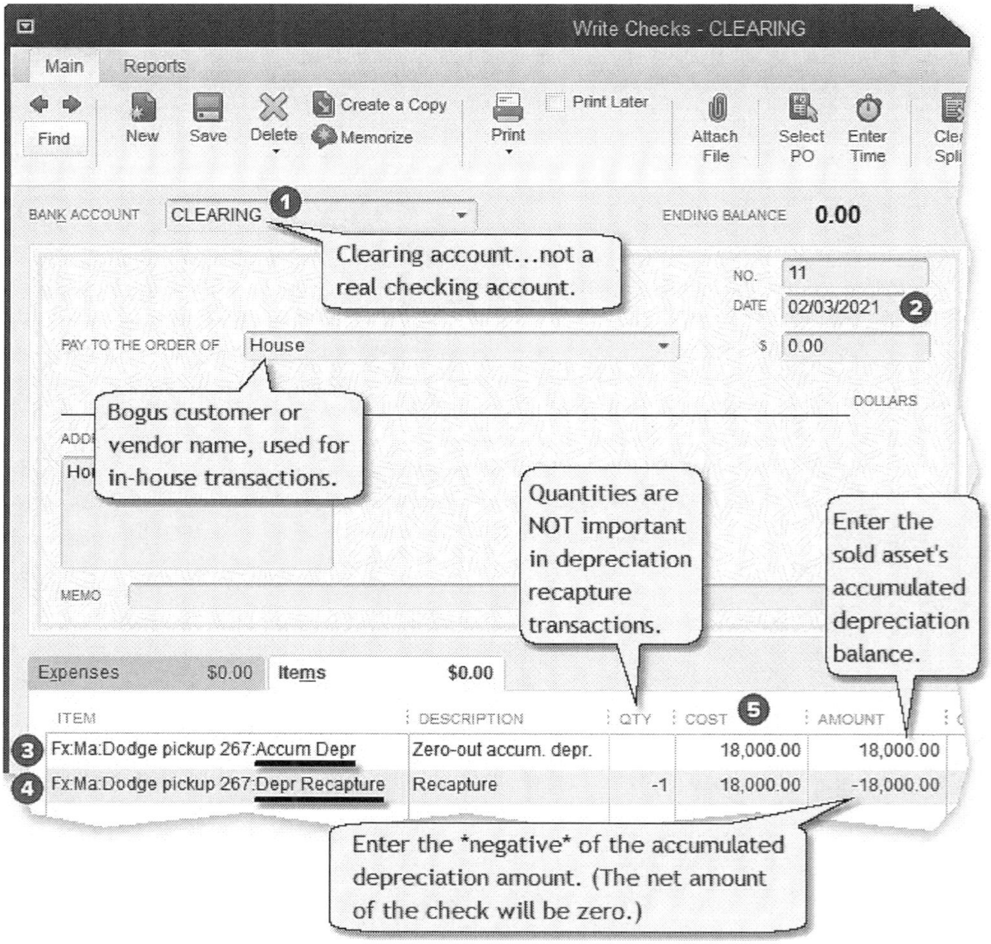

1. **Bank Account** should be a clearing bank account 38, because this is not an actual bank transaction.

2. **Date** should be the same as for the fixed asset's sale transaction, or at least within the same accounting period.

3. **Accum Depr.** The purpose of this line is to zero out the pickup truck's accumulated depreciation balance. Enter the Amount as a

positive number to offset (zero out) the Accum Depr Item's negative balance.

4. **Depr Recapture.** This line is an important part of the automatic calculation of gain or loss when a fixed asset has been sold outright. Enter *the negative of* the amount on the Accum Depr line.

5. **Cost.** *Do not* depend on using the *Cost* displayed by QuickBooks when you first select an Item. It *will often be wrong* for the Accum Depr subitem, because of how Items are configured for the S/S method 18. Just be sure the Amount on each line matches the accumulated depreciation total you looked up 113 for the asset.

3. **Click the Save & Close button** to save the transaction and close the Checks form, **or Save & New** to save the transaction and keep the form open for entering another check.

But I've heard "Never sell an Item if it will cause the Item to have a negative inventory quantity."

You've heard correctly. In the QuickBooks desktop editions you should avoid entering <u>*sale*</u> transactions which will result in a negative quantity on hand for an Item. If you do, QuickBooks can become confused about the order of purchases and sales, causing it to incorrectly calculate the Item's average cost —or worse, corrupt the QuickBooks database!

So is there a problem with having a negative quantity for Depr Recapture?

No, for several reasons:

- Depr Recapture subitems are only used in *purchase* transactions—never in *sale* transactions. (Because depreciation recapture is entered on the Checks form, QuickBooks handles it as a "purchase" even though nothing is actually being purchased.) Consequently, the Cost which QuickBooks calculates for a Depr Recapture subitem is never used for posting Cost of Goods Sold to any account.

- The timing of purchases and sales for a Depr Recapture subitem never affects how its Cost is calculated by QuickBooks—again, because *Depr Recapture subitems are never used in sale transactions*. So the way Depr Recapture subitems are used does not contribute to any risk of database corruption.

- Depr Recapture subitems post to an Other Income account, not to Cost of Goods Sold as Inventory Part Items normally do, so there is no chance of incorrectly calculating Cost of Goods Sold.

Seeing Results of the Sale

After entering the sale 110 and depreciation recapture 111 transactions, the pickup truck's basis and accumulated depreciation amounts should be zero, and any gain or loss on the sale should have been posted to the Other Income account you have set up for gains and losses 47.

Verifying that the sold asset's book value has been closed (zeroed out)

The Fixed Asset Book Values Report 217 is a good place to verify that the sold asset's basis and accumulated depreciation balances have been zeroed out, if you want to do that (it is optional). Here is the report, showing that the pickup truck's basis and accumulated depreciation balances are now zero.

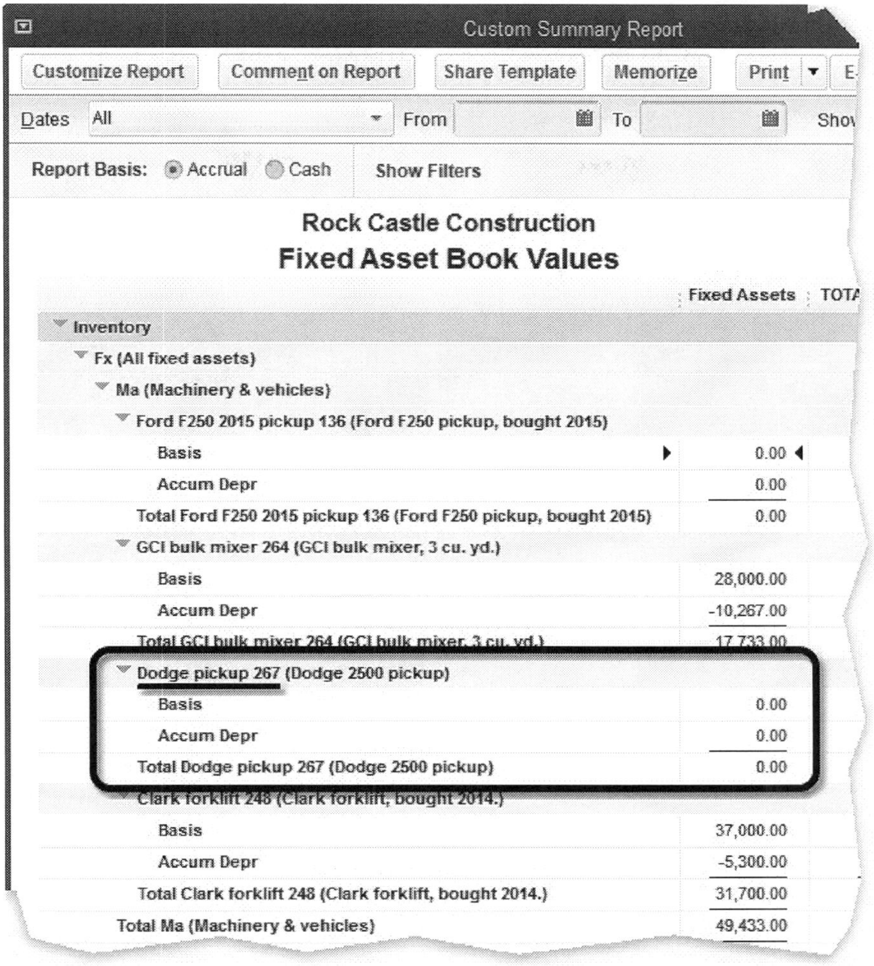

Could I have used an Item QuickReport instead?

No! After an asset has been sold, an Item QuickReport [211] will imply that the asset's Basis has not been zeroed out *even though it has been.* (This is because of how income accounts are used by Items in the S/S method [18].) Also, an Item QuickReport *will* show the amount of gain or loss on the sale *but the sign will be reversed*—i.e, a loss will show up as a positive amount; a gain will be negative.

To avoid confusion *only use reports recommended in this book for getting specific kinds of fixed asset information.*

Seeing the amount of gain or loss on the sale

QuickBooks' standard Item reports don't show fixed asset gains and losses in a very intuitive format. A better choice is to prepare a Fixed Asset Sales Report 228—a custom report which shows fixed asset sales during the accounting period, plus the gain or loss on each sale. Here is the report, filtered to only include the pickup truck's Items, showing that there was a $3,000 gain on the sale:

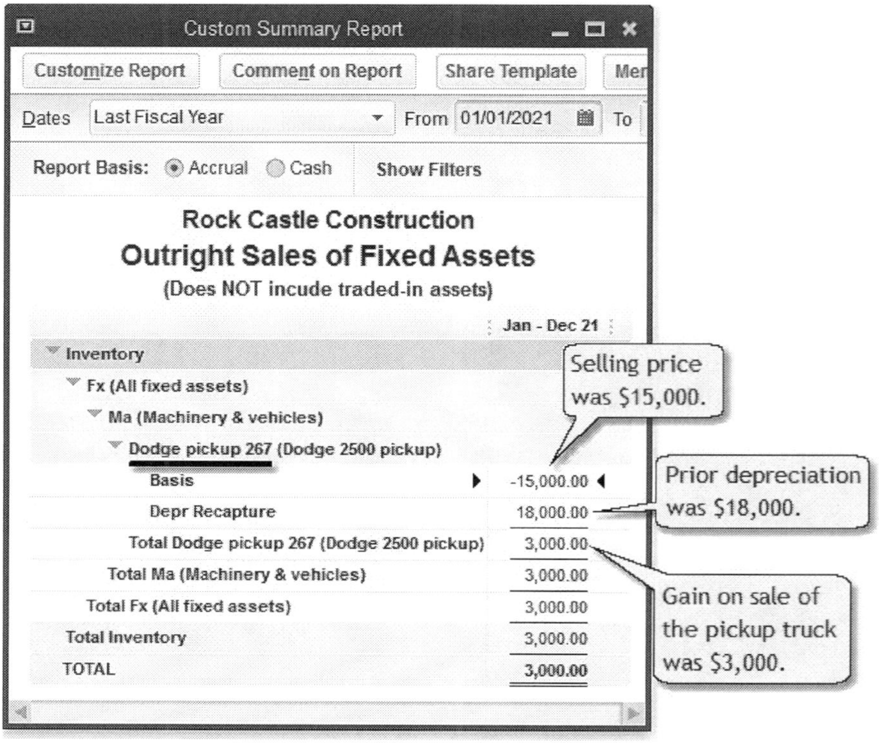

Gains and losses also show up in the Other Income section of Profit and Loss reports (Reports > Company & Financial > Profit & Loss Summary). Gains and losses for *all* fixed asset sales made during the period covered by the report will be provided as a single amount:

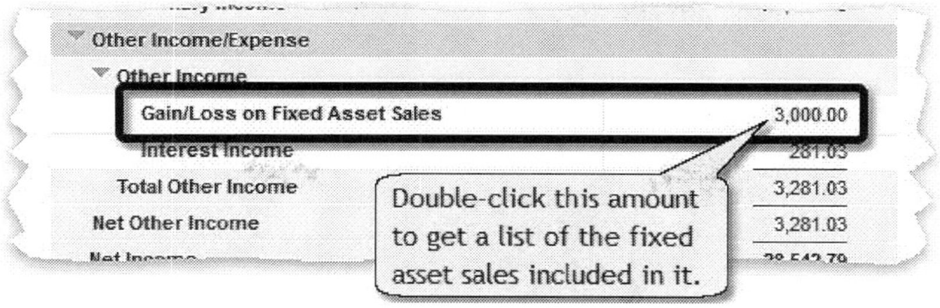

Retiring the Sold Asset's Item

After the year's accounting has been completed and income taxes have been prepared, it's a good idea to retire [121] Items representing fixed assets which were sold or disposed of during the year, so they will no longer appear in fixed asset reports.

Retiring Items for Sold/Disposed of Fixed Assets

After a fixed asset has been sold or disposed of and income taxes for the year have been prepared, you may not want to see that asset in reports any more. You may go to the Item List and mark the asset's main Item as inactive, but that still won't prevent the Item from showing up in reports. A better remedy is to "retire" fixed assets you no longer own, by assigning them to a different parent Item.

Wait until the year's income taxes have been filed before retiring fixed asset Items, to assure that the year's tax reports include all fixed assets sold or disposed of during the year.

The first step is to create an Inventory Part Item to use as a master parent Item for fixed assets you retire. Here is the setup window for an Item named FxRETIRED, created for that purpose. (An error indicator account [49] is selected in each of the account fields because this Item should not itself be used in transactions—it's sole purpose is to serve as a parent Item for retired fixed asset Items.)

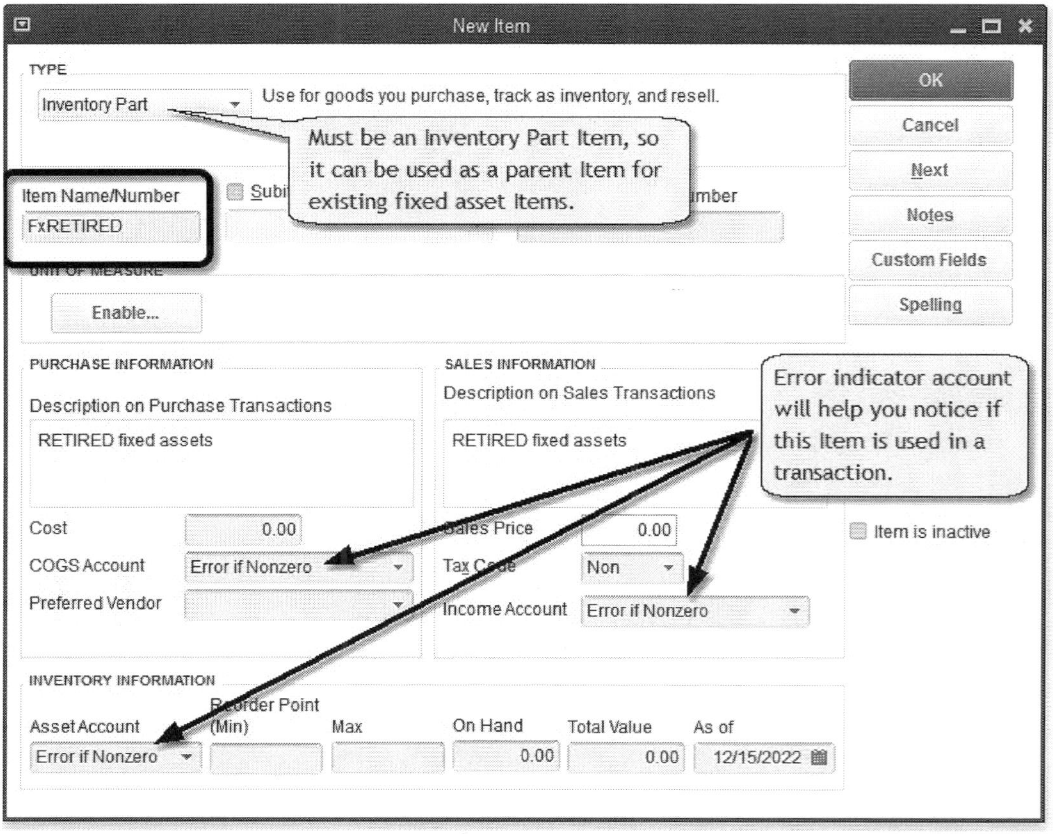

After creating FxRETIRED (or other Item of your choosing) you can use it to "re-parent" Items representing fixed assets you no longer own. For instance, suppose you have sold a pickup truck which has *Fx* as its master parent Item:

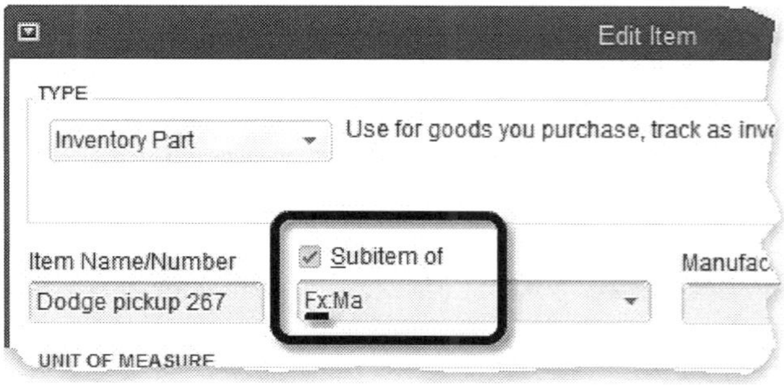

To retire the asset, edit its main Item, selecting FxRETIRED as the parent Item:

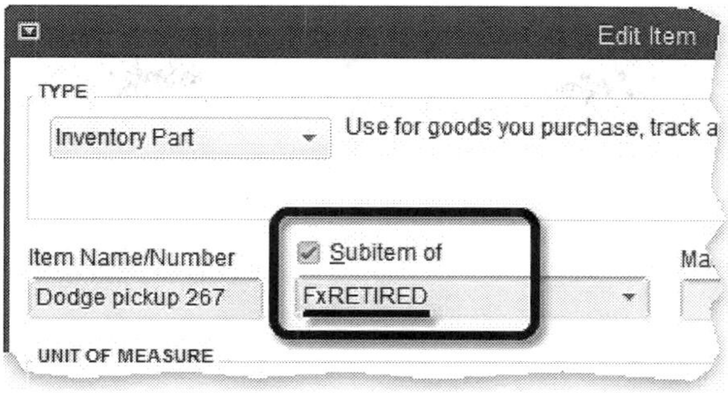

After saving this change, the Item will no longer appear in reports filtered for *Fx*. But you can still look up transactions and information about the Item in the Item List, as a subitem of FxRETIRED, and in reports filtered to show FxRETIRED and its subitems.

Entering Fixed Asset Damage, Salvage, or Disposals

Recording Major Damage to a Fixed Asset

Problem **We bought a number of pallet racks for our warehouse a couple years ago and began depreciating the entire lot as a fixed asset. Last week a tornado caved in a warehouse wall and part of the roof, destroying about half of them. The current book value of the pallet racks is $8,000...should I make an entry to reduce the book value for the ones that were destroyed? If so, how?**

Solution Record the lost value or usefulness of the pallet racks by making an entry similar to a depreciation expense entry, on the Checks form. However, don't use the Depreciation Expense account for recording the loss. Use an Other Expense type account, set up specifically for recording losses.

Only record permanent damage, not damage which was (or will be) repaired. Writing off the book value of damaged assets which will be repaired will "double count" expenses, assuming the repair costs are also deducted as a business expense.

Discussion

When a fixed asset sustains major damage which reduces its value and/or usefulness, and the damage won't be repaired, the estimated dollar amount of the damage is a loss to the business and should be entered as an expense. Failing to do so would cause balance sheet reports to overstate the remaining value of the business' assets.

Because damage of this type is an extraordinary expense—outside the realm of normal business expenses—the transaction *should not* post to Depreciation Expense. You might set up an Other Expense type account named Extraordinary Expense, for example, and use it. That way, the loss will appear on profit and loss reports separate from normal business expenses.

Though you may use the Extraordinary Expense account directly, on the Expenses tab of the Checks form, you may instead choose to create an Item for it so you can use it on the Items tab of the form:

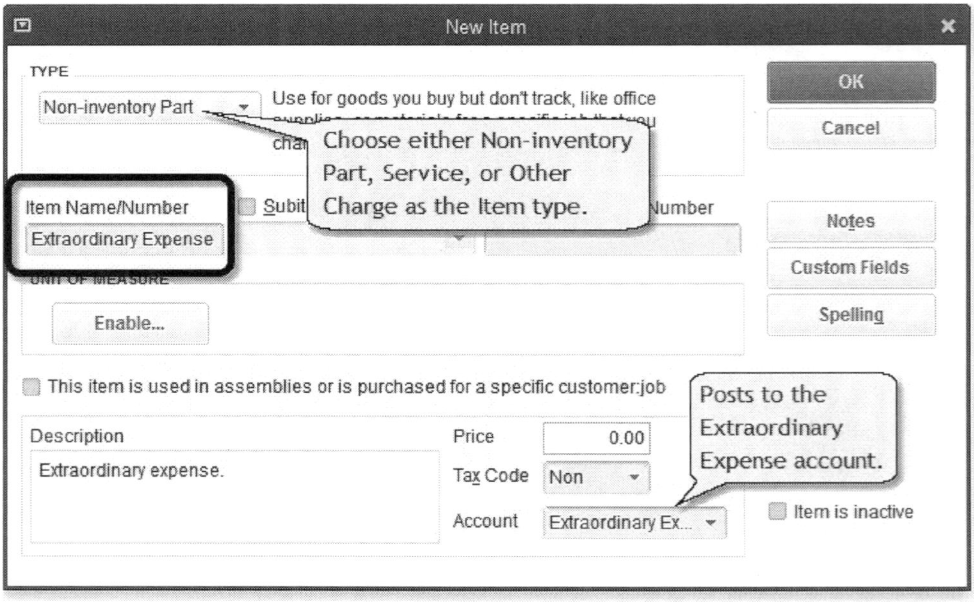

Below is a Check entry (Banking > Write Checks) which writes off 1/2 of the pallet rack's $8,000 book value as a loss, using the Extraordinary Expense Item created above.

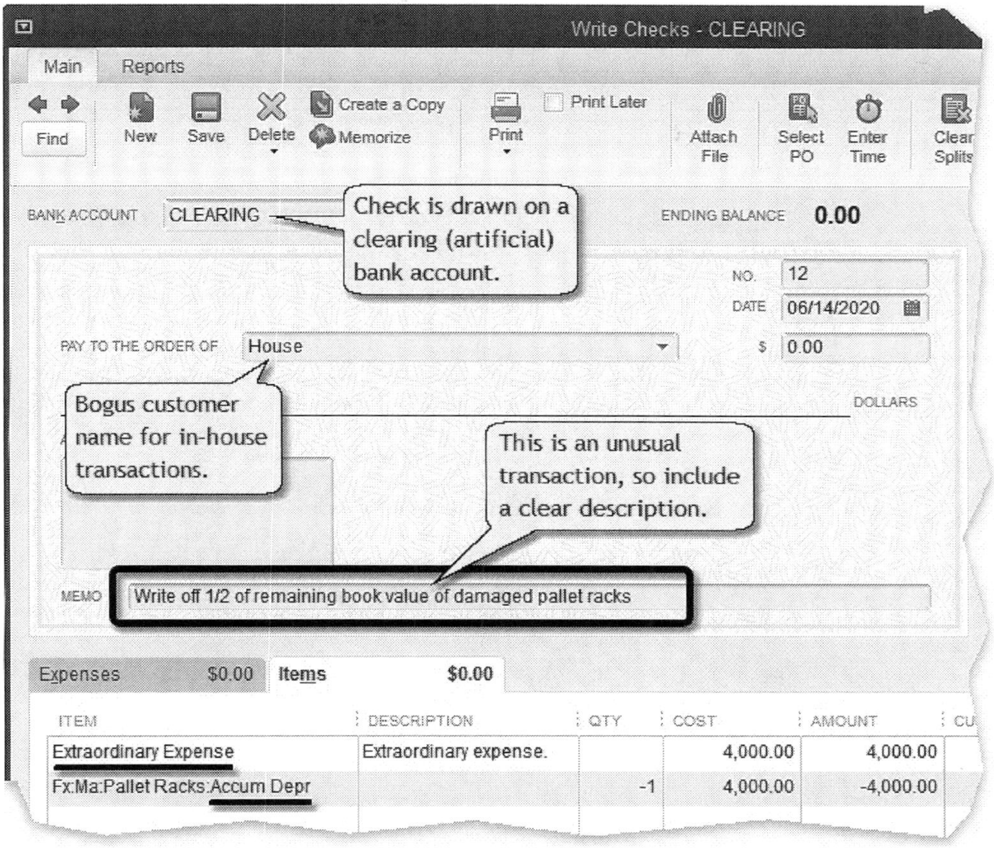

Recording the Salvage Sale of a Fixed Asset

Problem

We had some old overhead bins in our warehouse which were fully depreciated and had not been used for years, so we were glad when a local scrap steel dealer offered $500 for them, to be removed at his expense. He gave us a check for $500—how should we record it?

Solution

Enter the sale of the bins just like any other fixed asset sale, with the $500 amount received as the sale price.

Discussion

The sale of a fixed asset is recorded the same way regardless of the reason for the sale, how low the selling price was, or whether the asset was fully depreciated or not:

1. **Enter a Sales Receipt or Invoice for the sale** 110 (Customers > Enter Sales Receipts or Customers > Create Invoices) to record the amount received —$500 in this case—and to document the asset's removal from the business.

2. **Enter a $0 Check to recapture depreciation** 111 (Banking > Write Checks). This removes the asset's book value from the balance sheet and calculates gain or loss on the sale—a $500 gain in this case, because the bins were fully depreciated.

Because these steps are identical to the ones shown in *Entering a Sale* 109, they won't be repeated here.

Recording Disposal or Destruction of a Fixed Asset

When a fixed asset is disposed of without receiving any payment for it, the proper way to remove it from the list of fixed assets will depend on whether it had any book value when it was disposed of.

If the asset had *no* remaining book value (was fully depreciated, with no salvage value)...

Problem **We had a 30-year-old job site office trailer on our back lot which we had not used for years—the roof leaked and the structure was in poor condition. We gave it to an employee who offered to haul it away for free, to dismantle for some of the trailer parts. How do I remove the old trailer from our books?**

Solution Enter a zero-dollar check to zero out the trailer's original basis and accumulated depreciation balances, thereby removing it from the balance sheet.

★ ***Zero-dollar checks*** are a popular QuickBooks technique. They let you make transaction entries on the Checks form which otherwise would have to be made as journal entries, and allow Items to be used in those transactions (journal entries do not).

Discussion This approach is appropriate when disposing of fixed assets which have no remaining book value, because no gain or loss is involved. If an asset has any book value when disposed of, use the approach [129] described later.

Assuming the office trailer was fully depreciated:

1. **Look up the trailer's original basis and accumulated depreciation balances** in a Fixed Asset Book Values report [217] or Item QuickReport [211].

   For this example, assume the trailer's original basis (purchase price) was $22,000 and, because it is fully depreciated, it's accumulated depreciation balance is also $22,000, leaving it with a book value of $0.

2. **Enter a zero-dollar check** (Banking > Write Checks) **to cancel out the original basis and accumulated depreciation amounts.** The check should be

drawn on a clearing bank account[38], to avoid confusion with transactions in your real checking account:

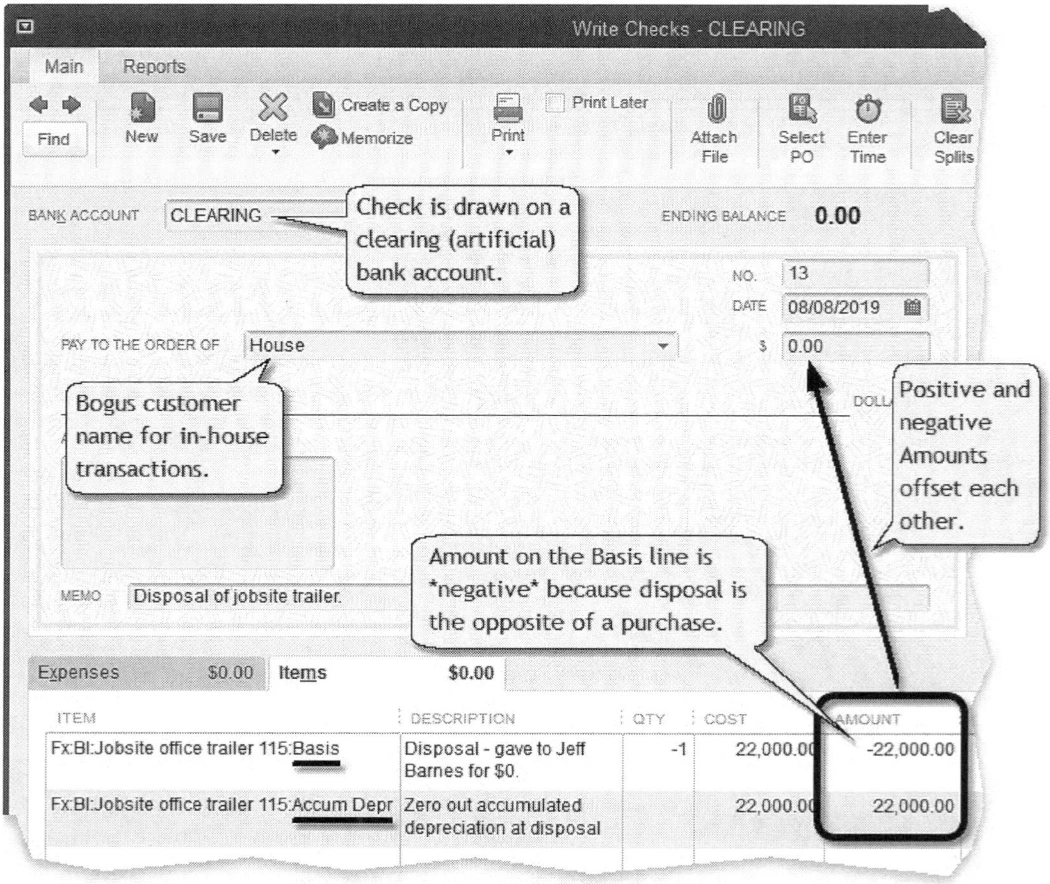

3. *Recommended:* **Retire**[121] **the trailer's Items** at the end of the tax year, so it will no longer appear in fixed asset reports.

If the asset had any book value...

Problem

We had an old skidsteer loader which was fully depreciated except for a salvage value of $2,000. With lots of oil leaks and a weak transmission it wasn't worth much, so we no longer carried insurance on it. Last month while an employee was using the loader it caught fire and was damaged beyond repair. A local salvage yard agreed to haul it away for free. How do I remove the skidsteer loader from our books?

Salvage value is an estimate of what the resale value of a fixed asset will be at the end of its useful life, and is not depreciated.

Solution

Use the Checks form to enter the disposal of the skidsteer loader as if it had been sold for a $0 amount. Enter a second zero-dollar check to recapture depreciation for the loader, so its salvage value will be recorded as a loss.

Discussion

Whenever a fixed asset with any amount of book value is disposed of for a $0 amount, the disposal should be entered as if the asset had been sold for $0, along with a depreciation recapture transaction to record the lost book value.

What about partial-year depreciation?

If a fixed asset has depreciable value when disposed of, proper fixed asset accounting calls for entering depreciation expense[147] for the part of the year it was owned before disposal. Enter partial-year depreciation *before* recording the disposal, so the asset's accumulated depreciation amount will be correct for the depreciation recapture[115] entry.

The *Calculate partial-year depreciation*[177] topic in Chapter 9 shows a simple way to figure the partial-year amount.

The reason for entering partial-year depreciation is to meet the accounting goal of matching fixed asset costs with the revenue those assets helped to produce. However, entering partial-year depreciation is an accounting choice —something to discuss with your accountant. It may be important to do if the business' financial statements are viewed by others outside of the business and are assumed to have been prepared using standard accounting practices. However, many small businesses—especially sole proprietorships and partnerships whose financial statements are mostly viewed internally—forgo entering partial-year depreciation to avoid the extra effort it requires.

In this example, the skidsteer loader's book value consists entirely of salvage value, which is not depreciable, so there was no partial-year depreciation to enter.

Here are the steps:

1. **Enter a Sales Receipt** (Customers > Enter Sales Receipts) to record the "sale"110 of the skidsteer loader for a $0 amount:

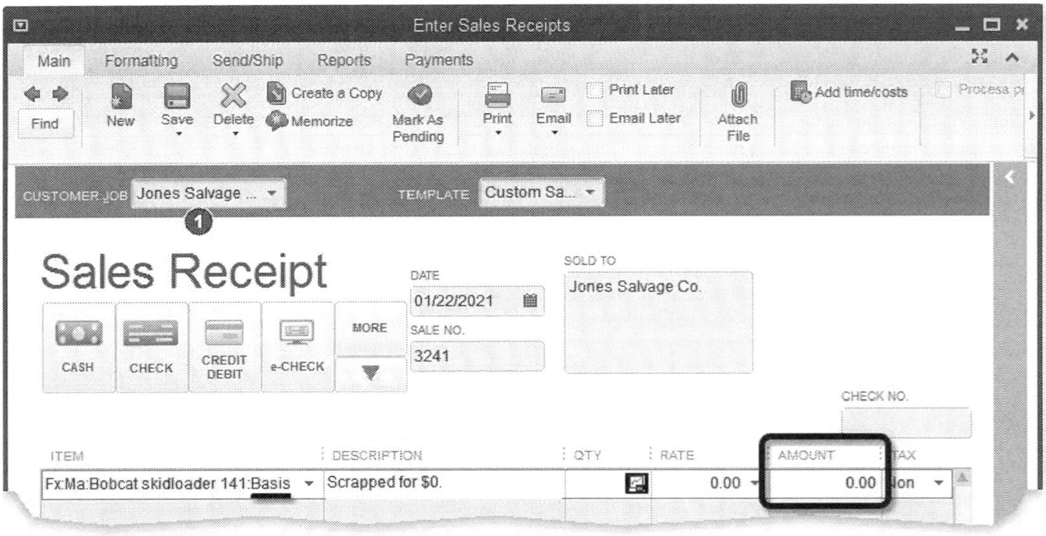

1 **Customer:Job.** The salvage company that hauled the loader away for free is selected here, just for reference. If the fixed asset is disposed of in house, so that no particular customer or business name is involved in the disposal, select a bogus customer name you have created for in-house transactions, such as *House* or *House Customer*.

This "sale" will be posted to the Undeposited Funds account, which is the default behavior for Sales Receipts. Because the amount is $0 however, QuickBooks will not make this transaction available to include in a bank deposit. That way, it cannot be accidentally included in a bank account, where it might cause confusion when reconciling the account.

2. **Enter a $0 Check** (Banking > Write Checks) **to recapture depreciation** 111 **for the asset.**

Before entering the Check, look up the skidloader's accumulated depreciation balance in either a Fixed Asset Book Values report 217 or an Item QuickReport customized to include the Amount column 211. If the accumulated depreciation balance is $18,000, the transaction would look like this:

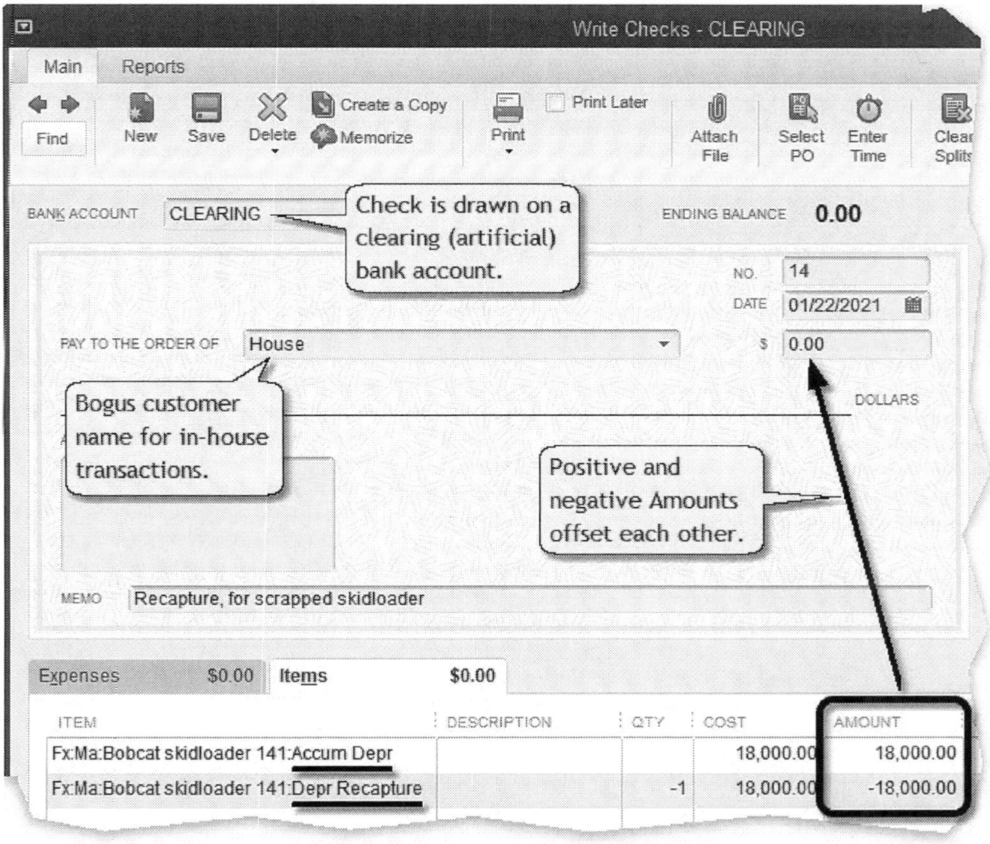

This transaction will zero out the skidloader's accumulated depreciation balance and will calculate the loss due to scrapping the machine —the skidloader's $2,000 salvage value—which will be shown on Fixed Asset Sales Reports 228 and profit and loss reports for the current accounting period.

3. *Recommended:* **Retire**[121] **the loader's Items** at the end of the tax year, so it will no longer appear in fixed asset reports.

Recording an Insurance Payout for the Loss of a Fixed Asset

Problem

One of our delivery vans was parked alongside a busy highway when a passing semi-truck driver lost control of his truck and plowed into the back of our van, pushing it into another car. No one was hurt, but the insurance company called our van a total loss and sent us a $17,500 check for it. How do I remove the van from our books, and also record the check from the insurance company?

Solution

Enter the insurance payout as if it were a sale of the van to the insurance company.

Discussion

When you receive an insurance payment for a fixed asset which was destroyed, essentially you are "selling" the fixed asset to the insurance company for the amount of the payout. The "sale" is recorded just like any other sale of a fixed asset, using two transaction entries, as shown in the examples below.

What about partial-year depreciation?

If a fixed asset has depreciable value when it is disposed of, proper fixed asset accounting calls for entering depreciation expense[147] for the part of the year it was owned before disposal. Enter partial-year depreciation *before* recording the disposal, so the asset's accumulated depreciation amount will be correct for the depreciation recapture[115] entry.

The *Calculate partial-year depreciation*[177] topic in Chapter 9 shows a simple way to figure the partial-year amount.

The reason for entering partial-year depreciation is to meet the accounting goal of matching fixed asset costs with the revenue those assets helped to produce. However, entering partial-year depreciation is an accounting choice—something to discuss with your accountant. It may be important to do if the business' financial statements are viewed by others outside of the business and are assumed to have been prepared using standard accounting practices. However, many small businesses—especially sole proprietorships and partnerships whose financial statements are mostly viewed internally—forgo entering partial-year depreciation to avoid the extra effort it requires.

1. **Enter a Sales Receipt** (Customers > Enter Sales Receipts) to record the "sale" [110] of the van to the insurance company.

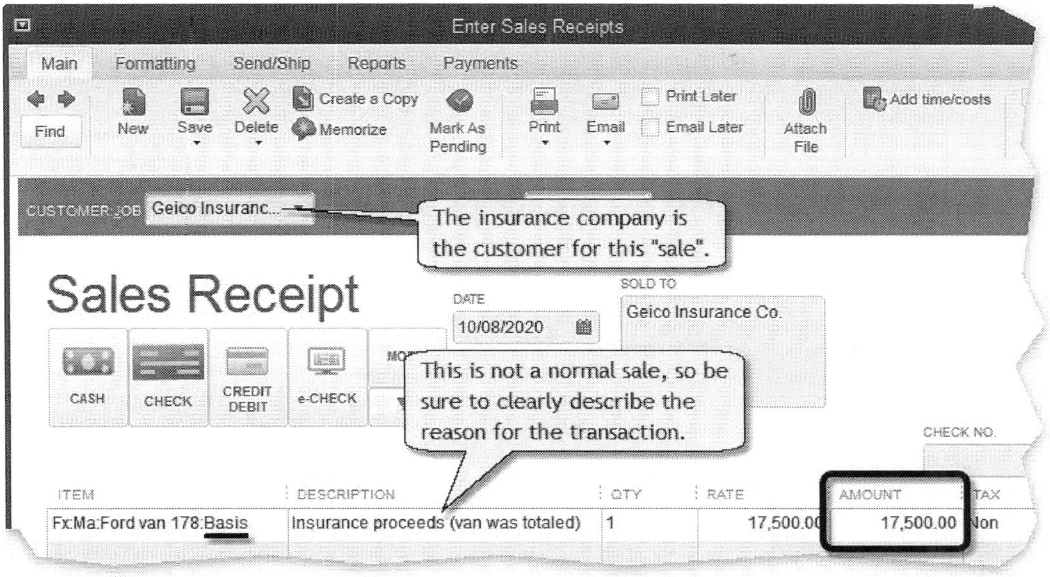

This "sale" will be posted to the Undeposited Funds account, where it will be available to include in a bank deposit (Banking > Make Deposits) via the Payments button:

2. **Enter a $0 Check** (Banking > Write Checks) **to recapture depreciation** [115] **for the van.** This will zero out its accumulated depreciation balance and calculate any gain or loss on the "sale" of the van.

   Before entering the Check, look up the van's accumulated depreciation balance in either a Fixed Asset Book Values report [217] or an Item QuickReport customized to include the Amount column [211]. If the accumulated depreciation balance is $24,000, the transaction would look like this:

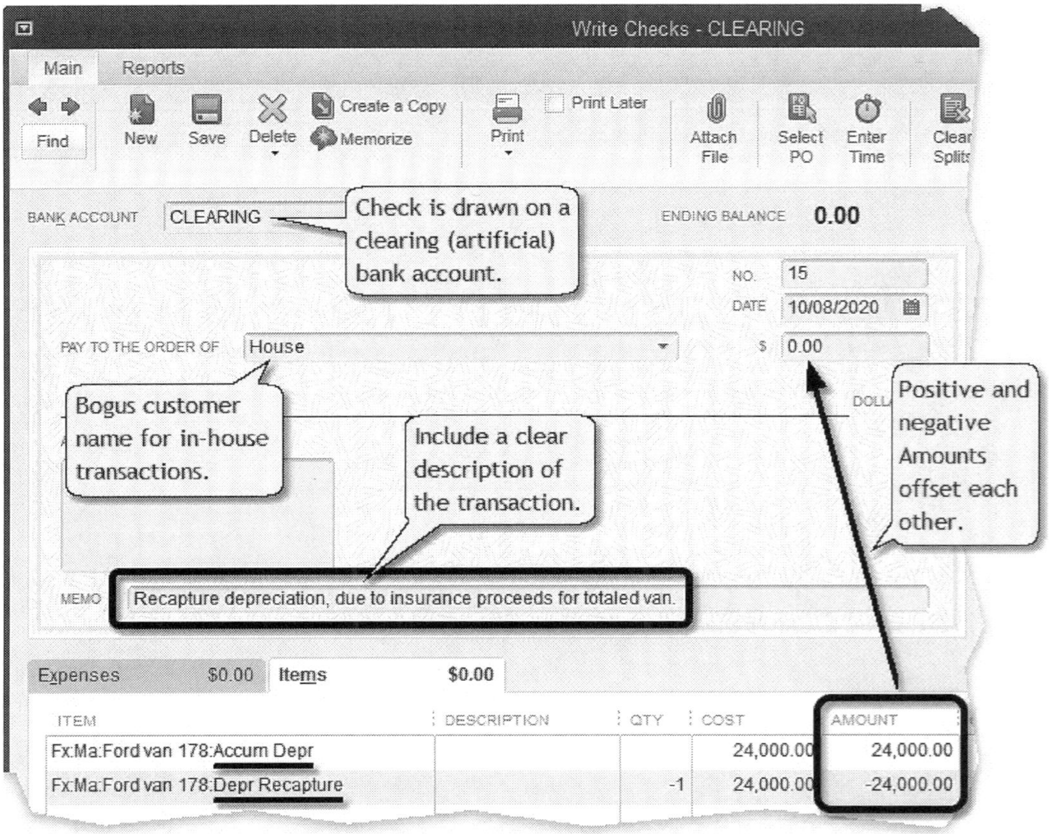

CHAPTER 7

Fixed Asset Swaps

About this chapter	This chapter shows how to enter transactions involving *swaps*—trading fixed assets your business owns, for fixed assets owned by someone else—including swaps where a payment was included as part of the deal.

This chapter deals with the *accounting book value* changes involved in swapping fixed assets. The *income tax* implications may be very different and should be handled by a tax professional.

How to Enter a Straight Swap (When No Payment is Involved)

Problem

We had a rough terrain forklift which we didn't really need any more. The storage company across the street was looking to buy a rough terrain forklift, and had a pickup truck that they were not using very much. The pickup and the forklift had about the same market value, so the storage company's manager and I worked out a straight swap of our forklift for their pickup truck. But how do I enter the swap in QuickBooks?

Solution

Enter a zero-dollar check to record the "purchase" of the pickup truck for a $0 amount, using the forklift as a trade-in.

Zero-dollar checks are a popular QuickBooks technique. They let you make transaction entries on the Checks form which otherwise would have to be made as journal entries, and allow Items to be used in those transactions (journal entries do not).

Discussion

A *straight swap* is when you trade an asset you own for an asset owned by someone else, without any payment being made by either party. This kind of transaction really is no different from trading in an asset [102] for another asset, except that the purchase price of the asset you are receiving is $0—hence the reason for entering the transaction as a zero-dollar check.

Before entering the check, look up the forklift's original basis and accumulated depreciation balances, which are needed for recording the forklift as a trade-in. You can find this information in a Fixed Asset Book Values report [217] or an Item QuickReport [211] customized to include the Amount column. Let's suppose the forklift's original basis was $28,000 and its accumulated depreciation balance is $24,000.

Armed with this information, the check would be entered this way:

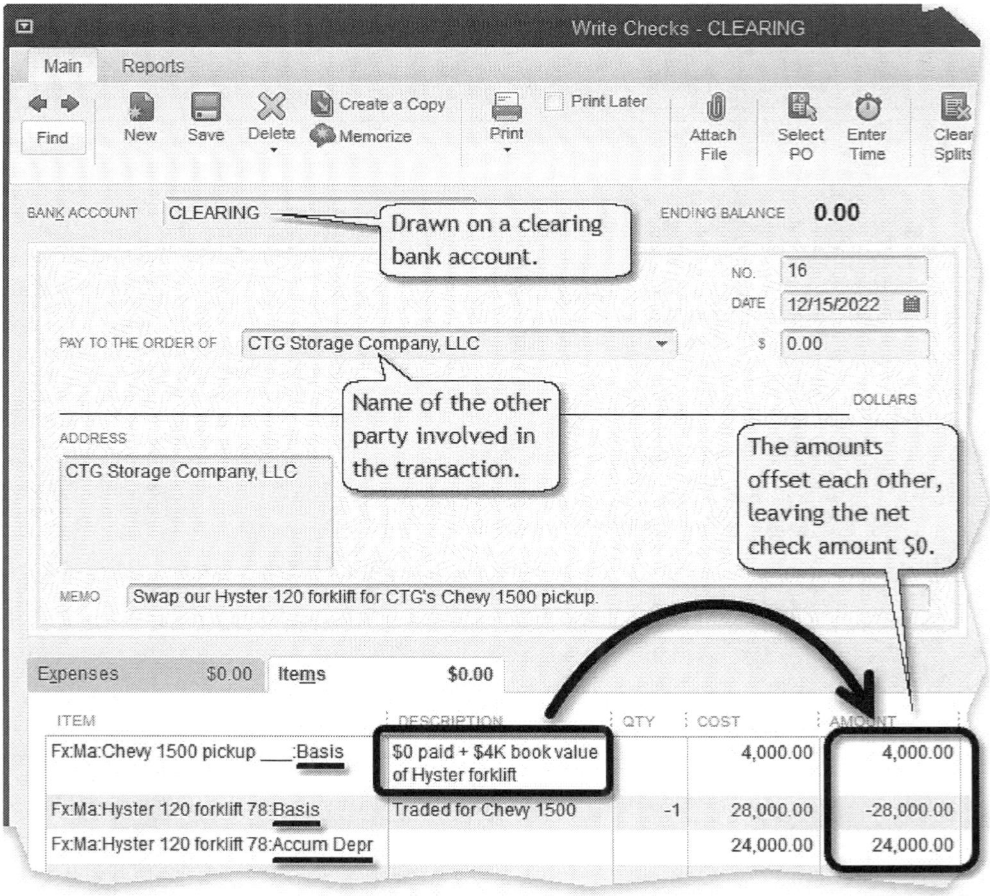

How to Enter a Swap which Involves a Payment

What if it's not a straight swap? That is, what if a payment is involved in addition to swapping assets with someone?

Swap assets, plus *making* a cash payment

Problem

Several years ago we bought a small telehandler to use on light construction jobs. More recently we have been needing a larger telehandler for lifting heavier loads. In talking with a job foreman with ABC Builders I learned that their needs were just the opposite: they had large telehandler and needed a smaller, lighter one. So we came to an agreement to swap telehandlers, with us also paying them $15,000 to make up for the higher value of the telehandler we are getting. How do we enter this in QuickBooks?

Solution

Enter a check (Banking > Write Checks) to record the purchase of the larger telehandler for the $15,000 amount you paid, listing your old, smaller telehandler as a trade-in.

Discussion

This kind of swap is essentially the same as any purchase involving a trade-in, as described in *Entering a Purchase with Trade-In* 102. And unlike the swap with no payment 135 described above, in this case you are entering a *real* check drawn on an actual bank account, not a clearing account 38.

Here is a Check entry for the cash amount paid, which also records other details of the fixed asset swap:

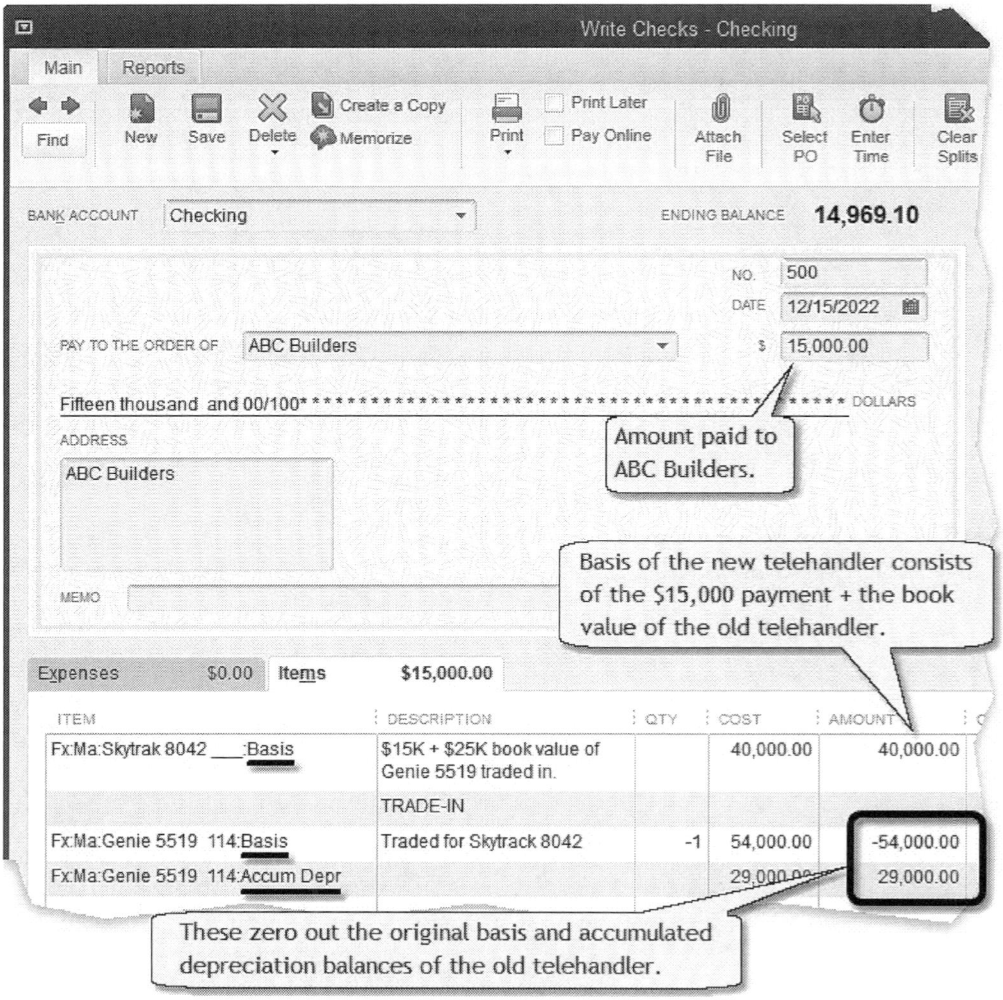

Swap assets, plus *receiving* a cash payment

Problem

We sell water well drilling rigs and provide sales support to our dealers. Until recently we had three trucks for servicing the rigs we sold, but our company is being reorganized and servicing will now be handled by a different operating division. That division needed our service trucks, so we swapped them for two SUVs—which our sales people will use—plus a $60,000 payment from the other division. How do I enter all of this in QuickBooks?

Solution

This situation is more complicated than most, because entering it in QuickBooks requires *four separate transaction entries,* each connected to a clearing bank account [38].

Discussion

The reason four entries are required is that QuickBooks will not allow entering Sales Receipts or Checks for *negative* dollar amounts.

Essentially, this swap involves "trading in" the three service trucks to acquire two SUVs. But instead of paying additional funds to purchase the SUVs, you are *receiving* a $60,000 payment. To record the purchase using a Sales Receipt as you normally would for a trade-in [102], the Sales Receipt would have to be entered for a *negative* amount (because funds are being received, not paid out). But QuickBooks won't allow that.

The workaround is to use separate transaction entries to "sell" the three service trucks and to "buy" the two SUVs, using a clearing bank account [38] as an intermediate place to temporarily hold funds being transferred between the various transaction entries, as shown below.

> ★ **This example deals with an asset group** [143]—multiple fixed assets of the same kind represented by a single main Item, with transaction quantities specifying the number of assets bought or sold.

1. **Enter a Sales Receipt (**Customers > Enter Sales Receipts**) to "sell" the service trucks *at their book value*.**

   Assume that a Fixed Asset Book Values report [217] shows the combined book value of the three service trucks as $90,000—$190,000 original basis, less $100,000 accumulated depreciation.

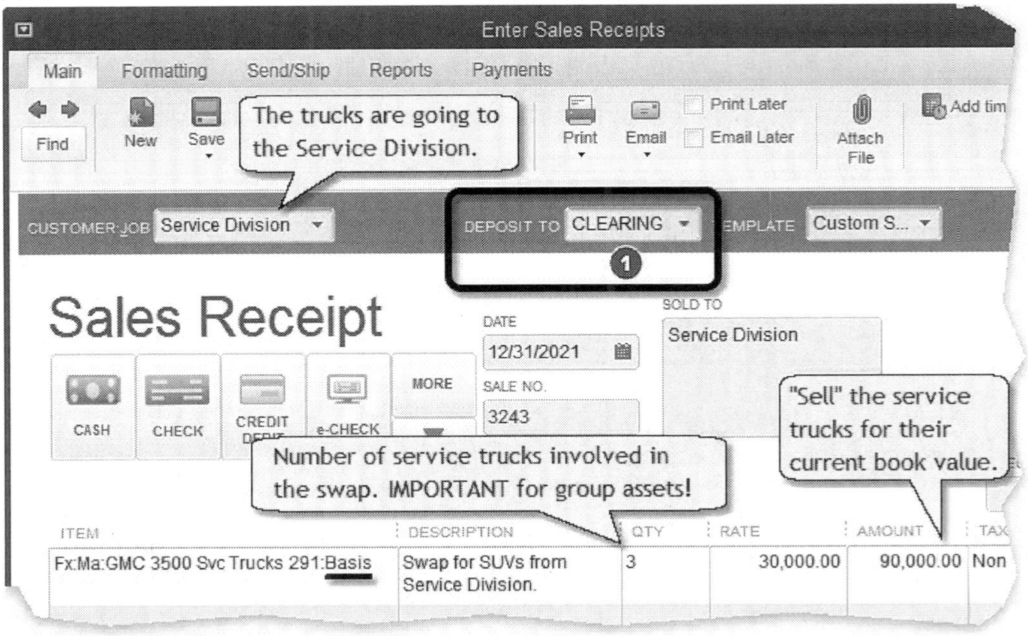

❶ **Deposit To.** If your Sales Receipts form has a *Deposit To* field, select the clearing bank account as the destination for the sale proceeds.

If the Sales Receipts form *does not* have a *Deposit To* field, QuickBooks will automatically post sale proceeds to the Undeposited Funds account. If that's the case, after entering the sale you *must* enter a deposit (Banking > Make Deposits) to move the sale proceeds from Undeposited Funds to the CLEARING bank account.

How to have a *Deposit To* field on your Sales Receipts forms, *turn off* the Preference setting at: Edit > Preferences > Payments > Company Preferences [tab] > Use Undeposited Funds as a default deposit to account.

The sale proceeds *must* be posted to the clearing bank account[38] (named CLEARING in the screenshot above). If your Sales Receipts form does not have a *Deposit To* field, you must enter a deposit (Banking > Make Deposits) to move the sale proceeds from Undeposited Funds to the CLEARING bank account. (*Do not* deposit them to a real-world bank account.)

2. **Enter a $0 Check** (Banking > Write Checks) **to recapture depreciation**[115] for the service trucks—to zero out their original basis and accumu-

lated depreciation balances. The check must be drawn on the CLEARING bank account 38. (Note that this transaction will not record a gain or loss on the sale, because the service trucks were "sold" at their book value.)

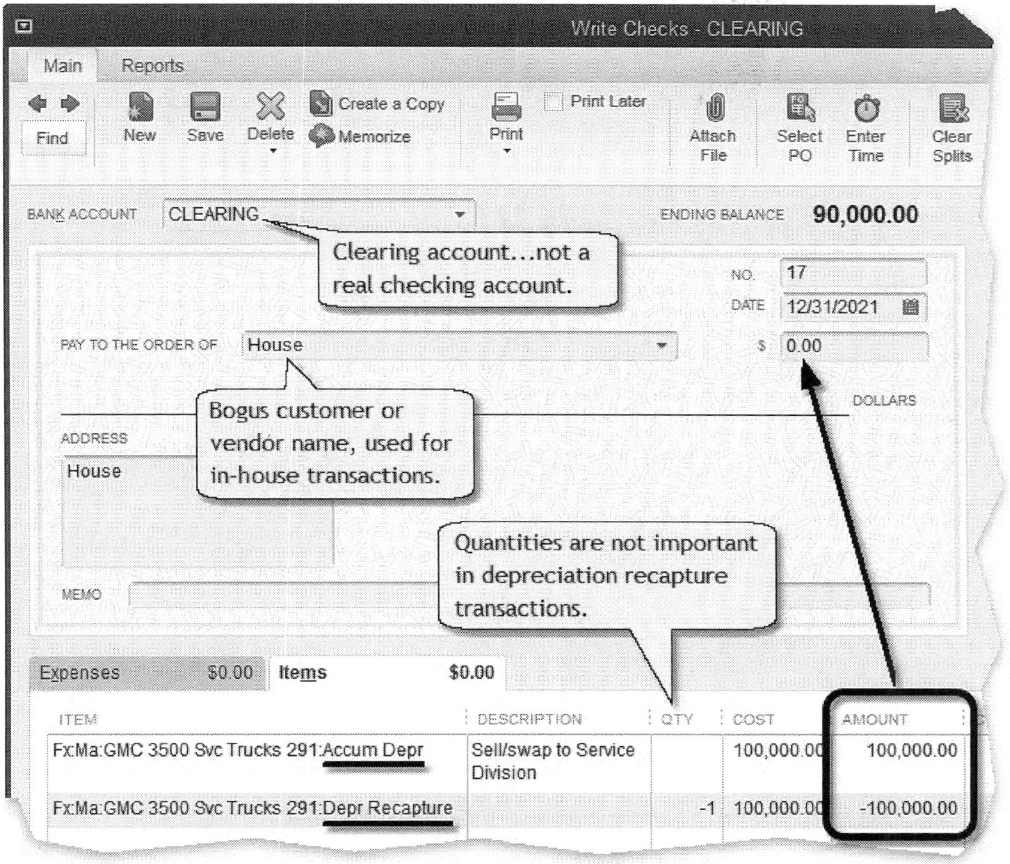

3. **Deposit (Banking > Make Deposits) the $60,000 payment you received** into the *regular* checking account, but select the CLEARING account as the source account for the deposit. This will have the effect of *withdrawing* $60,000 from the CLEARING account, leaving it with a $30,000 balance.

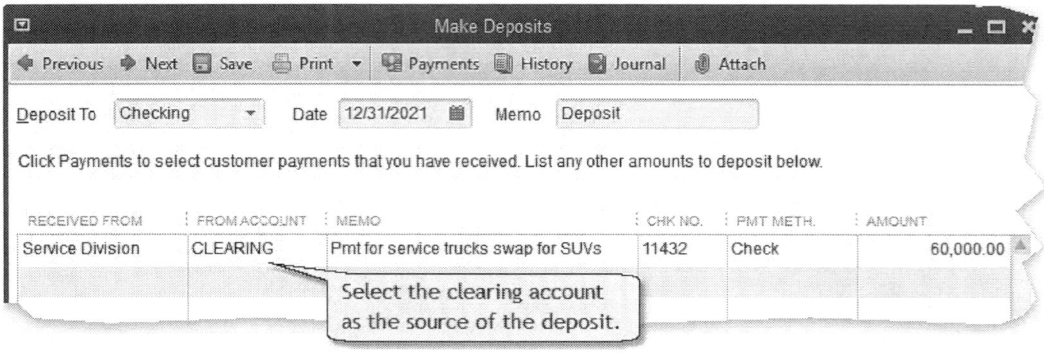

4. **Enter a check drawn on the CLEARING account to "purchase" the SUVs for $30,000.**

   The combined book value of the two SUVs will be $30,000—the difference between the $90,000 book value of the service trucks and the $60,000 payment received. This check should leave the CLEARING account with a $0 balance.

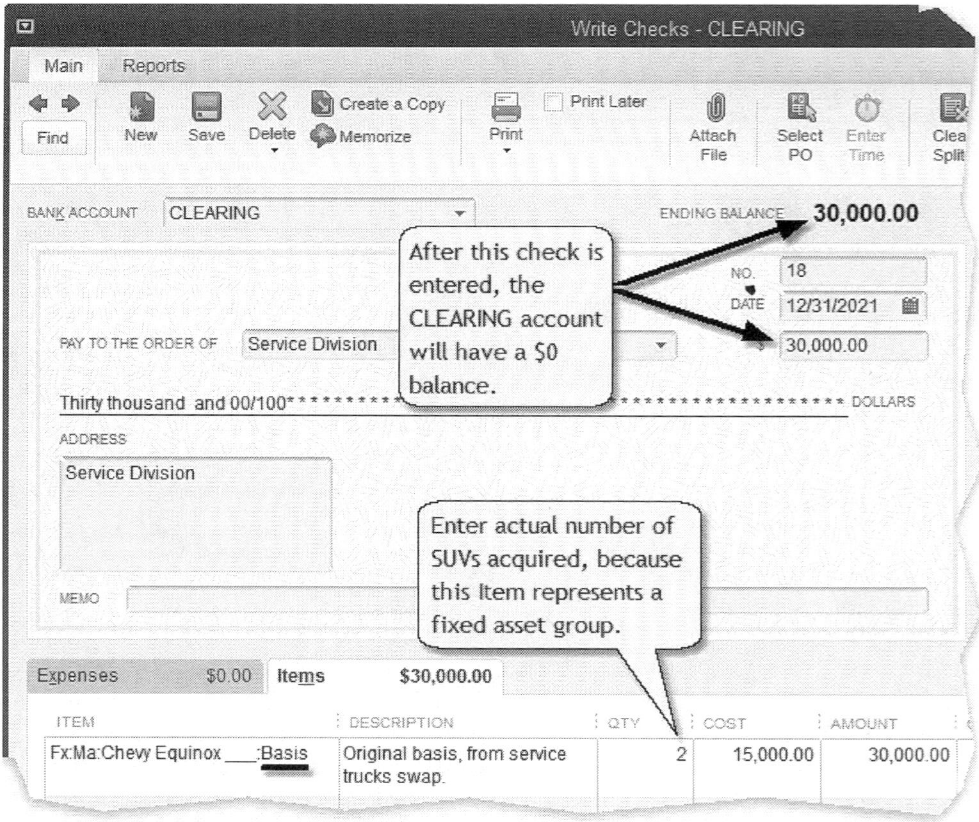

CHAPTER 8

Working with Fixed Asset Groups

About this chapter	This chapter provides tips for working with fixed asset groups—where a single main Item may represent any number of assets of the same kind.

About asset groups

For purposes of the S/S method [18], an *asset group* is a group of fixed assets of the same kind, usually acquired in the same transaction, which are represented by a single main Item. Common examples include:

- A group of vehicles acquired in a single purchase such as a fleet of trucks, delivery vans, or automobiles.
- Several machines of the same model acquired at the same time, such as a number of forklifts, or construction machines, or mixing vats, or portable storage units.
- A group of cows or other breeding livestock purchased by a rancher.

Some benefits of asset group Items include:

- **Asset groups save space** in the Item List because one set of Items (a main Item plus Basis, Accum Depr, and Depr Recapture subitems) may represent any number of fixed assets of the same kind.
- **Asset groups make sales and disposals of part of a group more intuitive,** because the sale or disposal transaction can specify the number (quantity) of assets which have been sold or disposed of.
- **Item reports can show the remaining inventory or count of assets in the group**, which is especially useful if part of the group has been sold or disposed of at different times.

Purchasing a Fixed Asset Group

The quantity of assets purchased as a group must be entered in the transaction which records the purchase [89]:

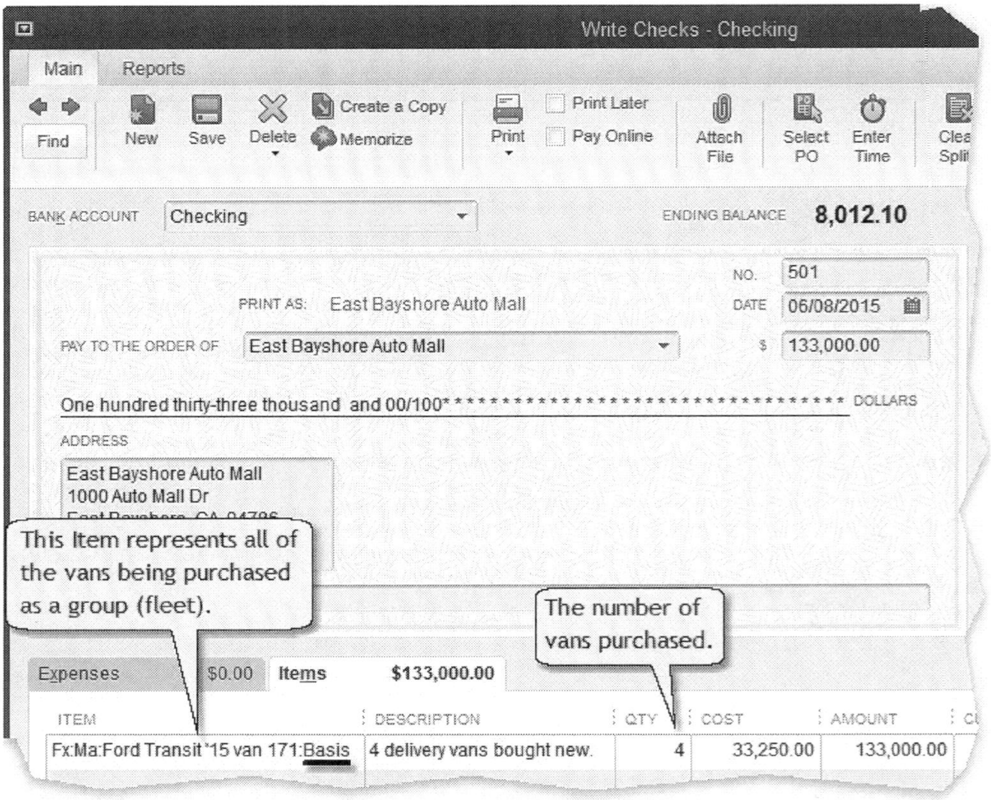

The quantity is important when entering fixed asset purchases and sales, especially for fixed asset groups. However, the quantity *is not* important in depreciation expense or depreciation recapture transactions.

Trading in All or Part of an Asset Group

When a fixed asset purchase involves trading in [103] all or part of an asset group, three things are especially important:

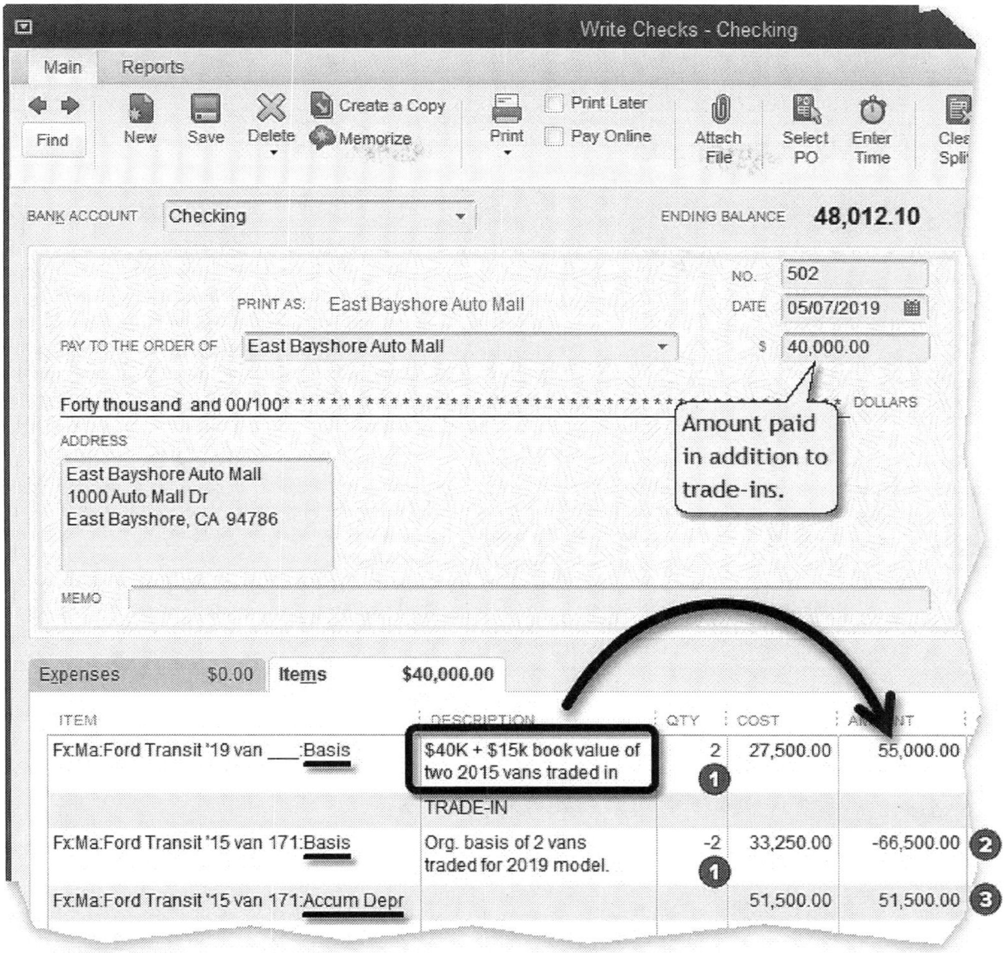

1. **Quantity.** The vans being purchased and the vans being traded in are both members of asset groups, so it's important to enter the actual number (quantity) of vans in each case—don't accept QuickBooks' default quantity of "1".

2. **Trade-in's Basis Amount.** The trade-in's Basis should be the original basis *of the portion of the group being traded in.* In this example, two mini-vans from a group of four are being traded in, so the Amount on this line is one-half of the entire group's original basis (compare this with the purchase example 144 farther above).

3. **Trade-in's Accum Depr Amount.** Likewise, the Accum Depr Amount should be one-half of the entire group's accumulated depreciation

balance, because one-half of the group is being traded in.

Entering Depreciation Expense for an Asset Group

Nothing is different or special about depreciation expense for an asset group. For details, see *Entering Depreciation Expense Manually* 156 in Chapter 9.

> **Quantities are never important** in entries for depreciation expense or accumulated depreciation recapture; only the Amounts are important. This is true both for single fixed assets and fixed asset groups.

Selling All or Part of an Asset Group

When you sell all or part of an asset group, the sale 109 transaction must indicate the number (quantity) of assets being sold from the group. If the group consists of three mini excavators and you are selling two of them, for example, the sale quantity should be entered as "2".

For the depreciation recapture 111 entry related to the sale, only recapture depreciation expense *for the portion of the group which has been sold.* If accumulated depreciation for the three mini excavators is $30,000, and two of them have been sold, the depreciation recapture amount should be $20,000.

You may sell different parts of the group at different times. If sale quantities have been entered correctly, the On Hand quantity for the group's Basis subitem (visible in the Item List) will always show the number of assets remaining in the group.

CHAPTER 9

Depreciation Expense

About this chapter	This chapter provides a brief explanation of depreciation expense and shows how to enter it for fixed asset Items.

Depreciation...Explored and Explained

If you are reading a book about fixed asset accounting (this one) it's likely that you already have a reasonably good understanding of depreciation and depreciation expense. But in case that isn't so—maybe your background in accounting is not very deep—let's take a brief side trip to consider some basics about depreciation and depreciation expense. The main purpose of this side trip will be to explore how your accounting goals relate to how—and whether—you should calculate depreciation expense, and whether or not you should enter depreciation expense in QuickBooks.

What is Depreciation?

Depreciation is the decline in value of an asset over time due to things like wear and tear, and obsolescence. Some like to say that depreciation is the decline in the *productive value* of an asset over time; the fact that an asset's usability or worth for producing things eventually gets "used up"—things wear out, become inefficient to operate, require more costly repairs, and become obsolete.

As a general definition, *fixed assets* are assets of the business which have a productive life of more than one year—things like machinery, buildings, and land. Because those assets are useful over a span of several years or more, writing off their purchase cost as an expense in just one year would misrepresent how those assets contribute value to the business. It would also make profits for that year appear to be small, due to large expense write-offs recorded in that year.

For these reasons, depreciation was developed into a formal accounting concept to allow a business' financial statements (profit and loss statement, and balance sheet) to more accurately reflect the cost of fixed assets —or, their contribution to productivity within the business—and their productive value over their useful lifetimes. *Depreciation expense* then, is an accounting entry which is used to write off part of an asset's purchase cost as a business expense in each year of the asset's expected useful life.

Depreciation expense is not charged for land. Unlike machinery, buildings, and similar fixed assets, the accounting assumption for land (borne out by real-world experience) is that its value is not "consumed" or "used up" over time. Land values may either rise or fall depending more on market conditions than on changes in the land's productive capability.

Salvage value is a concept related to depreciation. If you buy a machine for $10,000 and expect it to be worth $1,000 at the end of its useful life—its resale value for parts, scrap, or some other/lesser use—then the machine's salvage value is $1,000. The salvage value of a fixed asset *is not* depreciated because it is an amount you expect to be able to reclaim when the asset's useful life is over and you sell or scrap the asset. In this example, only $9,000 of the machine's purchase price would be depreciated, not the entire $10,000.

Your Assumptions Affect Depreciation Expense

An important thing to understand about depreciation expense is that *how* you choose to calculate it is based on a lot of assumptions, such as:

- **How quickly a fixed asset will be worn out or used up.** The asset's purchase cost will be written off as some amount of depreciation expense each year over the asset's *expected useful life,* but how long is that? Estimating the useful life of an asset requires making assumptions about how long the asset will last or will be useful.

- **How it contributes value or productive capabilities to the business.** Many assets contribute more productive value to the business when they are newer, compared to when they are older. A machine may have less downtime, lower repair costs, and may be more efficient (lower fuel costs, lower oil consumption, etc.) when it is new, compared to when it is several years old. Machines also decline in market value more quickly when they are newer, compared to when they are older.

For these reasons, accountants have devised "accelerated" depreciation methods which charge more of an asset's purchase cost as depreciation expense early in its useful lifetime, and less in later years—the goal being to mimic the asset's actual decline in value or productivity as it ages. Two of the commonly known accelerated depreciation methods are the Declining Balance and Sum-of-the-Years-Digits methods.

- **Your accounting assumptions—or really, your accounting goals.** The accounting profession has developed a body of standards for the accounting techniques, known as GAAP (Generally Accepted Accounting Principles). The GAAP guidelines prescribe how to record and report things like liabilities and owner's equity; how accounts receivable, inventories, and fixed assets are to be valued; and much more. Depreciation expense has a major effect on fixed asset values, and GAAP prescribes how it should be calculated in different situations.

  GAAP's primary goal is to standardize the reporting of financial information—especially important for publicly traded companies. (Shareholders need trustworthy information about the businesses financial situation, and standardized accounting practices make that possible.) But standardized financial reports are not a primary accounting goal for every business. The *Accounting Goals and Depreciation Expense* 151 topic will explore how your accounting goals relate to your choices about how—and whether—to calculate depreciation expense and enter it in QuickBooks.

Calculating depreciation expense

How you choose to calculate depreciation depends heavily upon your accounting goals for measuring business profits and asset value, and upon your understanding of how different kinds of fixed assets contribute to business productivity and profits. You may calculate depreciation expense very simply or by using more complex methods, and you can find plenty of details about calculating depreciation in any number of accounting textbooks and numerous Internet sites.

> Many paid commercial software products and free spreadsheet templates are available for doing the calculations, such as the spreadsheet template discussed in Chapter 9 - Depreciation Expense 167.

Kinds of Depreciation

Before thinking about how your accounting goals relate to depreciation expense, let's consider the three main kinds of depreciation.

- **Market value depreciation** is the decline in potential selling price or value of an asset... *"If I were to sell this asset today, what would it be worth?"*. Market values can decline for any number of reasons including overall economic conditions. However, an asset's age, condition, and degree of wear and tear are usually the main factors which determine its market value.

  Market value depreciation is not calculated based on the asset's original cost or useful life. Rather, it is *estimated* based on the selling prices of like assets of a similar age and condition. If you believe your delivery van was worth $30,000 last year but only $26,000 this year, then its market value has depreciated by roughly $4,000—but remember, market value depreciation is always just an estimate.

  An asset's market value can also *appreciate* (increase in value). For example, if the cost of buying a new asset rises steeply, buyers may suddenly be willing to pay more for older, used versions of the same asset than they were willing to pay a year or two ago.

- **Book value depreciation** is what most bookkeepers think of when they hear the term "depreciation". It is the gradual write-off of the purchase cost of fixed assets over their expected useful lifetimes, meant to mimic the gradual decline in value or usefulness of an asset as it ages, wears out, or becomes obsolete.

  If an asset cost $50,000 and you decide to depreciate it over a 10 year lifetime using the straight-line depreciation method, depreciation expense for the asset would be $5,000 each year.

  The term *book value* comes from how a fixed asset's remaining undepreciated value is represented on the company's "books"—i.e., in the company's accounting system. If an asset's purchase cost was $50,000 and it has been depreciated for three years at $5,000 per year, the accumulated depreciation for the asset would be 3 * $5,000 = $15,000, giving it a book value of: $50,000 - $15,000 = $35,000.

- **Tax depreciation** refers to depreciation calculated according to federal or state income tax regulations. Originally, depreciation methods specified by U.S. federal income tax rules were based on the same general accounting principles as book value depreciation: the gradual write-off of a fixed asset's cost as expense, over some number of years corresponding to its expected useful life.

  Over time however, the tax laws have increasingly been used for implementing economic and social policy. For fixed assets this has meant increased use of accelerated depreciation methods and special rules such as Section 179 deductions, aimed at stimulating purchasing by allowing the full cost of many fixed asset purchases to be written off as expense in a single year. Drastically accelerated write-offs of fixed asset costs are almost completely disconnected from the accounting idea of gradually writing off the cost of a fixed asset over its useful lifetime.

  > **Writing off fixed asset costs over a very short period of time** can greatly reduce a business' taxable income, at least in the short run. The prospect of reducing income taxes provides a strong incentive for continued purchases of more and newer fixed assets each year.

  Plainly stated, tax depreciation rules are just nutty. They bear no relationship to the useful life, remaining value, or remaining productive capacity of fixed assets, and should be used only to comply with the tax laws—not as a basis for evaluating costs or profitability of a business.

Accounting Goals and Depreciation Expense

Here are a few of the common financial accounting goals you will find among QuickBooks users in small businesses, not all of which conform to a "textbook" idea of accounting. They illustrate how different accounting and/or business goals affect decisions about how to handle fixed assets and depreciation within QuickBooks.

Most businesses have a range of other accounting goals in addition to these—such as goals for gathering more or better management information, or for analyzing the profitability of different departments of the business—but those are beyond the scope of this book.

Goal: Tax records...and not much else!

Some people mostly use QuickBooks to keep track of income, expenses, and fixed asset purchases and sales, mainly to have records acceptable for income tax preparation at year's end. In essence, this is like using QuickBooks as a significantly-more-convenient version of a paper accounting ledger book. Part of the convenience comes from QuickBooks' additional ease-of-use features for things like managing accounts payable (bills) and accounts receivable (invoiced sales, customer statements, etc.), reconciling bank statements, and so on.

Most people who use QuickBooks this way don't try to maintain "correct" (from an accounting standards perspective) balances for asset and equity accounts in QuickBooks, and therefore don't use QuickBooks for preparing balance sheets. (When needed, balance sheets are more often prepared ad hoc, outside of QuickBooks, usually with a spreadsheet.)

When tax compliance is the main goal, as if often the case, the business' only depreciation records (asset purchase costs, accumulated depreciation, etc.) may be those maintained by a tax preparer. In this situation, entering depreciation expense is usually pointless. Why? Because if accurate asset and inventory book values are not being maintained in QuickBooks, entering depreciation expense will not by itself allow QuickBooks to generate financial reports which are useful for evaluating profitability of the business.

> *Explanation:* If book values are not being maintained in QuickBooks, producing an accurate accrual profit and loss report is not possible without making a number of adjustments. There is little value in entering depreciation expense only to have it appear on a profit and loss statement which is not accurate from either a cash or accrual accounting standpoint.
>
> And if the depreciation expense was calculated for income tax purposes there is even less value in entering it, because tax-based depreciation expense is only loosely related to the real-world costs of oper-

> ating the business or to measuring the business' profits. This is especially true for small businesses, because the cap on directly expensing fixed asset purchases is generally a large amount. (For instance, the 2018 Tax Cuts and Jobs Act allows up to $1,000,000 in fixed asset purchases to be directly expensed as a Section 179 deduction.)

If tax compliance is your most important accounting goal, then consider using the Even Simpler method[233]. It will help you keep track of fixed asset purchases, sales, and trade-ins for income tax compliance, without the need to enter depreciation expense or track asset book values.

Goal: Tax records, plus market value balance sheets

In some industries, QuickBooks is commonly used for keeping records for tax compliance *but also* for preparing balance sheets based on market values (actually, *net realizable value*) rather than book values.

> ***Net realizable value*** is the estimated market value of an asset, less transportation and any other selling costs.

If this describes how you use QuickBooks, then for the reasons described above you don't need to be entering depreciation expense, and the Even Simpler method[233] would be appropriate for your business.

Accounting 101: Who uses market value balance sheets?

Trained accountants are often surprised to learn that financial reporting based on the market value of fixed assets and inventories is common practice in some industries—farming and fishing are examples, primarily because the IRS permits farmers and fishermen to keep cash basis tax records (the majority do) and to file taxes on a cash basis.

How does cash basis accounting promote using market valuation of fixed assets? Actually, by itself it doesn't. But cash basis accounting does promote market valuation of *inventories*—both inventories of finished goods and of production inputs (raw materials, supplies, fuel, etc.).

With cash accounting, production inputs are expensed at the time of purchase, not stored as asset value. This makes it difficult (nearly impossible in QuickBooks) to track those costs as Work in Progress (WIP) inventories. Consequently, hardly any QuickBooks users in agriculture or fishing industries maintain WIP inventories. And without production costs accumulated in WIP accounts, no cost information is available to transfer to Finished Goods as the value of finished goods inventories. For this reason, balance sheets are usually created by directly assigning an estimated market value (or net realizable value) to inventories and also to fixed assets.

If you have formal training in accounting you may recognize a wide range of problems with financial reporting based on market values, especially for business analysis. But it's important to note that the financial analysis practices in industries where it is commonplace have evolved over many decades to mitigate many of those problems. For example, most of the ratios and rules of thumb agricultural lenders use for loan analysis have been developed assuming that the underlying financial data was provided on a market value basis—which interestingly, is often the best data to use as the basis for making short-term lending decisions.

Goal: Records for tax compliance plus financial reporting

The common approach for meeting this goal is to make an effort to maintain standard accrual accounting records in QuickBooks, including fixed asset book values based on reasonable assumptions about the useful lives of assets—or in other words, with depreciation expense calculated based on economic assumptions, not income tax rules.

Accrual accounting matches revenue with the expenses involved in generating that revenue. Likewise, maintaining fixed asset book values which are based on the declining value and usefulness of assets helps match fixed asset costs with revenue generation. This makes profit and loss reports and balance sheet reports useful for analyzing the profitability and financial position of the business based on earnings (the amount by which revenue exceeds cost recovery) rather than on the changing market value of assets.

If GAAP-compliant financial reports are desired, adjustments may be made to produce them directly from QuickBooks. For example, some fixed asset book values may need to be adjusted downward if the assets' market values have declined more quickly than book values.

For income tax preparation, a tax preparer may gather tax data by directly accessing the QuickBooks company file or from reports provided by the business—a profit and loss report or one of QuickBooks' Income Tax reports, a list of fixed asset purchases and sales for the year, and possibly others.

If this describes your accounting goals, then handling fixed asset transactions as described for the regular S/S method 19—which occupies most of this book—will help you meet those goals.

Can I maintain fixed asset book values based on income tax depreciation?

Yes, but it's not a great idea...

Author's comments:

From time to time I used to encounter people who wanted to enter tax depreciation in QuickBooks, individually for each fixed asset. They wanted to be able to look up an asset and see how much tax basis remained for it, to aid in planning for the tax consequences of selling or trading in assets.

This has never been a very good idea. It requires a lot of effort for minimal benefits: the same information is usually available from an asset list provided by your tax preparer. And depreciation expense calculated according to income tax rules is mostly useless for any purpose other than taxation—it bears little relationship to the cost of fixed asset ownership over time, and skews the financial picture provided by both profit and loss reports and balance sheet reports. This is especially true of the accelerated depreciation write-offs allowed by recent tax law changes.

Entering Depreciation Expense Manually

Problem

We used a spreadsheet to calculate depreciation for our vehicles, machinery, and buildings, but how do we enter the depreciation expense in QuickBooks?

Solution

Enter depreciation expense on the Checks form for each of the fixed assets involved, offset to the Depreciation Expense account, resulting in a zero-dollar amount for the check.

Zero-dollar checks are a popular QuickBooks technique. They let you make transaction entries on the Checks form which otherwise would have to be made as journal entries, and allow Items to be used in those transactions (journal entries do not).

Discussion

You can record depreciation expense for any number of fixed assets with a single Checks form entry. Or, you may make multiple entries (using separate checks), which you might want to do to record depreciation expense separately for different asset categories, for instance.

By the way, the example in this section shows how to enter depreciation transactions manually, to give you an overall understanding of what is involved. But later sections of the chapter will show a much easier approach: how to calculate depreciation using a spreadsheet [167], and import depreciation transactions from the spreadsheet into QuickBooks.

Setting Up a Depreciation Expense Item

Before recording depreciation you need to have an account set up for depreciation expense as described in the Setting Up Accounts [46] section of Chapter 4.

Setting up an Item to represent that account is also useful, because it lets you make all of the depreciation entries on the Items tab of the Checks form if you want, instead of having to split them between the Expenses tab and the Items tab.

Here's how to set up an Item to represent the Depreciation Expense account:

1. **Open the Item List window** (Lists > Item List).
2. **Select** Item > New from the button menu at the bottom of the window.

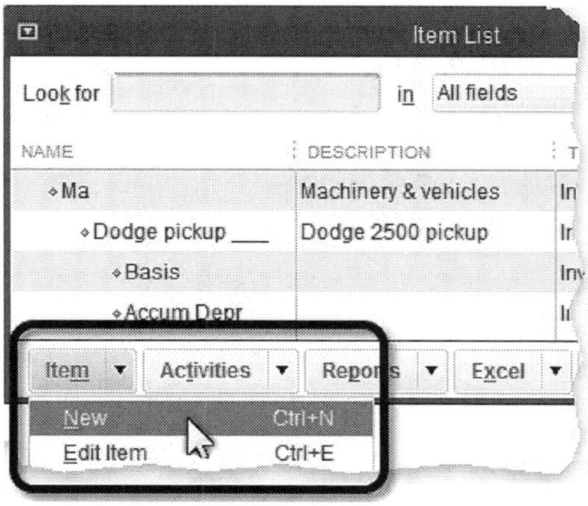

The New Item window will open.

3. **Fill in details for the Item** as shown below.

   The Depreciation Expense Item should be set up as either a Non-inventory Part or Service type Item. *Do not* set it up as an Inventory Part Item.

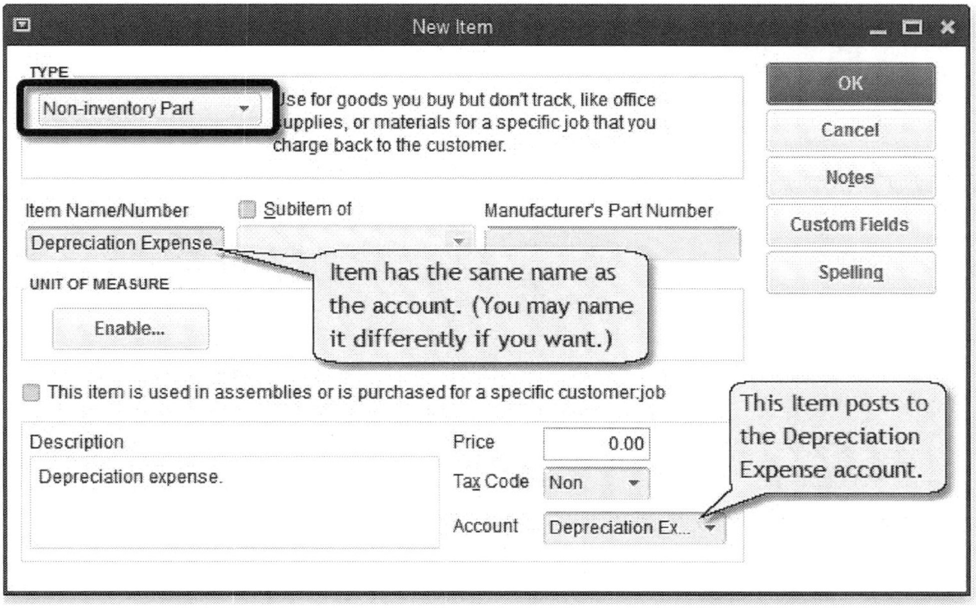

4. **Click the OK button** to save the new Item and close the window.

How to Enter Depreciation Expense

With a single Checks form entry you can record depreciation expense for any number of fixed assets, as demonstrated below. To enter depreciation expense for a larger number of Items, see the Automating Depreciation Expense sections later in this chapter.

1. **Open the Checks form** (Banking > Write Checks).

2. **Fill out the top part of the check** as shown below.

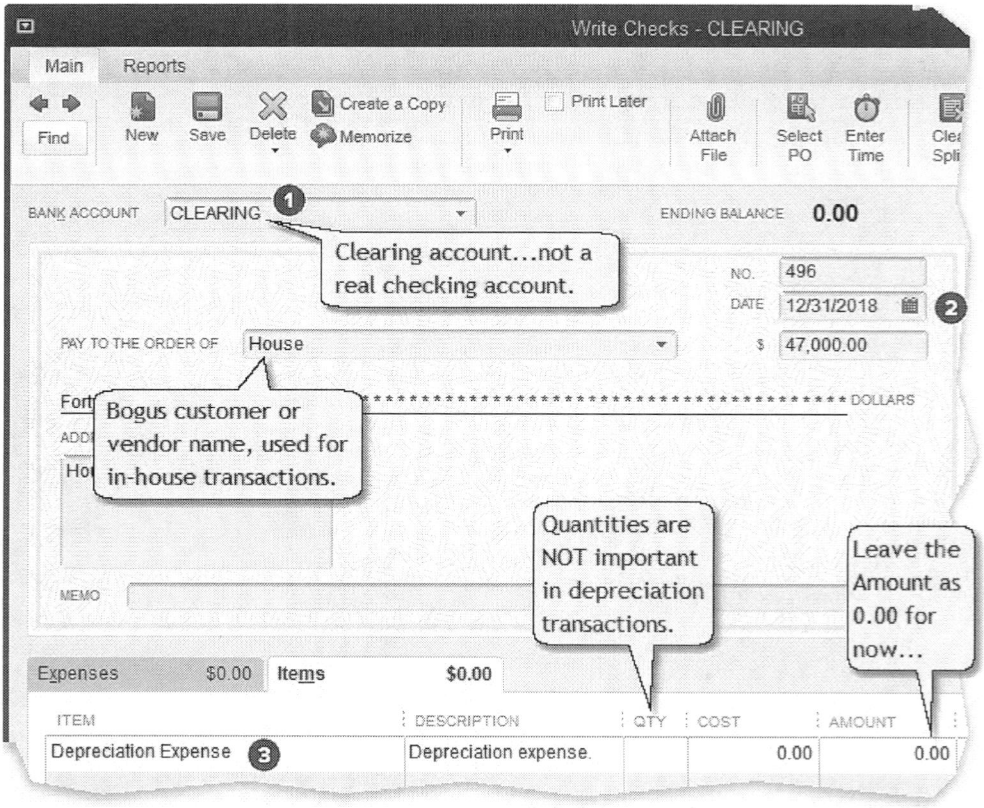

❶ **Bank Account** should be a clearing bank account 38, because this is not an actual bank transaction.

2. **Date** the check with the date on which you want the depreciation expense recorded.

3. **Item.** Select the Depreciation Expense [156] Item on the first line of the Items tab, but leave its Amount as 0.00 for now

   Using an Item to represent depreciation expense is optional. If you don't want to use an Item, you can select the Depreciation Expense account on the Expenses tab instead.

3. To add an asset's depreciation expense to the check, **select its accumulated depreciation subitem**, then **enter the depreciation expense *as a negative number*.** You may include as many assets on the check as you want—there are three in this example:

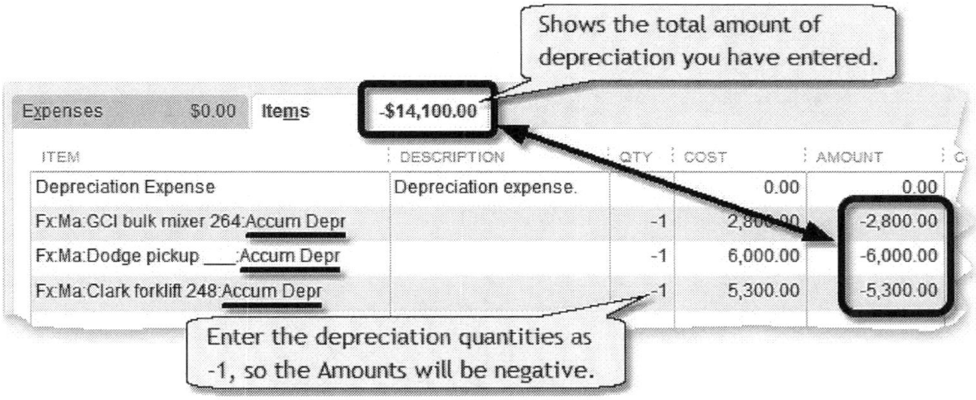

Where did the depreciation amounts come from?

QuickBooks does not calculate depreciation. You may use a spreadsheet or other third-party software application, or you might have your accountant calculate depreciation for each of your fixed assets and provide you with a list of amounts to enter into QuickBooks. (As mentioned earlier [150], generally the depreciation expense you enter in QuickBooks should be calculated for accounting book value purposes, not income tax purposes.)

Calculating Depreciation with a Spreadsheet [167], later in this chapter, describes a free spreadsheet template you can use for calculating depreciation.

Another alternative, if you use straight-line depreciation, is to calculate the annual depreciation amount for an asset and set up a recurring memorized transaction [163] to have QuickBooks enter it automatically.

4. **Enter the depreciation total on the Depreciation Expense line,** as a *positive* number.

   Simply enter the total from the Items tab on the Depreciation Expense line, but as a *positive* number, replacing the 0.00 Amount:

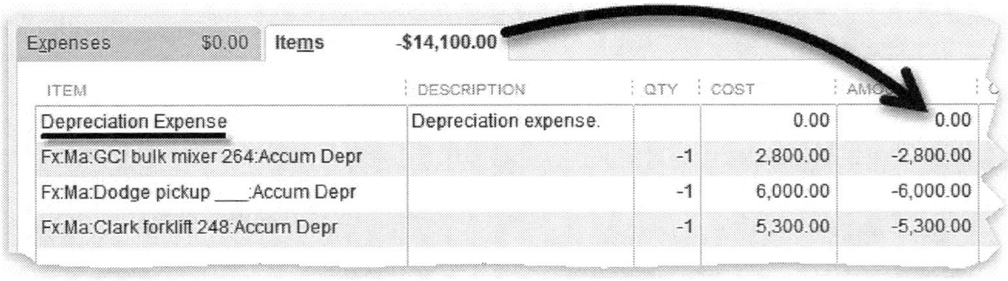

   Doing that will exactly offset all of the negative depreciation expense amounts, making the net amount on the Items tab—and for the entire check—$0.00.

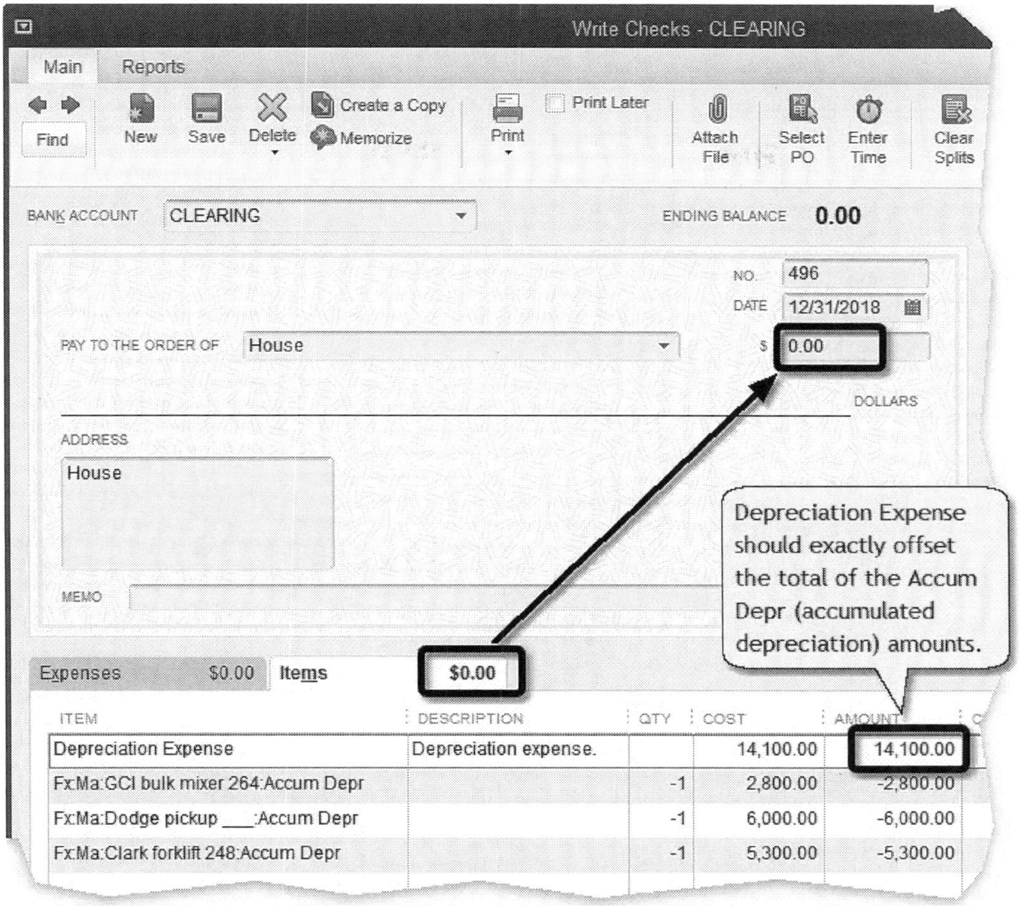

5. **Click the Save & Close button** to save the check and close the form, **or Save & New** to save the check and keep the form open for entering another check.

Experienced accountants will recognize that this entry accomplished the same thing as a journal entry for depreciation expense. The difference is that the Checks form allows using Items, to record depreciation expense for individual assets, while a journal entry does not.

Could I enter depreciation expense with an inventory adjustment?

If you know how Inventory Part Items work "under the hood", you might think that depreciation expense could be entered using an inventory adjustment (Vendors > Inventory Activities > Adjust Quantity/Value on Hand) offset to the Depreciation Expense account. But for a number of reasons, including the unique Item setup used with the S/S method, you _cannot_ correctly enter depreciation expense with an inventory adjustment.

Seeing the results

An Item QuickReport 211 customized to include the Amount column is a good place to see all of the depreciation expense transactions which have been entered for an Item. Here is an example:

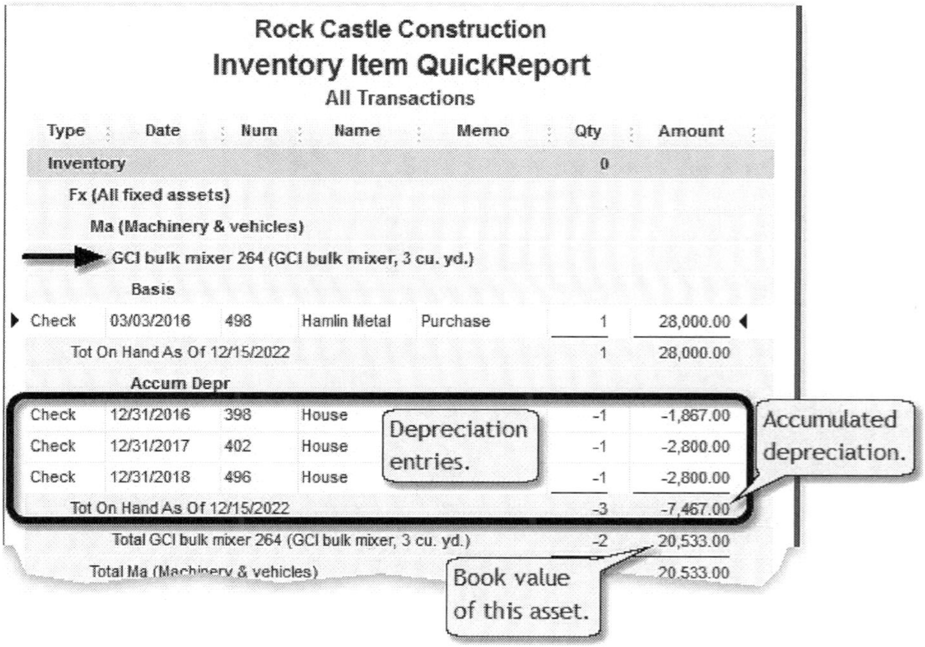

Rock Castle Construction
Inventory Item QuickReport
All Transactions

Type	Date	Num	Name	Memo	Qty	Amount
Inventory					0	
Fx (All fixed assets)						
Ma (Machinery & vehicles)						
GCI bulk mixer 264 (GCI bulk mixer, 3 cu. yd.)						
Basis						
Check	03/03/2016	498	Hamlin Metal	Purchase	1	28,000.00
Tot On Hand As Of 12/15/2022					1	28,000.00
Accum Depr						
Check	12/31/2016	398	House		-1	-1,867.00
Check	12/31/2017	402	House		-1	-2,800.00
Check	12/31/2018	496	House		-1	-2,800.00
Tot On Hand As Of 12/15/2022					-3	-7,467.00
Total GCI bulk mixer 264 (GCI bulk mixer, 3 cu. yd.)					-2	20,533.00
Total Ma (Machinery & vehicles)						20,533.00

Entering Depreciation Expense with Memorized Transactions

Problem **Is there a way for QuickBooks to automatically enter depreciation expense for me?**

Solution If you are willing to use the straight-line depreciation method you can set up a memorized transaction to automatically enter depreciation expense in each year of an asset's expected useful life.

Discussion The *straight-line depreciation* method writes off the purchase cost of a fixed asset in even amounts over the asset's expected lifetime. If you purchase an asset for $20,000 and depreciate it over a 10-year useful life, depreciation expense for the asset will be $2,000 each year for 10 years.

Because the depreciation amount is the same each year, this makes it feasible to set up a memorized transaction to automatically enter that amount each year. (The automatic entries will stop at the end of the asset's useful life.)

How to Set Up an Automatic Entry for Depreciation Expense

1. **Prepare a Check for depreciation expense for the asset,** using the steps shown in *Entering Depreciation Expense Manually* 156.

   Include *only one fixed asset* on the check. For example:

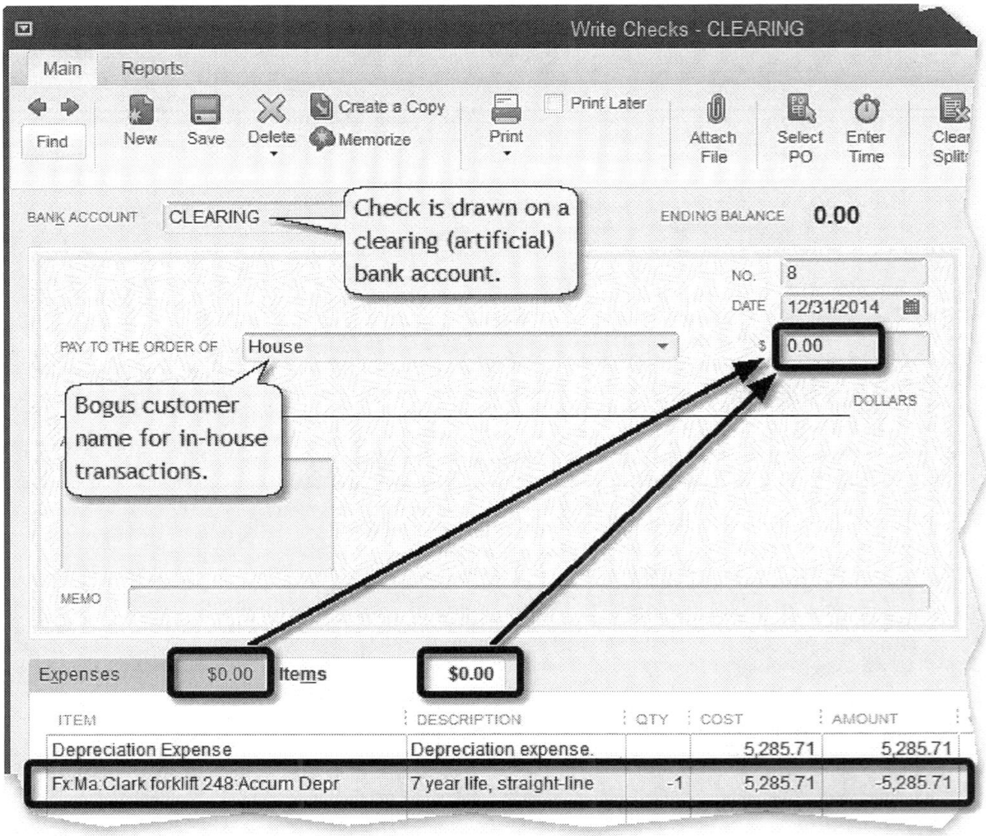

2. **Click *Memorize*** in the Main ribbon bar of the Checks form.

The Memorize Transaction window will open.

3. **Choose memorized transaction settings** as shown below.

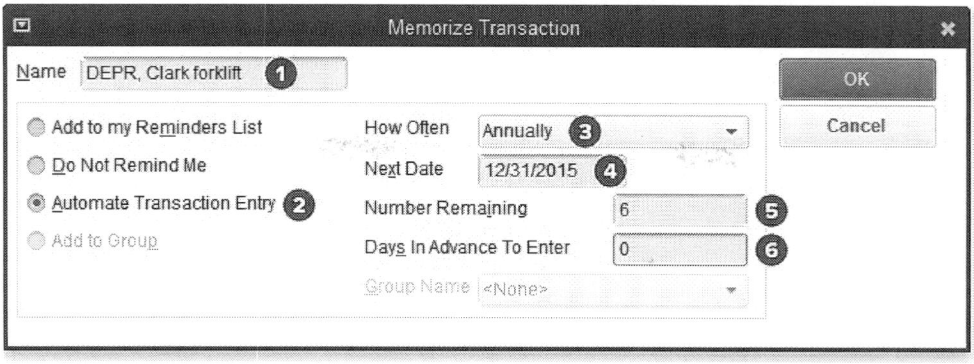

❶ **Name** the memorized transaction in a way that clearly identifies the fixed asset. This will make it easy to find if you need to delete it—which will be necessary if the asset is sold or traded-in 167 before the end of its useful life, to stop the automatic depreciation entries.

★ **Using the same name prefix for all depreciation memorized transactions,** like "DEPR" in the example above, makes them easier to find in the memorized transactions list.

❷ **Automate Transaction Entry.** Select this option so the transaction will be re-entered automatically on the dates and for the number of times you set.

❸ **How Often** indicates how often you want the transaction to be re-entered in QuickBooks.

❹ **Next Date** indicates the next date in the future when you want the transaction to be re-entered.

❺ **Number Remaining** indicates the number of automatic entries to make in the future. For a 7-year asset the Number Remaining would be 6, because *it does not include the current entry* (the Check being memorized) which will be the asset's first depreciation expense entry.

❻ **Days in Advance to Enter** is the number of days ahead of the Next Date that you want the memorized transaction to be re-entered. If the Next Date is the actual date you want to use for the memorized transaction, Days in Advance to Enter should be 0.

4. **Click OK to save the settings** and close the Memorize Transaction window.

5. **Click the Save & Close button** to save the transaction and close the Checks form, **or Save & New** to save the transaction and keep the form open for entering another check.

That's it! This year and for the next 6 years (in this example), a depreciation expense entry will be made on the 31st day of December for the fixed asset identified as *Clark forklift 248*.

Why only one fixed asset per Check?

Suppose you have purchased a dozen different fixed assets this year, with expected useful lives of 5, 7, and 10 years. At year's end you set up a single memorized transaction to enter depreciation expense for all of those assets, and set it to repeat annually for 10 years.

Five years later, the annual depreciation entry for the 5-year assets needs to stop. But the memorized transaction is set up to work for 10 years! You would have to edit the memorized transaction and delete all of the 5-year assets from it to prevent additional depreciation expense from being posted for them.

"Aha!" you think, "I'll just set up *three* different memorized transactions—one for 5-year assets, one for 7-year assets, and one for 10-year assets—and have each of them repeat for the correct number of years—5, 7, or 10. That way, depreciation for the 5-year assets will automatically stop after the fifth year."

Correct, but there's still a problem: what if you sell one of the 5-year assets after owning it for only three years (two years short of its useful life)? Depreciation expense needs to be stopped for that asset but must continue for the other 5-year assets. So again, one way to fix this problem would be to edit the memorized transaction for 5-year assets and delete the sold Item, but that's a bit messy and prone to making errors.

So, the most sensible approach is to set up <u>one</u> memorized transaction for <u>each</u> fixed asset. Then if the asset is sold or disposed of before the end of its useful life you can simply delete the memorized transaction, preventing any more depreciation expense from being recorded for it.

What to Do if You Sell, Trade, or Dispose of the Fixed Asset

When the asset is gone—sold, traded-in, destroyed—the annual depreciation expense entry for it needs to be stopped. To do that, simply delete the asset's memorized transaction.

To delete a memorized transaction:

1. **Open the Memorized Transactions List** (Lists > Memorized Transactions List).
2. **Click on the memorized transaction you want to delete,** to select it.
3. **Type** *Ctrl-D* to delete the memorized transaction, or select *Delete Memorized Transaction* from the Memorized Transaction list's button menu at the bottom of the window.

Calculating Depreciation with a Spreadsheet

This section tells how to get and use a Microsoft Excel template for calculating depreciation, available as a free download from the publisher's Web site. Later sections of the chapter show how to import depreciation transactions prepared by the template, into QuickBooks.

Author's note: *You can find spreadsheet templates for calculating depreciation all over the Internet. As this is written, a Google search for "free depreciation schedule template" returns about 8,000 search hits! As you might guess, the usefulness of these free templates varies a lot. Some are quite good, but the majority produce a single "textbook ex-*

ample" depreciation schedule for one fixed asset at a time. Those are useful for learning how different depreciation methods work but not for creating depreciation transactions for dozens or hundreds of assets.

I wanted to provide you with something more robust and more useful—a depreciation template which is free but would:

1. ***Accommodate real-world circumstances** like the need for partial first-year depreciation, and non-calendar fiscal years.*
2. ***Maintain a list of all of your fixed assets,** and calculate depreciation expense for each asset for any given year.*
3. ***Prepare depreciation transactions for importing into QuickBooks,** to make the entire process simple and automated.*

So, this section is all about the template I designed to meet these goals, which works in Microsoft Excel and many other spreadsheet programs.

About the Depreciation Template

How to get the software you need (it's free)

The depreciation template is a free download, available from the ***FREE Stuff*** page at goflagship.com. Visit the following page in your Web browser (Google Chrome, Firefox, Internet Explorer, etc.), scroll down to find the template file, and then click the link to download the file.

www.goflagship.com/free-stuff.html

You can download either of two file types to get the template:

***.xlsx** This file type is compatible Microsoft Excel 2007 and later versions, on both Microsoft Windows and Apple Macintosh computers.

***.xls** The .xls file type should be compatible with most Excel-compatible spreadsheet programs, including older versions of Microsoft Excel and free spreadsheets such as OpenOffice Calc and LibreOffice Calc—so **Microsoft Excel is not required!**

If you use a spreadsheet other than a desktop edition of Excel, some of the instructions and menu selections shown in this chapter may need to be adjusted a bit for your particular spreadsheet, but adapting them should be easy.

How to open it

With appropriate spreadsheet software installed (Microsoft Excel or a compatible spreadsheet), you can open the template by (1) starting your spreadsheet program, then (2) selecting File > Open from its menu, (3) navigating to the location where the downloaded file was saved (on Microsoft Windows, typically a folder named *Downloads*), and (4) selecting the file you downloaded. You may also be able to open the file directly from within your Web browser by clicking on the file name in a list of downloaded files.

If you use a Web-based spreadsheet like the Google Sheets or the Microsoft Office 365 version of Excel, you should be able to upload or import the file into that spreadsheet as well.

How it is organized

The template has several worksheets, but you will use the *Asset List* more than any other worksheet in the template, so let's see how it is organized:

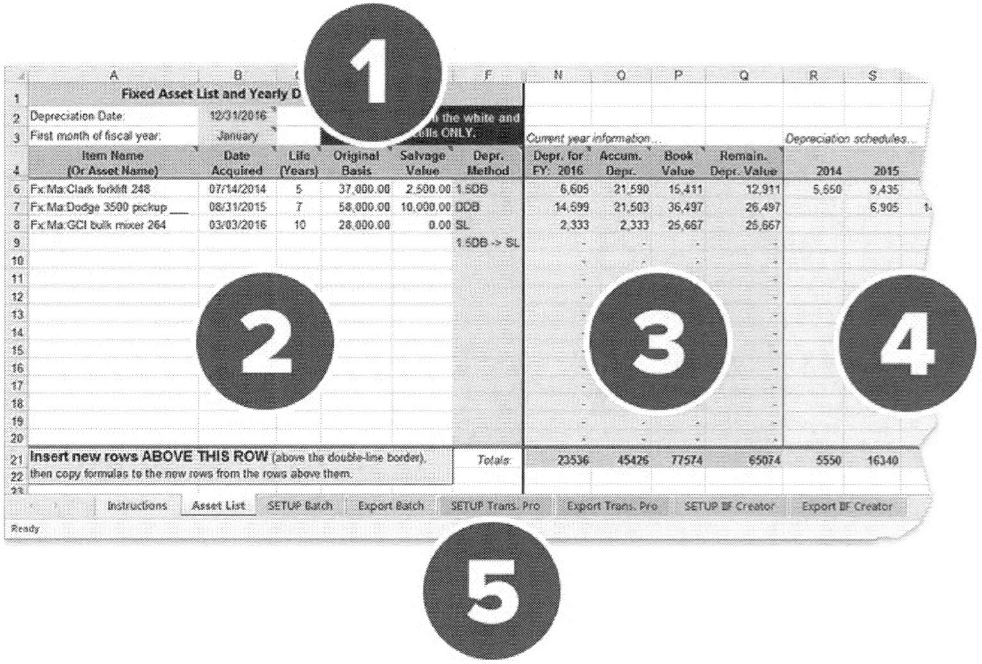

❶ **General information.** Fields near the top of the sheet give you a place to enter general information, such as the Depreciation Date.

❷ **Fixed asset list.** This is where you will enter information for each fixed asset to allow calculating depreciation for it, and creating a permanent list of your fixed assets which you can reuse for depreciation calculations every year.

❸ **Current year depreciation information** columns show calculated information for the current year (based on the Depreciation Date you have entered at the top of the worksheet).

❹ **Depreciation schedules** provide annual depreciation amounts for each asset over its useful lifetime.

The template only calculates yearly (not monthly) depreciation.

❺ **Tabs** at the bottom give you access to the template's various worksheets:

- **Instructions** provides an overview of the template and general instructions for using it.

- **Asset List** lets you maintain a list of fixed assets and calculates depreciation for them as described above.

- **Export tabs** build transactions for exporting to QuickBooks. The template supports several ways to export depreciation transactions to QuickBooks, and each tab conforms to requirements of a particular exporting method.

- **SETUP tabs.** Each export tab has an associated setup tab of the same color, where you can enter information needed for building transactions on the associated export tab. *SETUP Batch*, for instance, is the setup tab for the *Export Batch* tab.

Using the *Asset List* Worksheet

Here are basics of using the *Asset List*, which is where most of your time will be spent with the template. (The Export worksheets will be discussed later in the chapter.)

Entering basic depreciation information

Besides the details you will enter for each asset, two pieces of general information are needed for calculating depreciation:

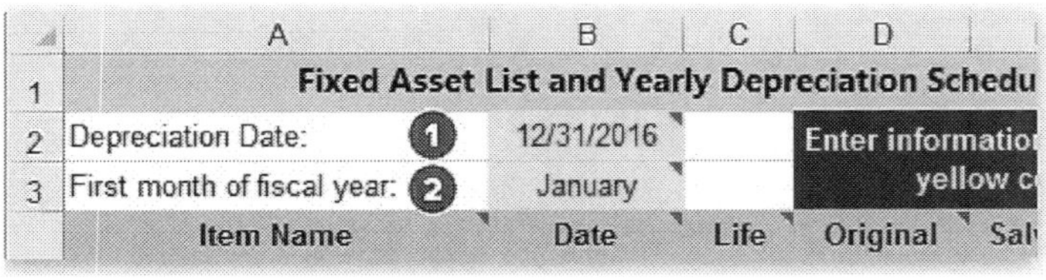

❶ **Depreciation Date** is the date for which you want depreciation expense to be calculated. It is used as the transaction date on depreciation transactions you export to QuickBooks. Also, depreciation is always calculated for the *fiscal year* in which the Depreciation Date falls:

Example 1: If you use the calendar year as your fiscal year, you might normally want depreciation transactions dated December 31st each year—12/31/2019 for the year 2019, for example. But the same depreciation amounts will be calculated if you enter December 20th or even July 4th, 2019 as the Depreciation Date...because these dates all fall within the 2019 fiscal year. (The template only calculates depreciation for individual years, not months.)

Example 2: If your fiscal year begins September 1 and the Depreciation Date is 08/31/2019 (the last day of August), depreciation expense will be calculated for the period September 1, 20<u>18</u> through August 31, 2019.

2 **First month of fiscal year.** Select the month in which your fiscal year begins—January if the calendar year is your fiscal year. This determines how much partial-year depreciation is calculated for the first and last years of the asset's life.

Adding assets to the *Asset List*

You may add assets to the list at any time, but its common to add them at year's end just prior to importing depreciation transactions into QuickBooks. Unless you have acquired very many fixed assets during the year, simply typing their Item names into the list may be the easiest way to add them.

How do you figure out which assets need to be added to the list? You could prepare a *Fixed Asset Purchases & Trade-ins* 223 report, which will show all newly acquired fixed assets for the entire year or other period you select for the report.

Another way is to simply compare the Item List with the *Asset List* worksheet to see which Items are missing from the *Asset List*. If you use special characters such as underscores [56] to identify newly acquired assets (ones which have not yet been assigned an asset number), finding their Item names in the Item List should be easy:

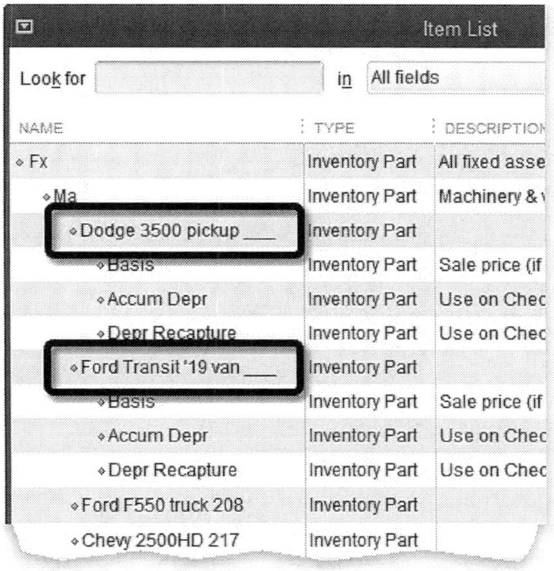

You need to add each asset's main Item name to the *Asset List*—*without* any subitems like Basis or Accum Depr—and be sure to enter the Item's *full name* (i.e., including its parent Items). For example, do *not* enter:

Dodge 3500 pickup ___

Instead, enter it this way (emphasis added to the parent Item names):

Fx:Ma: **Dodge 3500 pickup ___.**

- **A way to reduce typing mistakes** is to open an Item for editing in QuickBooks, Copy its name to the Windows clipboard, Paste the name into the *Asset List* sheet, then insert the parent Item names.

- Another way to find newly acquired assets is with a Fixed Asset Purchases & Trade-ins report.

In addition to Item names you need to enter depreciation information for each asset:

	A	B	C	D	E	F
1	Fixed Asset List and Yearly Depreciation Schedule					
2	Depreciation Date:	12/31/2016		Enter information in the white and yellow cells ONLY.		
3	First month of fiscal year:	January				
4	Item Name (Or Asset Name)	Date Acquired	Life (Years)	Original Basis	Salvage Value	Depr. Method
6	Fx:Ma:Clark forklift 248	07/14/2014	5	37,000.00	2,500.00	1.5DB
7	Fx:Ma:Dodge 3500 pickup	08/31/2015	7	58,000.00	10,000.00	DDB
8	Fx:Ma:GCI bulk mixer 264	03/03/2016	10	28,000.00	0.00	SL
9						

- **Date Acquired** is the asset's purchase date or acquisition date—acquired in a swap or barter transaction, for instance. This date is needed for calculating the asset's depreciation schedule (including partial first-year depreciation for assets purchased in any month other than the first month of the fiscal year). To find the date an asset was acquired you can open a QuickReport 211 for the Item, then double-click its purchase transaction to open the transaction to see the date it was acquired.

- **Life** is the asset's estimated useful life: the number of years over which you want to depreciate the asset.

- **Original Basis** is the total of the purchase price paid for the asset plus the book value of any trade-ins.

- **Salvage Value** is the expected salvage value of the asset at the end of its useful life, often 0.

- **Depr. Method.** This column contains a a dropdown list which lets you select a depreciation method for each asset. These methods are supported:

SL	Straight Line
SumYD	Sum of Years Digits
DB	Declining Balance
DB -> SL	Declining Balance with switch to Straight Line
1.5DB	150% Declining Balance
1.5DB -> SL	150% Declining Balance with switch to Straight Line
DDB	Double Declining Balance (200%)

DDB -> SL Double Declining Balance w/ switch to Straight Line

If you need to add a lot of assets to the list you can use a more mechanized approach. Prepare a QuickBooks report which includes full name paths for Items, and customize the report to include only the columns you need (Item, Purchase Date) and only transactions for the desired year. Then export the report to Microsoft Excel, where you can Copy Item names to the clipboard for Pasting into the *Asset List* sheet.

The Purchases by Vendor Detail report (Reports > Purchases > Purchases by Vendor Detail) is a good report to use for this, because it includes the transaction date—the Date Acquired for the Item.

Just a simple asset list/depreciation calculator?

Though the template was designed to support exporting transactions, as needed for the Simple/Smart method 18, there is no requirement to use it that way. Anyone who is *not* using the Simple/Smart method can use the template simply as an asset list with depreciation calculation abilities. If you choose to use it that way, you don't need to enter Item names: just enter asset names in the Item Name column of the *Asset List* sheet.

Calculated results

As you add assets and depreciation information to the list, calculated results for the current year (determined by the Depreciation Date entered at the top of the worksheet) will appear to the right:

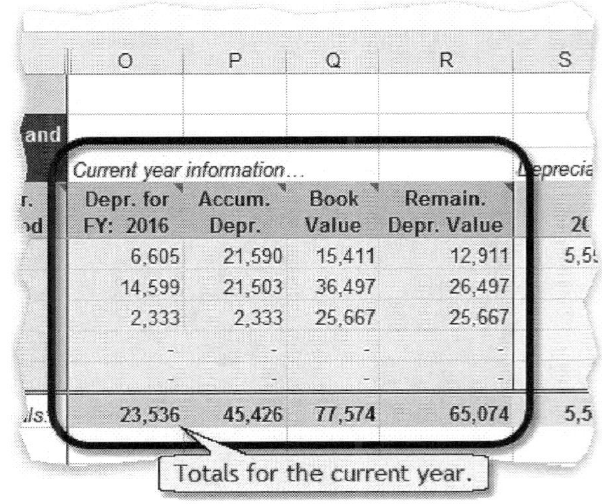

O	P	Q	R
Current year information...			
Depr. for FY: 2016	Accum. Depr.	Book Value	Remain. Depr. Value
6,605	21,590	15,411	12,911
14,599	21,503	36,497	26,497
2,333	2,333	25,667	25,667
-	-	-	-
-	-	-	-
23,536	45,426	77,574	65,074

- **Depr. for FY XXXX** is the amount of depreciation calculated for the current fiscal year, for each asset. (Actually, calculations are for the fiscal year which includes the Depreciation Date entered at the top of the worksheet.)

- **Accum. Depr.** is the accumulated depreciation amount for each asset, including the **Depr. for FY: XXXX** amount.

- **Book Value** is the book value of each asset: its Original Basis minus Accum. Depr. (accumulated depreciation).

- **Remain. Depr. Value** is an asset's remaining depreciable value: Book Value minus Salvage Value.

Farther to the right, are annual depreciation schedules for each asset, covering their entire useful lives:

S	T	U	V	W	X	Y
Depreciation schedules...						
2014	2015	2016	2017	2018	2019	2
5,550	9,435	6,605	4,623	3,236	5,051	
	6,905	14,599	10,428	7,448	5,320	2
		2,333	2,800	2,800	2,800	2,
5,550	**16,340**	**23,536**	**17,851**	**13,485**	**13,171**	**5,**

Column totals = depreciation expense for each year.

How To...

Calculate partial-year depreciation

If you sell a fixed asset 109 you may choose to enter depreciation expense for the part of the year it was owned before being sold. To calculate that amount:

- **Look up the asset's depreciation amount for the full year** in the Depreciation schedules section of the *Asset List*, then multiply that amount by the fraction of the year that the asset was owned.

  Example: Suppose you sell an asset in March of 2019, and find that its full-year depreciation amount for 2019 would have been $5,320:

Depreciation schedules...					
2014	2015	2016	2017	2018	2019
5,550	9,435	6,605	4,623	3,236	5,051
	6,905	14,599	10,428	7,448	5,320
		2,333	2,800	2,800	2,800

March is the 3rd month (of a calendar fiscal year), so the partial-year amount would be: $5,320 * 3/12 = $1330.

- In QuickBooks, **enter the $1,330 of depreciation expense** manually[156].

This would also be a good time to disable[178] the sold asset, as described next, to prevent including it in future depreciation expense transactions.

Disable an asset without deleting it from the list

Disabling an asset keeps it in the *Asset List* but prevents including it in depreciation expense transactions and displays it with a grayed background to show that it is disabled. To disable an asset, insert two asterisks (**) *at the beginning* of its Item name. The second asset in the list has been disabled in this example:

3	First month of fiscal year:	January		yellow cells ONLY.		
4	Item Name (Or Asset Name)	Date Acquired	Life (Years)	Original Basis	Salvage Value	Depr. Method
5	Fx:Ma:Clark forklift 248	07/14/2014	5	37,000.00	2,500.00	1.5DB
	**Fx:Ma:Dodge 3500 pickup	08/31/2015	7	58,000.00	10,000.00	DDB
8	Fx:Ma:GCI bulk mixer 264	03/03/2016	10	28,000.00	0.00	SL
9						

Handle an asset sale or trade-in

Assets which are sold or traded in need to either be deleted from the *Asset List* or disabled as described above[178]. Generally you should delete assets you no longer own. Keeping them in the *Asset List* is unnecessary, because important details—an asset's purchase date and amount, prior depreciation, sale date and amount, etc.—are available in QuickBooks.

You can delete assets throughout the year if you like, or wait until year's end. A good approach is to disable assets during the year as they are sold or traded in, then delete them after the year's business has been closed.

The best way to delete an asset is to delete its entire row from the worksheet rather than just erasing the asset's Item name and depreciation data but leaving the , to avoid clutter in the *Asset List*.

Compare depreciation methods

Sometimes you may want to compare depreciation methods for an asset before choosing one. You can do that by entering the same depreciation information on several rows of the *Asset List* but selecting a different depreciation method on each row.

You may label the rows with any text you want, or not at all. If you do label them, put two asterisks (**) at the beginning of the text to avoid having these "test" rows included in transactions exported to QuickBooks. For example:

	A	B	C	D	E	F	
1	**Fixed Asset List and Yearly Depreciation Schedule**						
2	Depreciation Date:	12/31/2016		Enter information in the white and yellow cells ONLY.			
3	First month of fiscal year:	January					Curr.
4	**Item Name (Or Asset Name)**	**Date Acquired**	**Life (Years)**	**Original Basis**	**Salvage Value**	**Depr. Method**	**De FY**
6	Fx:Ma:Clark forklift 248	07/14/2014	5	37,000.00	2,500.00	1.5DB	
7	Fx:Ma:Dodge 3500 pickup ___	08/31/2015	7	58,000.00	10,000.00	DDB	
8	Fx:Ma:GCI bulk mixer 264	03/03/2016	10	28,000.00	0.00	SL	
10	**Ditch Witch trencher	01/01/2019	7	73,000.00	5,000.00	SL	
11	**Ditch Witch trencher	01/01/2019	7	73,000.00	5,000.00	SumYD	
12	**Ditch Witch trencher	01/01/2019	7	73,000.00	5,000.00	DDB	

■ ■ ■

2018	2019	2020	2021	2022	2023	2024	2025	202
3,236	5,051							
7,448	5,320	2,843	457	0				
2,800	2,800	2,800	2,800	2,800	2,800	2,800	2,800	
	9,714	9,714	9,714	9,714	9,714	9,714	9,714	
	17,000	14,571	12,143	9,714	7,286	4,857	2,429	
	20,857	14,898	10,641	7,601	5,429	3,878	4,695	

Making the template work more quickly

As provided, the template automatically recalculates formulas whenever you change any data. If you have a lot of assets this can cause a noticeable lag in the template's responsiveness. If it is bothersome you can turn off automatic recalculation in Excel by selecting File > Options > Formulas > Workbook Calculation > Manual.

While automatic calculation is turned off (in Excel and most other spreadsheets) you must press the *F9* function key to have formulas recalculated.

The template's error messages *will not be displayed nor cleared* while automatic calculation is turned off. You must recalculate formulas to update the error message cells.

Save often!

It is a good idea to save the spreadsheet often as you add assets or make other changes. Otherwise, you risk losing your changes in the event of a sudden power failure or computer hardware problem.

Another good idea is to save the spreadsheet file to a new file name at least annually. That way, if you make a big mistake such as accidentally erasing some assets from the *Asset List* worksheet, you'll have prior-year worksheets available as backups, such as:

DepreciationTemplate2019.xlsx
DepreciationTemplate2018.xlsx
DepreciationTemplate2017.xlsx

Importing Depreciation Expense: Batch Enter Transactions

This discussion is intended for intermediate to advanced QuickBooks users.

It is less "step-by-step" than much of the rest of this book and skips details which most experienced QuickBooks users already understand.

Even if you automate depreciation calculations with a spreadsheet or with some other software application, you still face the job of getting depreciation transactions *entered* into QuickBooks. One option is to enter depreciation transactions manually 156, and that is reasonable to do for a small number of fixed assets. But what if you have several dozen fixed assets? Or several hundred?

This section shows how to import a batch of depreciation transactions—for all of your fixed assets at once—from the spreadsheet template [167] described earlier in the chapter, into QuickBooks' Batch Enter Transactions window.

But I have QuickBooks Pro or Premier, so I don't have the Batch Enter Transactions feature...do I? As you will see below, you probably <u>do</u> have it; you just need to know to access it.

If you use a spreadsheet other than a desktop edition of Microsoft Excel, the instructions and menu commands in this section will need to be adjusted a bit for your particular spreadsheet program, but adapting them should be easy.

One great thing about the Batch Enter Transactions window is that it *costs nothing to use*. The importing methods described later require purchasing additional software.

About Depreciation Expense Entered as a Batch

In *Entering Depreciation Expense Manually* [156], depreciation for individual assets was entered as multiple Item lines on the Checks form. To automate that process, you might reasonably assume that the details of a Check transaction could be prepared with a spreadsheet, Copied to the Windows clipboard, then Pasted into the Batch Enter Transactions window to create a Check entry. But not so! The Batch Enter Transactions window only supports entering *single-line* Checks—where only one expense account or one Item is involved.

If you are familiar with the Batch Enter Transactions window you might say "But hold on...why not just use the Split window?", and you would be *almost* correct. The Split window, accessible with a button click from Batch Enter Transactions, *does* let you enter multiple lines of a Check. Unfortunately, it *does not* allow them to be *pasted in* from the Windows clipboard—a necessity for importing transactions from a spreadsheet.

Fortunately there is an alternative: Batch Enter Transactions has a Bills & Bill Credits option which *will* allow multiple transaction lines to be pasted in all at once from the clipboard.

But I don't see *Batch Enter Transactions* in the QuickBooks menus...where is it?

Batch Enter Transactions is *advertised* as a feature of only the Accountant and Enterprise editions, but it has been available for several years in QuickBooks Pro and Premier—if you know where to look!

The availability of this feature in Pro and Premier may be due to an oversight by QuickBooks' programmers, so it could "go away" at any time in a future QuickBooks release. But it's just as likely to stay, as a bit of goodwill cast in the direction of Pro and Premier users by the makers of QuickBooks.

To see if Batch Enter Transactions is available in your edition of QuickBooks:

1. **Right-click on the icon bar** at the top or left side of QuickBooks' main window, **then select the option to customize it.**

   If your icon bar is at the top it may look like this:

   If your icon bar is at the left it may look like this:

   The Customize Icon Bar window will open.

2. **Click the Add button.**

The Add Icon Bar Item window will open.

3. **Scroll through the list of available icons** and **select the one named Batch Transactions** (if available)

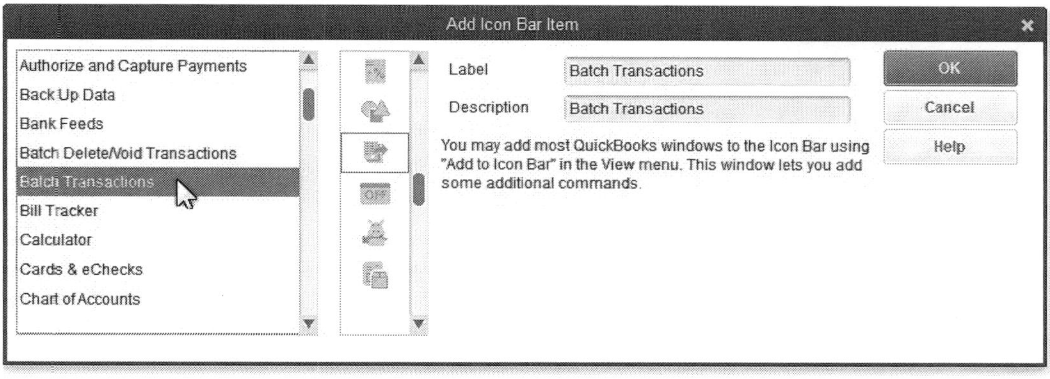

4. **Click OK** to close the Add Icon Bar Item window.

5. **Click OK** to close the Customize Icon Bar window.

After this, the icon should appear in QuickBooks' icon bar:

Unless something changes in a future QuickBooks release, the *only* way for Pro and Premier users to access the Batch Enter Transactions feature is by adding it to the icon bar—because *no menu selection is avail-*

able for it (unless you have QuickBooks Accountant or QuickBooks Enterprise, that is).

Configuring the Batch Enter Transactions window

1. In QuickBooks, **open the Batch Enter Transactions window** by clicking on its icon 182 in the icon bar.

2. **Select Bills & Bill Credits** as the transaction type.

3. **Customize the column layout** to include only the Item, Amount, Date, Vendor, Memo, and Account columns, *in that order.*

   Use the *Add* and *Remove* buttons to select columns, and the *Move Up* and *Move Down* buttons to change their order, as needed.

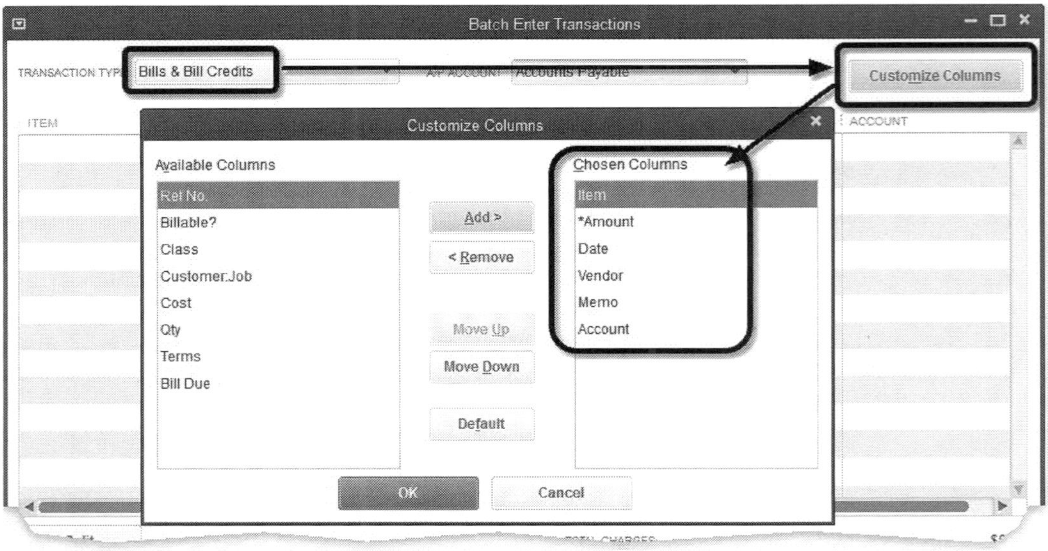

The main point is that the columns must match those on the *Export Batch* tab of the worksheet.

The Account column is an exception! It is not used in the worksheet but QuickBooks won't let you remove it, so put it last after the other columns.

Importing Depreciation Transactions

Here are some things to check before importing transactions from the spreadsheet into QuickBooks:

Spreadsheet checklist

- ❑ Enter the Depreciation Date and select the correct fiscal year first month, at the top of the *Asset List* sheet.
- ❑ Make sure Item names, purchase dates, and depreciation information for fixed assets acquired during the year have been entered in the *Asset List*, and that Item names are spelled exactly as they are in QuickBooks.
- ❑ Make sure all assets sold, salvaged, or traded in during the year have been either deleted from the *Asset List* or disabled[178].
- ❑ Examine calculated results on the *Asset List* sheet—book values, depreciation schedules, etc.—to see if they appear reasonable. If not, check the depreciation information you have entered, looking for problems.
- ❑ Enter information on the *SETUP Batch* tab, or review the information to see that it is correct.
- ❑ Look for warning messages on the *Export Batch* tab. (Each of the export tabs displays a warning message if it does not have enough rows for building transactions for all of the fixed assets in the *Asset List*.)
- ❑ Examine transactions on the *Export Batch* tab to see if they appear complete and reasonable. If not, look for problems on the *Asset List* sheet.
- ❑ Don't forget to save the spreadsheet file if you make any changes to the template or its data.

QuickBooks checklist

- ❑ Make sure each of the Items representing fixed assets has an Accum Depr subitem (or other name you have chosen to use for accumulated depreciation subitems). All fixed asset Items must use *the same* accumulated depreciation subitem name, and it must match the name you enter on the template's *SETUP Batch* tab.

- ❑ Open the Batch Enter Transactions window, select the Bills & Bill Credits transaction type, and make sure the columns are configured to match those on the *Export Batch* sheet as described earlier 184.

Importing transactions

1. In QuickBooks, **open the company file** which is to receive the depreciation transactions.

2. On the *Export Batch* tab of the spreadsheet, **highlight just the cells containing transaction details**. *Do not include the row of column names at the top.*

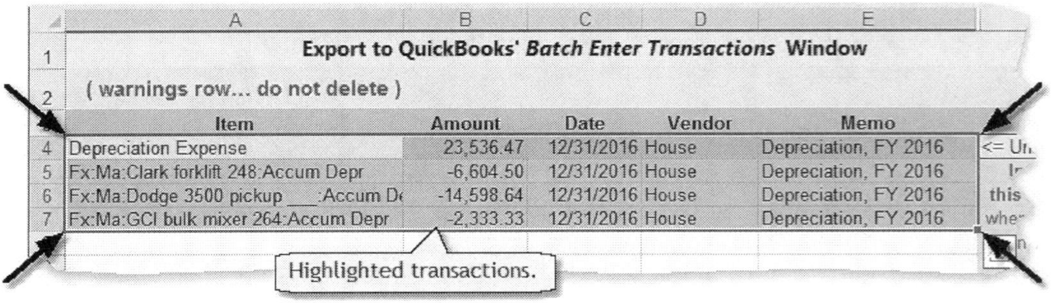

3. **Copy the highlighted transactions to the Windows clipboard,** by:

   - ❖ Typing *Ctrl-C*, or
   - ❖ Right-clicking in the highlighted area to display a pop-up menu, then selecting Copy from the menu, or
   - ❖ In Excel, selecting Home > Copy.

4. In QuickBooks, **open the Batch Enter Transactions window** by clicking on its icon 182 in QuickBooks' icon bar, if it is not already open.

5. **Click in the Item column** of the Batch Enter Transactions window, **then Paste the transactions** from the clipboard into the window by:

   - ❖ Typing *Ctrl-V*, or
   - ❖ Right-clicking in the Item column to display a pop-up menu, then selecting Paste from the menu, or

- ❖ In Excel, selecting Home > Paste.

Here are the transactions, after pasting them into the Batch Enter Transactions window:

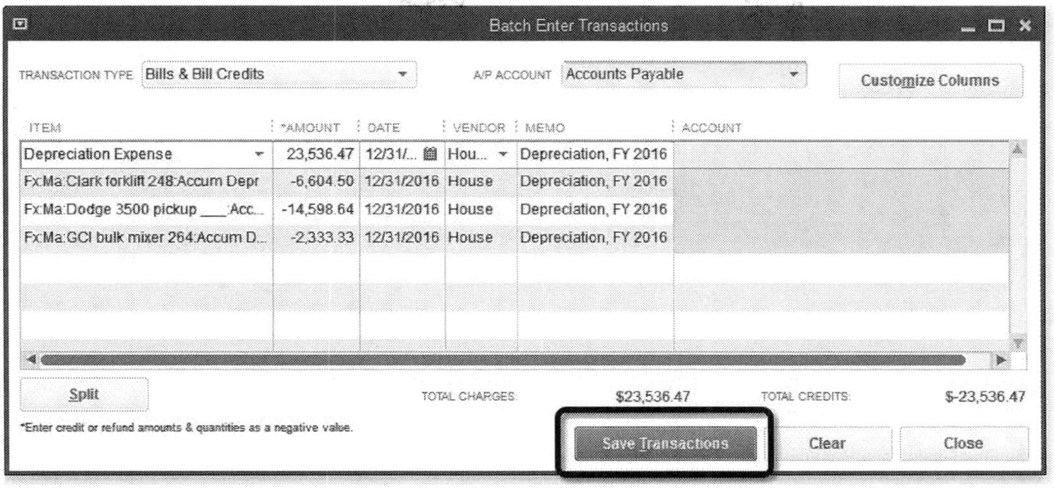

> **Depreciation amounts are different here** than shown earlier in the chapter, because different depreciation methods have been used.

6. **Click the Save Transactions button** to save the transactions.

   If there are problems with any of the transaction data QuickBooks will display it in red and give you an opportunity to make corrections before allowing the transactions to be saved.

   > **See *Questions & Problems*** 189 for details on handling problems with the pasted-in transactions.

7. **Click the Close button** to close the Batch Enter Transactions window.

Applying the Bill Credits to the Bill

The imported transactions consist of a number of Bill Credits—one for each asset's depreciation amount—and a single Bill for the total amount of depreciation expense. The Bill Credits must be applied to the Bill to offset (cancel out) the amount "owed" on the Bill. QuickBooks won't do that automatically: *you have to do it*, in the Pay Bills window.

1. **Open the Pay Bills window** (Vendors > Pay Bills).

2. **Select the Bill** created by the imported transactions, **by checkmarking it.**

   The Bill will likely be the only one for the vendor named "House" (or other name you use for in-house transactions), making the Bill easy to find.

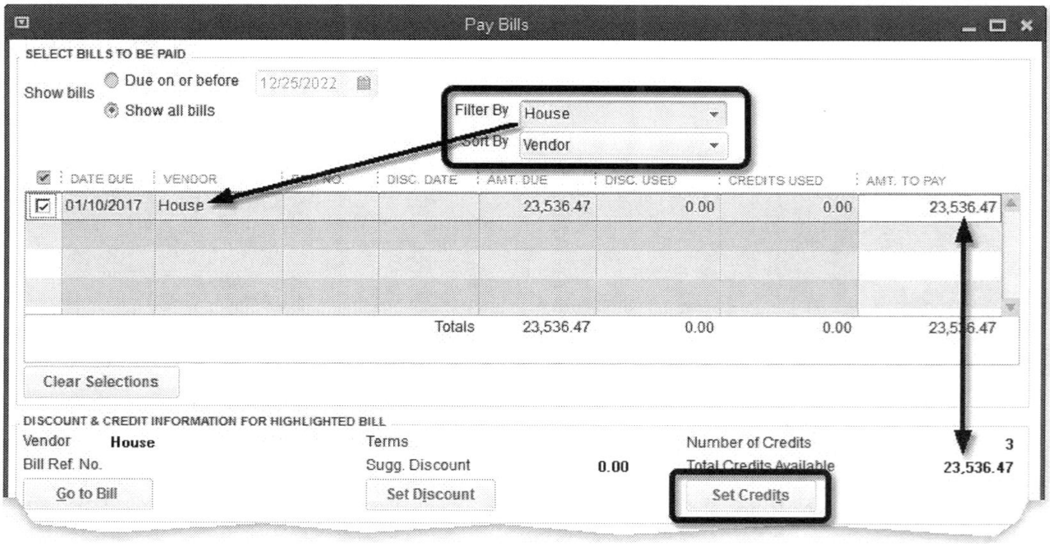

3. **Click the Set Credits button** to see the credits available for offsetting the Bill.

4. **Select each of the imported Bill Credits** by checkmarking them, **then click the Done button.**

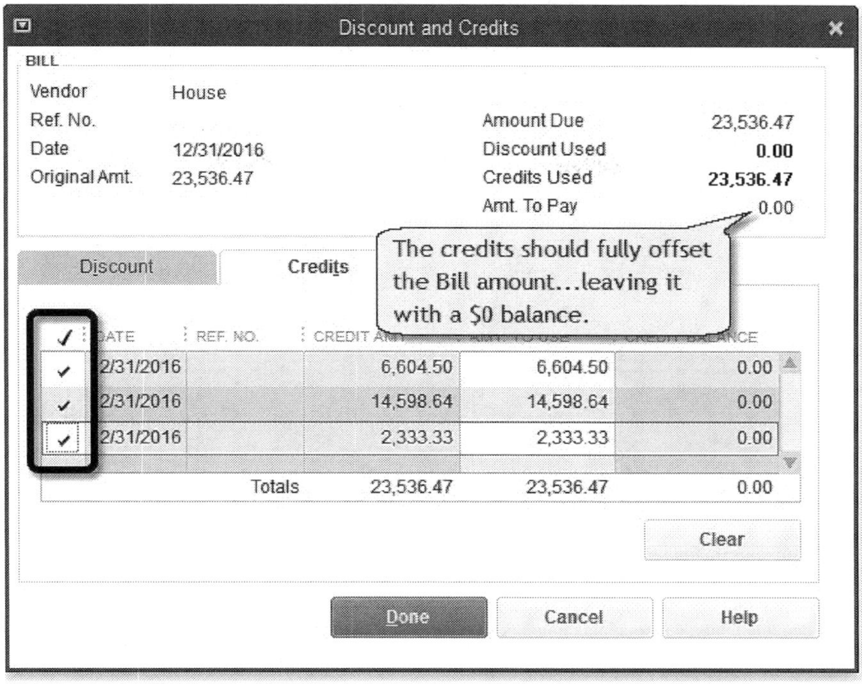

5. **Finally, click the Pay Selected Bills button** at the bottom of the Pay Bills window, to apply the Bill Credits to the Bill and close the window.

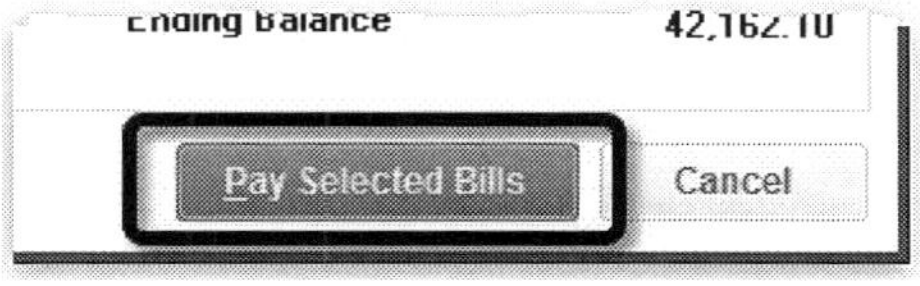

Questions & Problems

Why did QuickBooks reject one (or all) of my Item names?

QuickBooks will reject an Item name if any part of it is misspelled, so…

- Did you enter the Item name(s) correctly in the *Asset List* worksheet?
- Did you include the Item's full name path; that is, include its parent Items?

- Did you correctly spell the accumulated depreciation subitem name you entered on the *SETUP Batch* tab?

Why did QuickBooks reject my Vendor name?

Either you misspelled or failed to enter the Vendor name on the *SETUP Batch* tab.

I applied all of the Bill Credits to the Bill, but that didn't completely offset the Bill amount. Why not?

This is only likely to happen if the *Export Batch* worksheet does not have enough rows for creating transactions for all of your fixed assets. If a warning message like the following appears in the *Export Batch* worksheet, you need to insert more rows. After adding a sufficient number of rows (by following instructions on the worksheet), the error message will go away.

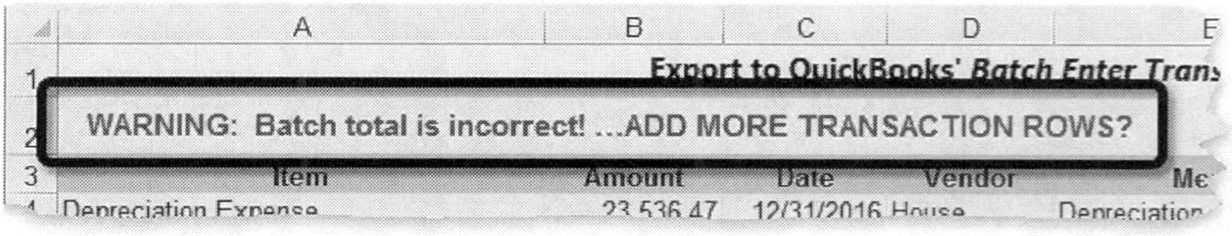

Importing Depreciation Expense: Transaction Pro Importer

> ***This discussion is intended for intermediate to advanced QuickBooks users.***
>
> It is less "step-by-step" than much of the rest of this book and skips details which most experienced QuickBooks users already understand.

Transaction Pro Importer (TPI) is a data importing utility which can import transactions and other data (Customers, Items, etc.) from a variety of file types into QuickBooks, available from Baystate Consulting at transactionpro.com. This section shows how to use TPI to import depreciation transactions into QuickBooks from the spreadsheet template [167] described earlier.

TPI lets you import a batch of depreciation entries as a single Check transaction, so it avoids the need to manually offset Bill Credits against a Bill as is necessary when using the Batch Enter Transactions [180] window.

> **If you use a spreadsheet other than a desktop edition of Microsoft Excel,** the instructions and menu commands in this section will need to be adjusted a bit for your particular spreadsheet program, but adapting them should be easy.

Importing Depreciation Transactions with Transaction Pro Importer (TPI)

Here are some things to check before using TPI to import transactions.

Spreadsheet checklist

❑ Enter the Depreciation Date and select the correct fiscal year first month, at the top of the *Asset List* sheet.

❑ Make sure Item names, purchase dates, and depreciation information for fixed assets acquired during the year have been entered in the *Asset List*, and that Item names are spelled exactly as they are in QuickBooks.

❑ Make sure all assets sold, salvaged, or traded in during the year have been either deleted from the *Asset List* or disabled [178].

❑ Examine calculated results on the *Asset List* sheet—book values, depreciation schedules, etc.—to see if they appear reasonable. If not, check the depreciation information you have entered, looking for problems.

❑ Enter information on the *SETUP Trans. Pro* tab, or review the information to see that it is correct.

❑ Look for warning messages on the *Export Trans. Pro* tab. (Each of the export tabs displays a warning message if it does not have enough rows for building transactions for all of the fixed assets in the *Asset List*.)

- ❑ Examine transactions on the *Export Trans. Pro* tab to see if they appear complete and reasonable. If not, look for problems on the *Asset List* sheet.
- ❑ Don't forget to save the spreadsheet file if you make any changes to the template or its data.

QuickBooks checklist

- ❑ Make sure each of the Items representing fixed assets has an Accum Depr subitem (or other name you have chosen to use for accumulated depreciation subitems). All fixed asset Items must use *the same* accumulated depreciation subitem name, and it must match the name you enter on the template's *SETUP Trans. Pro* tab.

TPI checklist

- ❑ Download and install the Transaction Pro Importer program, available at transactionpro.com. A free trial is available, so you can try TPI for a while before purchasing it.

Importing transactions

1. In QuickBooks, **open the company file** which is to receive the depreciation transactions.
2. In your spreadsheet program (Excel or other), **save the depreciation template file** (File > Save) if you have made any changes, **then close the file** (File > Close).

   TPI cannot import from the file while it is open in your spreadsheet program.

   You can view transactions on the *Export Trans. Pro* tab prior to closing the file:

	A	B	C	D	E	F	G	H	I
1	Bank Account	Payee	Transaction Date	RefNumber	Memo	Items Item	Items Qty	Items Description	Items Cost
2	CLEARING	House	12/31/2016	1234	Total depreciation expense, FY 2	Depreciation Expense	1	Depreciation,	23,536.47
3	CLEARING	House	12/31/2016	1234	Depreciation expense, FY 2016	Fx:Ma:Clark forklift 248:Accum Depr	-1	Depreciation,	6,604.50
4	CLEARING	House	12/31/2016	1234	Depreciation expense, FY 2016	Fx:Ma:Dodge 3500 pickup ___:Accum Depr	-1	Depreciation,	14,598.64
5	CLEARING	House	12/31/2016	1234	Depreciation expense, FY 2016	Fx:Ma:GCI bulk mixer 264:Accum Depr	-1	Depreciation,	2,333.33
6									

3. **Start TPI** by clicking on its icon in the Windows Start Menu, Windows desktop, or other location.

4. In TPI, **fill in information about the worksheet** to be imported.

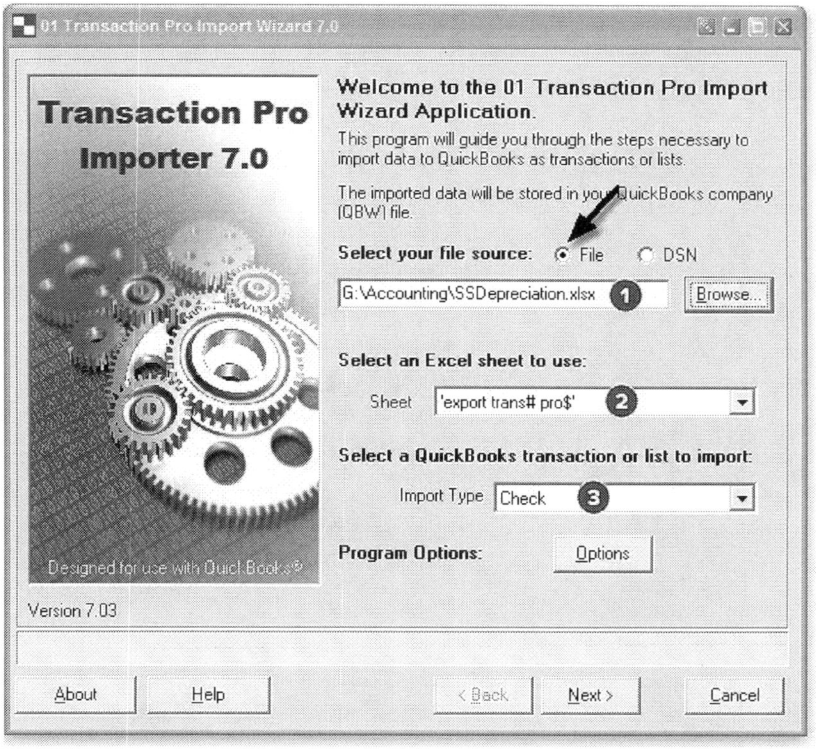

❶ **Select File** as the file source, **then select or enter the name of the template file.**

❷ **Select the name of worksheet** within the template **which contains transaction data to be imported.** Worksheet names appear a bit differently here than in the spreadsheet. The *Export Trans. Pro* worksheet should appear something like:

'export trans# pro$'

3 **Select Check as the import type,** because the depreciation entries will be imported into QuickBooks as a check.

5. **Click the Options button** (below the Import Type box) to open TPI's Options window.

6. **Select options** as shown below, **then click the Save button** to return to the main TPI window.

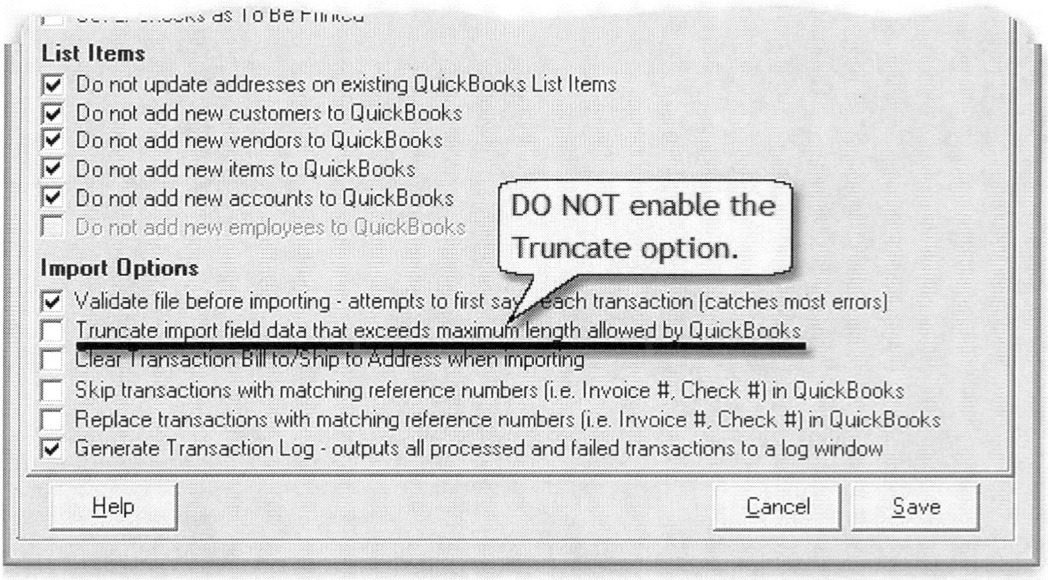

7. In the main TPI window, **click the Next button.**

   TPI will display a preview of the data to be imported.

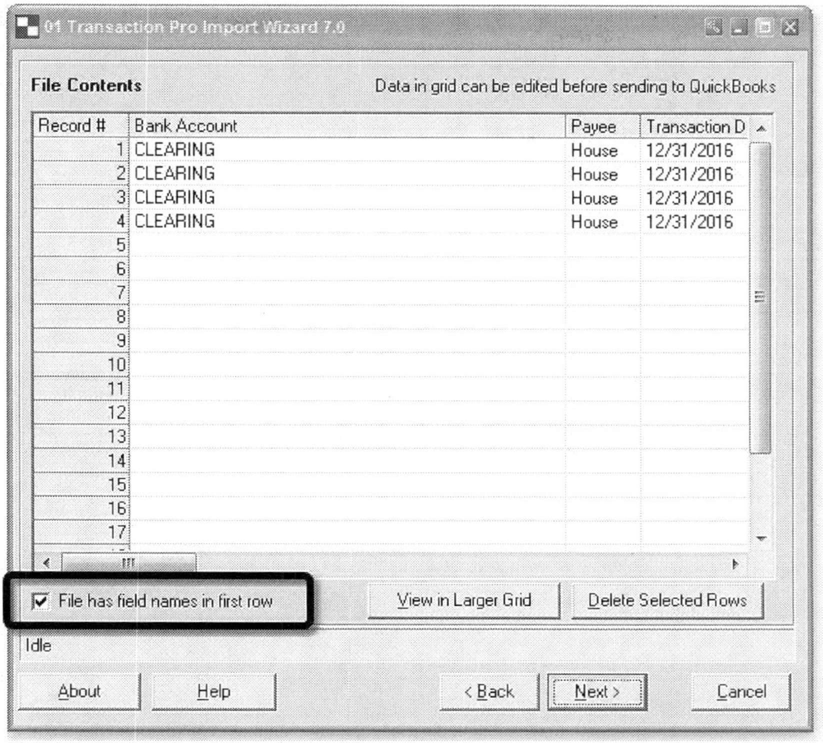

8. **Checkmark the *File has field names in first row* option** as shown above.

9. **Highlight *all* of the rows below the last actual transaction row.**

All rows where the *Bank Account* field is empty or which contain non-transaction messages or text should be highlighted:

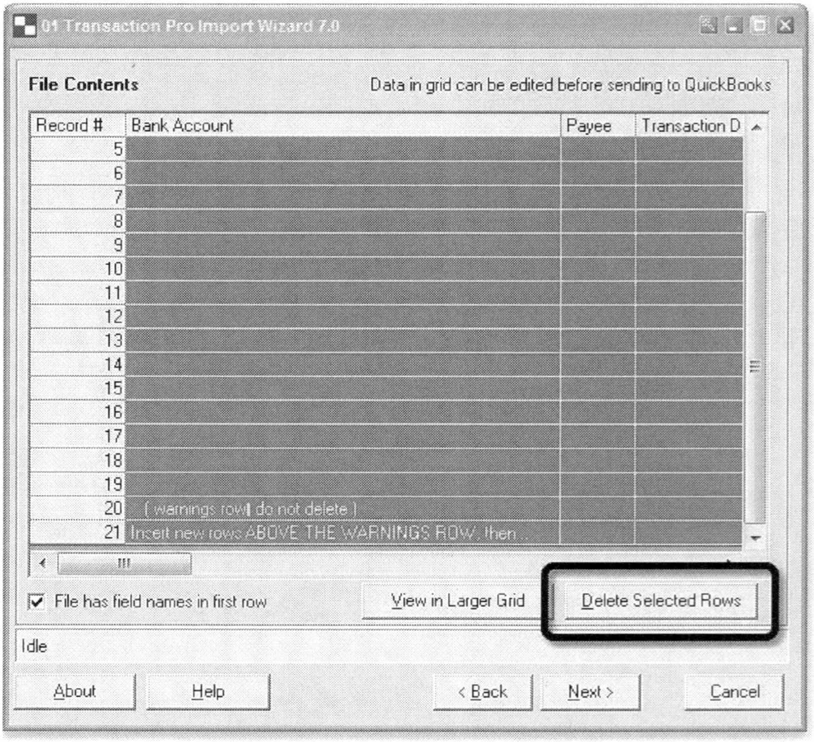

10. **Click the *Delete Selected Rows* button** to delete the highlighted rows.

The window should then contain only transaction rows:

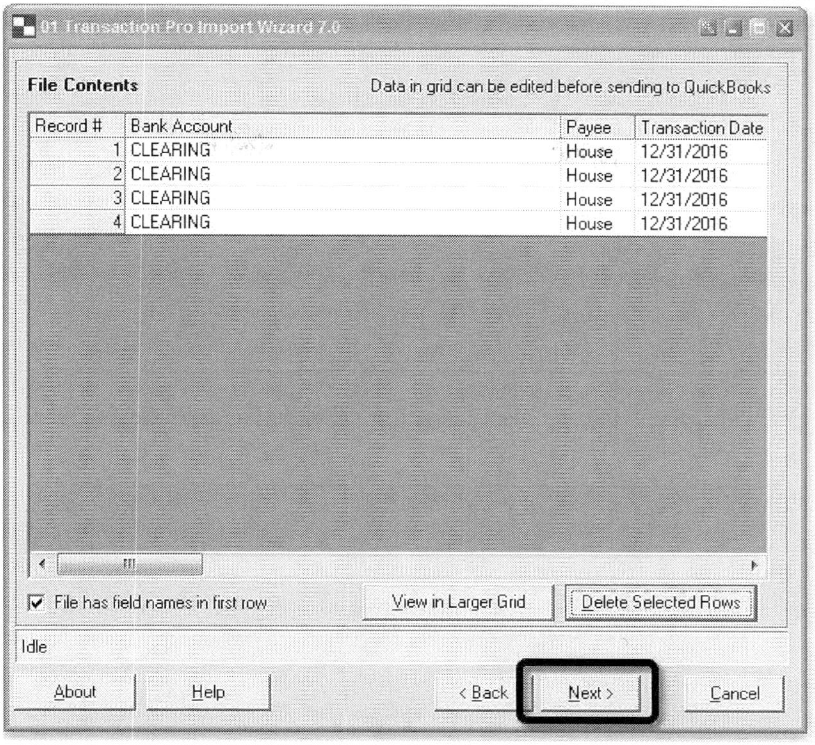

11. **Click the Next button** to move to the field name mapping window.

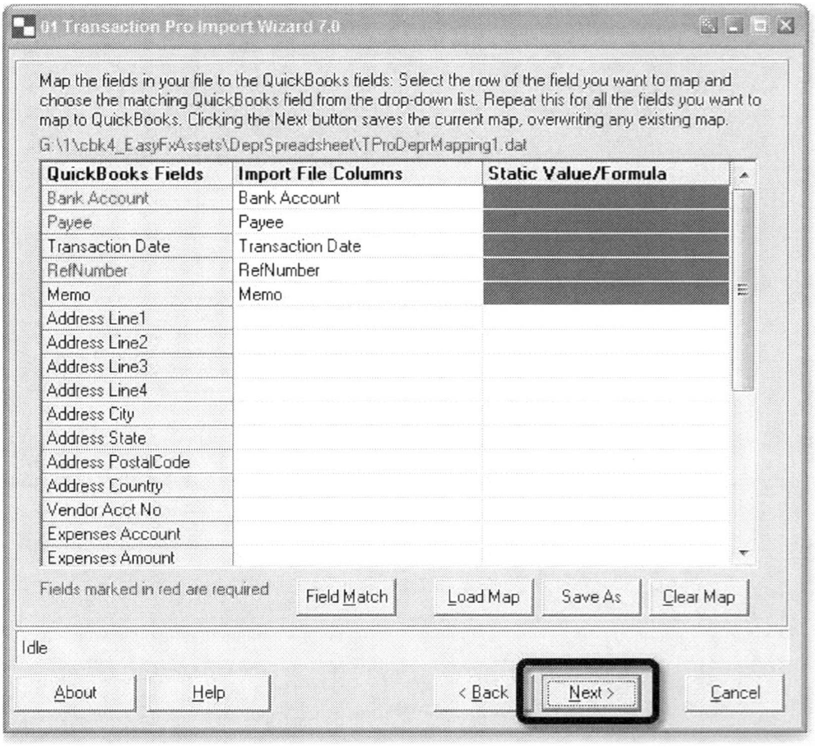

This window allows you to manually associate QuickBooks field names with field (column) names present in the import file. If you selected the correct spreadsheet file and the correct worksheet within the file however, no manual field name matching should be necessary. (The template's column names are designed to match QuickBooks field names.)

12. **Click the Next button.**

    If you get a message asking to overwrite your existing message grid, click on the Yes button. (If you also use TPI for importing other kinds of data, you may want to save the field mapping for each kind, using the *Load Map* and *Save As* buttons.)

13. At the next window (not shown), which allows editing the transaction data, **click the Next button again.**

    A window will be displayed for gathering information TPI can use to set up new QuickBooks Items—which should only be necessary if unknown Item names are detected in the import data. You may select any information you like here; the following is an example.

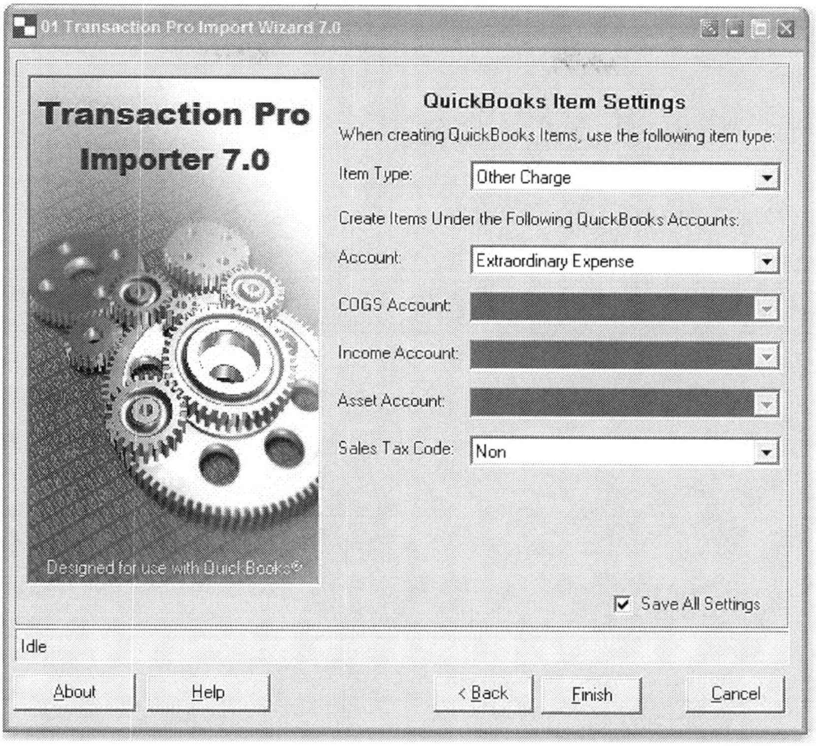

14. Click the Finish button.

TPI will ask if you want to begin the check transfer to QuickBooks.

15. Click OK to allow the transfer to take place.

The import data will then be sent to QuickBooks as a check.

16. You may view the imported Check in QuickBooks if you want, by finding it in the Register window for the CLEARING account (or other Bank type account you use for clearing transactions):

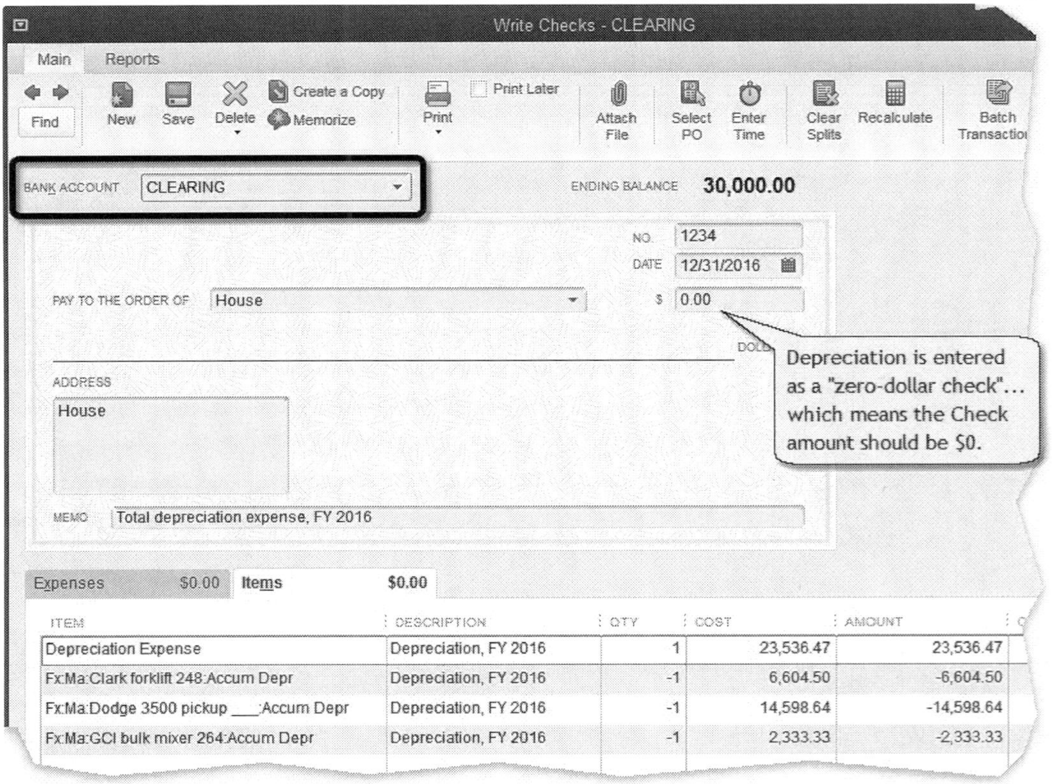

Questions & Problems

Why did QuickBooks reject one (or all) of my Item names?

QuickBooks will reject an Item name if any part of it is misspelled, so...

- Did you enter the Item name(s) correctly in the *Asset List* worksheet?
- Did you include the Item's full name path; that is, include its parent Items?
- Did you correctly spell the accumulated depreciation subitem name you entered on the *SETUP Trans. Pro* tab?

Why did QuickBooks reject my Vendor name?

Either you misspelled or failed to enter the Vendor name on the *SETUP Trans. Pro* tab.

The Check amount is not zero in QuickBooks, as it should be. Why not?

This is only likely to happen if the *Export Trans. Pro* worksheet does not have enough rows for creating transactions for all of your fixed assets. If a warning message like the following appears in the *Export Trans. Pro* worksheet, you need to insert more rows. After adding a sufficient number of rows (by following instructions on the worksheet), the error message will go away.

Importing Depreciation Expense: IIF Transaction Creator

> ***This discussion is intended for intermediate to advanced QuickBooks users.***
>
> It is less "step-by-step" than much of the rest of this book and skips details which most experienced QuickBooks users already understand.

IIF Transaction Creator (IIFTC) is a data importing utility which can import transactions and other data (Customers, Items, etc.) into QuickBooks from Microsoft Excel, available from Big Red Consulting at bigredconsulting.com. This section shows how to use IIFTC to import depreciation transactions into QuickBooks from the spreadsheet template 167 described earlier.

IIFTC lets you import a batch of depreciation entries as a single Check transaction, so it avoids the need to manually offset Bill Credits against a Bill as is necessary when using the Batch Enter Transactions 180 window.

If you use a spreadsheet other than a desktop edition of Microsoft Excel, the instructions and menu commands in this section will need to be adjusted a bit for your particular spreadsheet program, but adapting them should be easy.

Importing Depreciation Transactions with IIF Transaction Creator (IIFTC)

Here are some things to check before importing transactions using IIFTC.

Spreadsheet checklist

- ❑ Enter the Depreciation Date and select the correct fiscal year first month, at the top of the *Asset List* sheet.
- ❑ Make sure Item names, purchase dates, and depreciation information for fixed assets acquired during the year have been entered in the *Asset List*, and that Item names are spelled exactly as they are in QuickBooks.
- ❑ Make sure all assets sold, salvaged, or traded in during the year have been either deleted from the *Asset List* or disabled 178.
- ❑ Examine calculated results on the *Asset List* sheet—book values, depreciation schedules, etc.—to see if they appear reasonable. If not, check the depreciation information you have entered, looking for problems.
- ❑ Enter information on the *SETUP IIF Creator* tab, or review the information to see that it is correct.
- ❑ Look for warning messages on the *Export IIF Creator* tab. (Each of the export tabs displays a warning message if it does not have enough rows for building transactions for all of the fixed assets in the *Asset List*.)
- ❑ Examine transactions on the *Export IIF Creator* tab to see if they appear complete and reasonable. If not, look for problems on the *Asset List* sheet.

- ☐ Don't forget to save the spreadsheet file if you make any changes to the template or its data.

QuickBooks checklist

- ☐ Make sure each of the Items representing fixed assets has an Accum Depr subitem (or other name you have chosen to use for accumulated depreciation subitems). All fixed asset Items must use *the same* accumulated depreciation subitem name, and it must match the name you enter on the template's *SETUP IIF Creator* tab.

IIFTC checklist

- ☐ Download and install the IIF Transaction Creator program, available at bigredconsulting.com. A free trial is available, so you can try IIFTC for a while before purchasing it.

- ☐ If the IIFTC installation is successful, a menu item for controlling the importing process will be added in Microsoft Excel:

Importing transactions

> **Before beginning...***start <u>both</u> QuickBooks and Microsoft Excel in Administrator mode:* right-click on the icon you use for starting each program, and select *Run as administrator*. This should prevent connection problems in step 4, below.

1. In QuickBooks, **open the company file** which is to receive the depreciation transactions.

2. In Excel, **open the depreciation template** 167**, then click on the** *Export IIF Creator* **tab.**

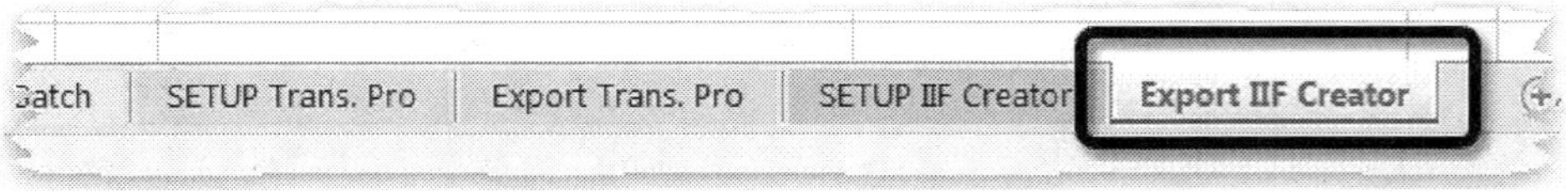

3. **Select** IIF Creator > Step 2. Integrate QuickBooks Lists from Excel's main menu.

The Integrate QuickBooks Lists window will open.

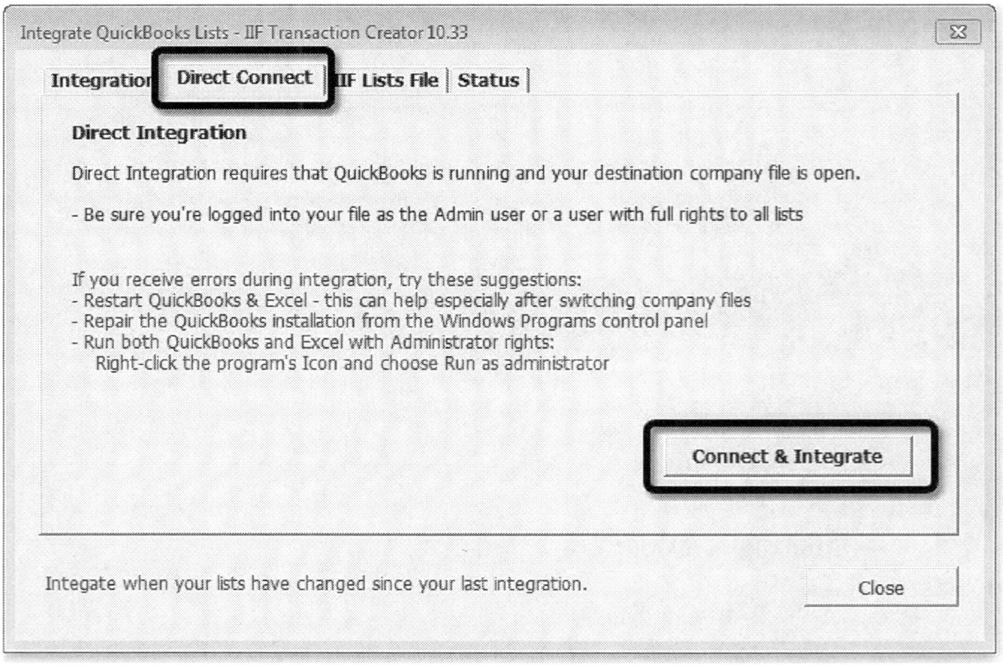

4. **Click on the *Direct Connect* tab, then on the *Connect & Integrate* button.**

IIFTC will connect to QuickBooks and retrieve QuickBooks lists, etc., to be used later for verifying information in the transactions before importing them).

5. **Select** IIF Creator > Step 3. Check Worksheet from Excel's main menu.

IIFTC will check the *Export IIF Creator* worksheet for problems. You may receive informational messages but the worksheet should be OK for exporting. **Press the Continue button** to dismiss the messages.

The Check Worksheet window will be displayed. It should not list any "new" names, items, etc. (list items found in the spreadsheet but not in QuickBooks).

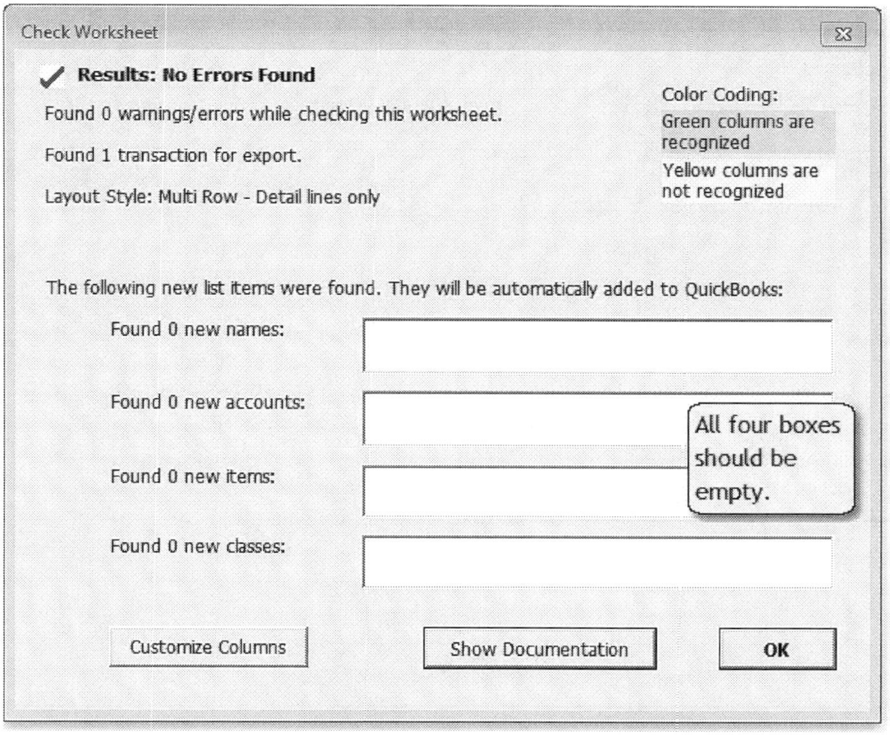

6. **Click the OK button** to close the Check Worksheet window.

7. **Select** IIF Creator > Step 4. Create IIF File from Excel's main menu.

The Create IIF File window will open. It gathers information needed for creating an IIF file, which is a file type QuickBooks accepts for importing transactions and lists (customers, vendors, items, etc.).

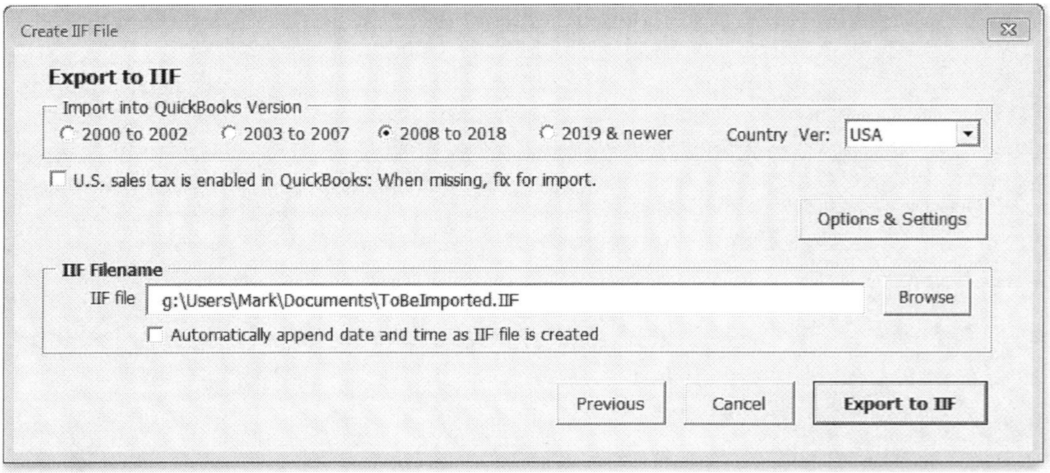

8. **Select the QuickBooks version, and a file name/location** for the IIF file.

   The filename extension should be .IIF (the file name should have .IIF at the end) as shown in the illustration above.

9. **Click the *Export to IIF* button.**

10. **Select** IIF Creator > Step 5. Import your IIF File from Excel's main menu.

The Import IIF File window will open, providing instructions about how to import the file into QuickBooks.

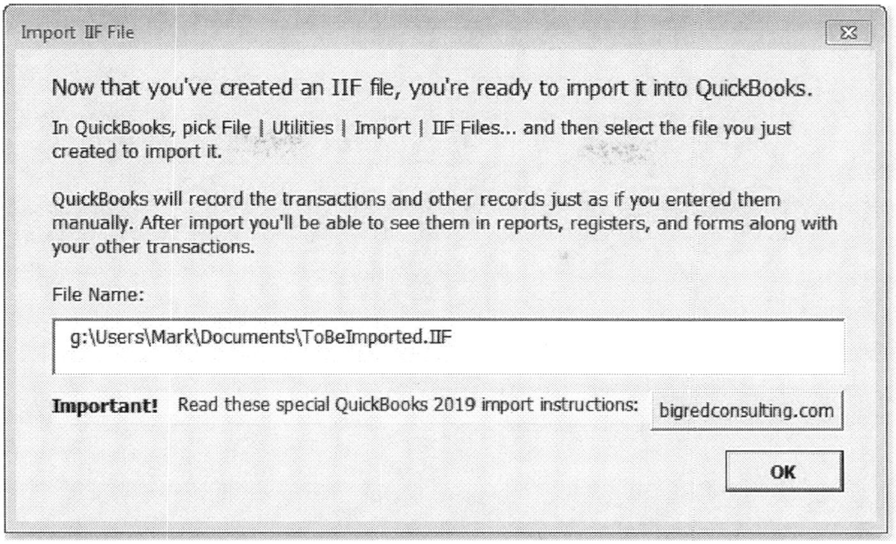

11. **Click the OK button** to close the window. **Or, you may leave it open until you have imported the .IIF file into QuickBooks,** as a reminder of the file's location.

    You may also Copy the file's name to the Windows clipboard by highlighting the entire file name and path, then pressing *Ctrl-C*, so you can Paste it into the file open dialog in QuickBooks, in step 13 below.

12. In QuickBooks, **select** File > Utilities > Import > IIF Files.

    A window will open for selecting an IIF to import.

13. **Enter the file's name, then click on the Open button.**

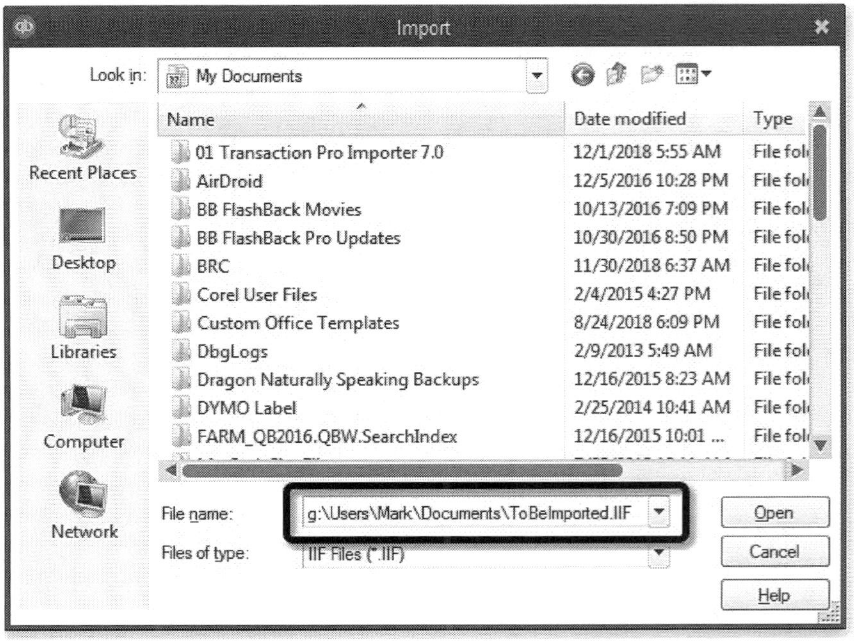

QuickBooks will import the file, creating a Check transaction.

14. **You may view the imported Check in QuickBooks if you want,** by finding it in the Register window for the CLEARING account (or other Bank type account you use for clearing transactions):

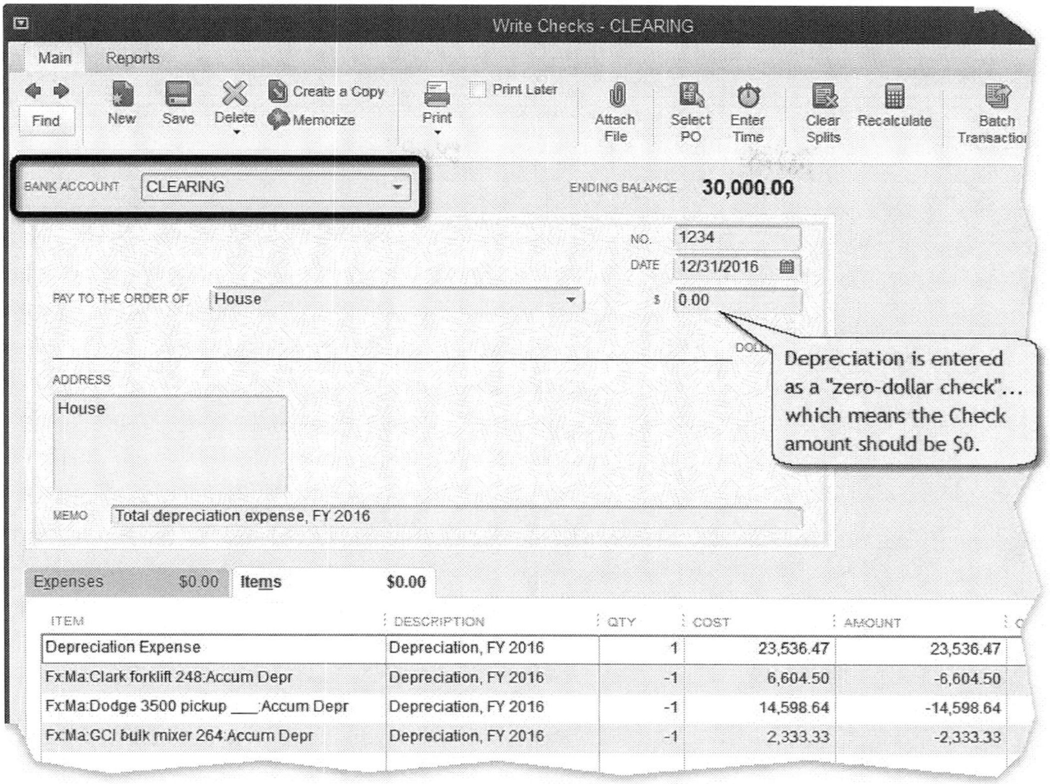

Questions & Problems

Why did IIFTC say that one (or several) of my Item names were "new"?

Any Item name for which an exact match is not found in QuickBooks will be seen as a "new" Item by IIFTC, so...

- Did you enter the Item name(s) correctly in the *Asset List* worksheet?
- Did you include the Item's full name path; that is, include its parent Items?
- Did you correctly spell the accumulated depreciation subitem name you entered on the *SETUP IIF Creator* tab?

Why did QuickBooks say my Vendor name was "new"?

Either you misspelled or failed to enter the Vendor name on the *SETUP Trans. Pro* tab.

The Check amount is not zero in QuickBooks, as it should be. Why not?

This is only likely to happen if the *Export IIF Creator* worksheet does not have enough rows for creating transactions for all of your fixed assets. If a warning message like the following appears in the *Export IIF Creator* worksheet, you need to insert more rows. After adding a sufficient number of rows (by following instructions on the worksheet), the error message will go away.

CHAPTER 10

Reports for Fixed Assets

About this chapter	This chapter shows how to prepare fixed asset reports for day-to-day activities as well as for income tax preparation.

Everyday Reports

Two reports are especially useful for working with the S/S-method 18 of handling fixed assets:

- The Item QuickReport 211 will likely be your "workhorse" report for fixed assets, because it provides quick access to all of the transactions involving a single asset, or all fixed assets in a particular category such as machinery or buildings.
- The Fixed Asset List report 211 is useful for seeing the original basis, accumulated depreciation, and current book values of fixed assets.

Item QuickReports

For one fixed asset...

1. **Open the Item List window** (Lists > Item List).
2. **Click on the desired Item,** to highlight it.

   To get the report for a specific fixed asset, click on its main Item. (The asset's subitems will automatically be included in the report.)

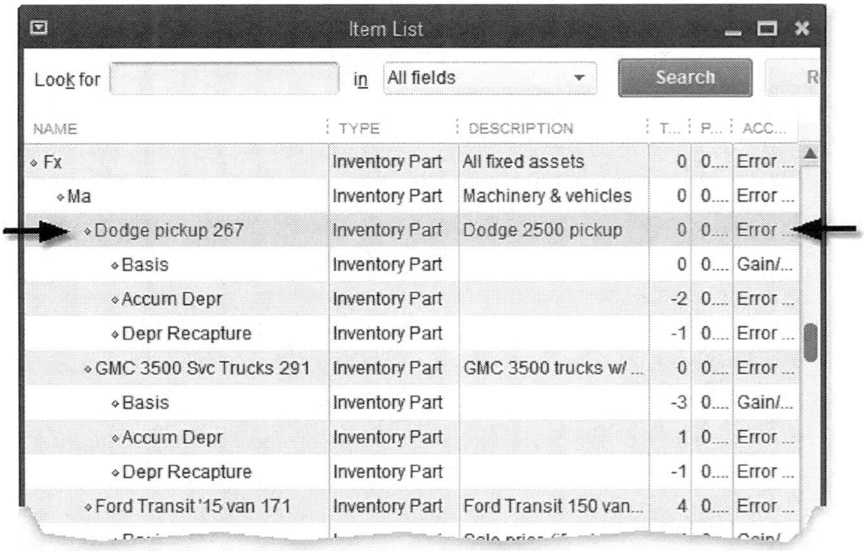

3. **Type** *Ctrl-Q* to open a QuickReport window for the Item, or select *Quick-Report* from the Reports button menu at the bottom of Item List window:

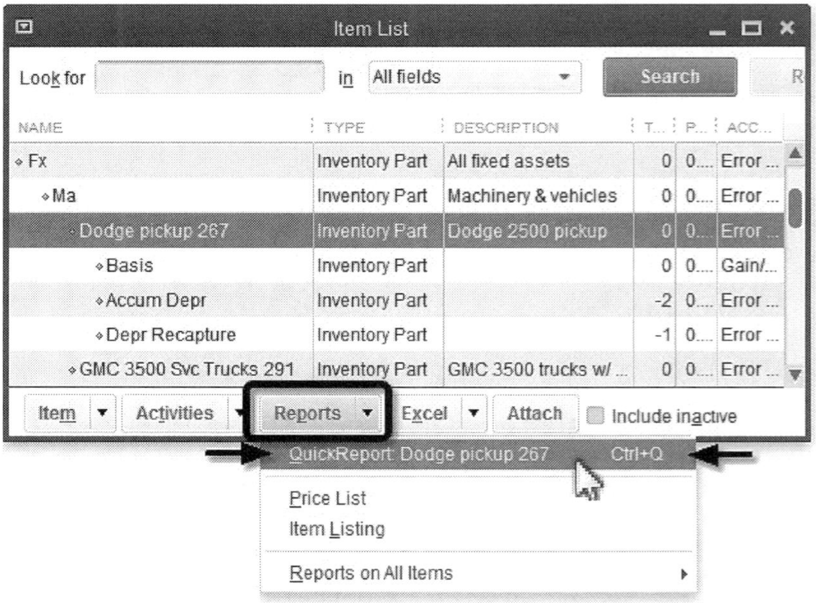

A QuickReport window will open for the Item you selected. By default, it will list the Item's transactions *for the current fiscal year*.

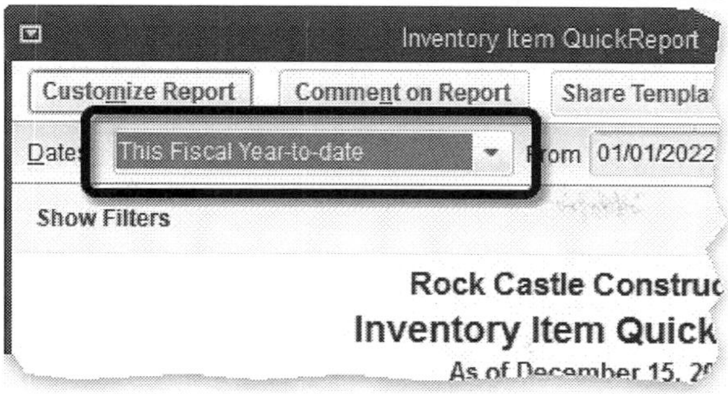

4. *Optional.* Most of the time you should change the report's Date setting to *All*, to include all of the asset's transactions (some may be from other years):

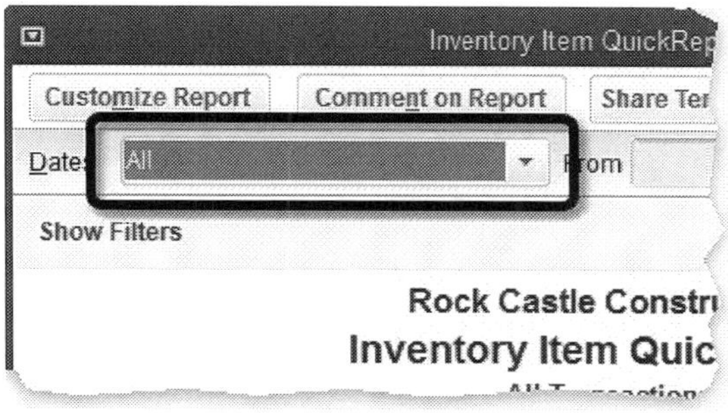

Adding the Amount column

Unfortunately, by default an Item QuickReport does not include any financial amounts! The report will be more useful for fixed asset information if you customize it to include the Amount column:

5. **Click the Customize Report button** at the top of the QuickReport window.

The Modify Report window will open.

6. On the Display tab of the Modify Report window, **select *Amount* in the Columns area,** by checkmarking it.

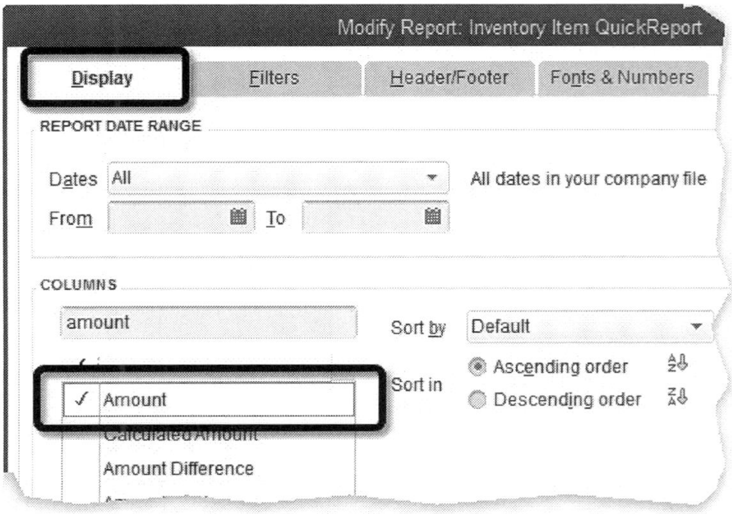

7. **Click the OK button** to close the Modify Report window and update the report.

With the Amount column included, the report now shows an amount for each of the asset's transactions.

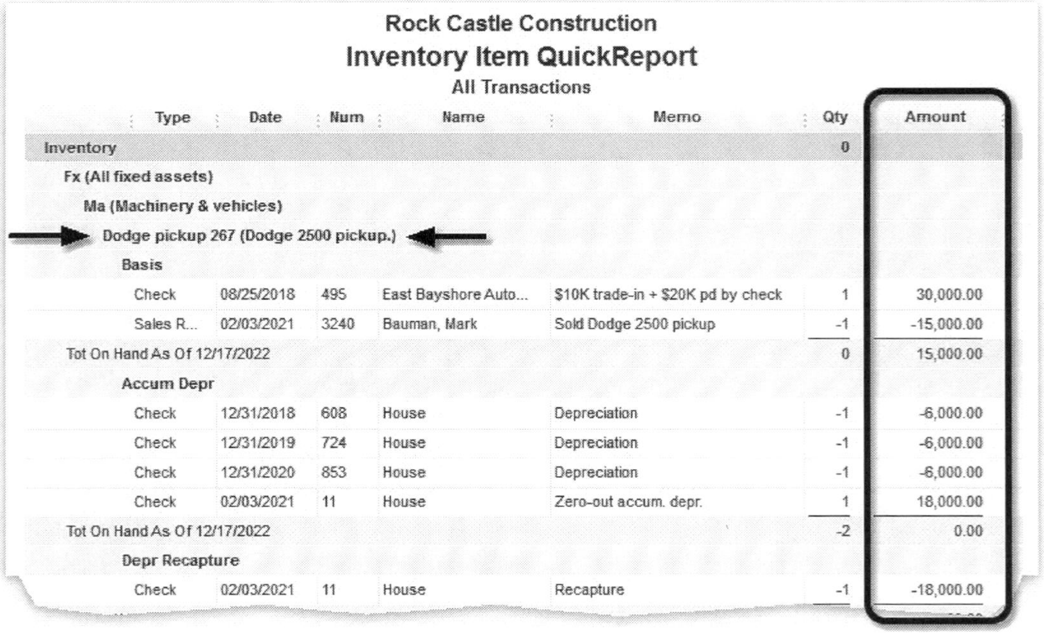
Rock Castle Construction

Inventory Item QuickReport

All Transactions

Type	Date	Num	Name	Memo	Qty	Amount
Inventory					0	
Fx (All fixed assets)						
Ma (Machinery & vehicles)						
Dodge pickup 267 (Dodge 2500 pickup.)						
Basis						
Check	08/25/2018	495	East Bayshore Auto...	$10K trade-in + $20K pd by check	1	30,000.00
Sales R...	02/03/2021	3240	Bauman, Mark	Sold Dodge 2500 pickup	-1	-15,000.00
Tot On Hand As Of 12/17/2022					0	15,000.00
Accum Depr						
Check	12/31/2018	608	House	Depreciation	-1	-6,000.00
Check	12/31/2019	724	House	Depreciation	-1	-6,000.00
Check	12/31/2020	853	House	Depreciation	-1	-6,000.00
Check	02/03/2021	11	House	Zero-out accum. depr.	1	18,000.00
Tot On Hand As Of 12/17/2022					-2	0.00
Depr Recapture						
Check	02/03/2021	11	House	Recapture	-1	-18,000.00

Should you memorize this Item QuickReport? ...Yes!

Because Item QuickReports don't automatically include the Amount column —and it really needs to be there to make the report useful for fixed asset information—you should memorize the customized report so that it can be recreated easily.

To memorize the customized QuickReport (i.e., with the Amount column included), click on the Memorize button in the upper part of the report window.

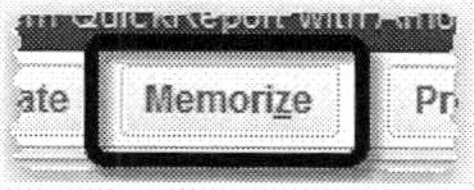

Then whenever you want to create the report for a specific fixed asset(s), select it from the Memorized Reports List (Reports > Memorized Report) and change the report filter 215 to include the Item(s) you want to know about.

***Filtering* a report** means controlling or limiting the information included in it.To filter a report, click the Customize Report button in the upper part of the report window. That will open the Modify Report window, where you can use the Filters tab to set a filter(s) for the report.

For multiple fixed assets...

Item QuickReports also work well for getting information about your entire list of fixed assets, or only part of it if you want. All you need to do is change the report filter to include a wider (or narrower) range of Items in the report:

1. **Open an Item QuickReport and** customize it to **include the Amount column** as described above 211.

   If you have memorized the report, simply select it from the memorized reports list (Reports > Memorized Reports).

2. **Click the Customize Report button** at the top of the QuickReport window.

The Modify Report window will open.

3. On the Filters tab, **select *Item* in the Filter panel, then select the desired parent Item** in the dropdown list in the center of the window.

   If you want the report to include all fixed assets, select the master parent Item 55 (assuming you are using one).

   If you want the report limited to a narrower category, select the Item representing that category. This example sets a filter for *Fx:Ma*, limiting the report to Machinery fixed assets.

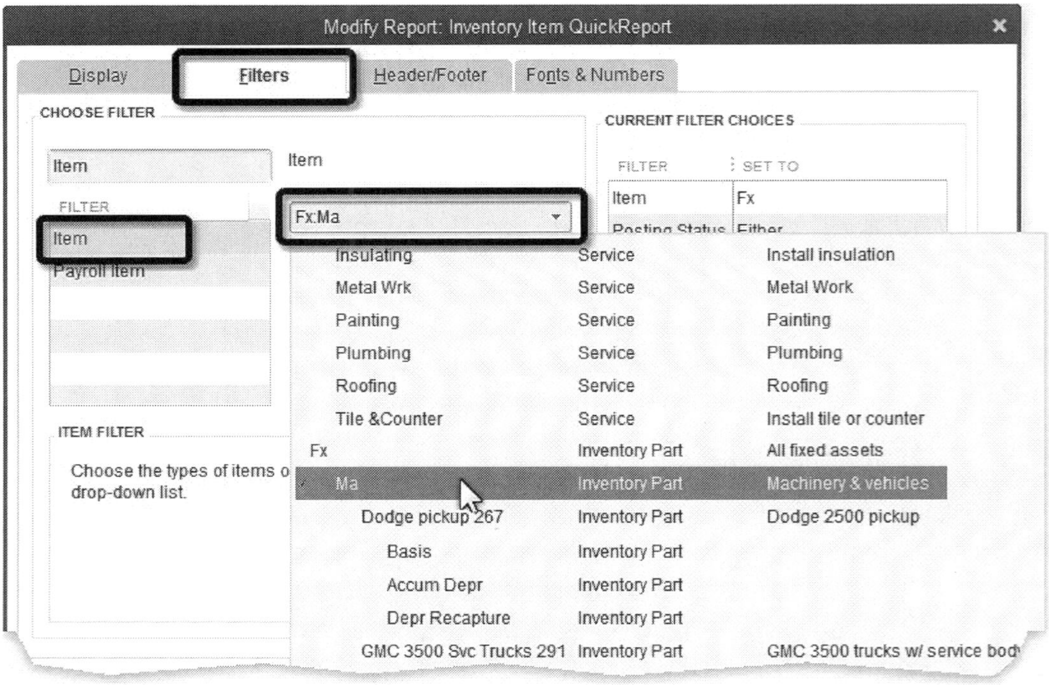

4. **Click the OK button** to close the Modify Report window and update the report.

   Now instead of a single Item the report will show information for all Items included by the filter; in this case, all fixed assets which happen to be subitems of *Fx:Ma* (Machinery fixed assets):

Rock Castle Construction
Inventory Item QuickReport
All Transactions

	Type	Date	Num	Name	Memo	Qty	Amount
Inventory						0	
Fx (All fixed assets)							
Ma (Machinery & vehicles)							
Dodge pickup 267 (Dodge 2500 pickup.)							
Basis							
	Check	08/25/2018	495	East Bayshore Auto...	$10K trade-in + $20K pd by check	1	30,000.00
	Sales R...	02/03/2021	3240	Bauman, Mark	Sold Dodge 2500 pickup	-1	-15,000.00
Tot On Hand As Of 12/17/2022						0	15,000.00
Accum Depr							
	Check	12/31/2018	608	House	Depreciation	-1	-6,000.00
	Check	12/31/2019	724	House	Depreciation	-1	-6,000.00
	Check	12/31/2020	853	House	Depreciation	-1	-6,000.00
	Check	02/03/2021	11	House	Zero-out accum. depr.	1	18,000.00
Tot On Hand As Of 12/17/2022						-2	0.00
Depr Recapture							
	Check	02/03/2021	11	House	Recapture	-1	-18,000.00
Tot On Hand As Of 12/17/2022						-1	-18,000.00
Total Dodge pickup 267 (Dodge 2500 pickup.)						-3	-3,000.00
GMC 3500 Svc Trucks 291 (GMC 3500 trucks w/ service body.)							
Basis							

And many others...

Fixed Asset Book Values Report

Sometimes you may want a list of fixed assets and their book values; for example, to include as supplemental documentation with a balance sheet report. Here are the steps for preparing a report which shows the book values (original basis minus accumulated depreciation) of all fixed assets. If you prefer, you can limit the report to a single asset or group of assets.

If part of a fixed asset group 143 **has been sold,** the report lists the original basis and accumulated depreciation *of the remaining group members* (i.e., the part of the group which has not been sold), not the original basis of the entire group.

1. **Open a Custom Summary report** (Reports > Custom Reports > Summary).

When the report window opens, the Modify Report window will also open. (If it doesn't open automatically, click the Customize Report button in the upper part of the report window.)

2. In the Modify Report window, **select the Display tab options shown below**.

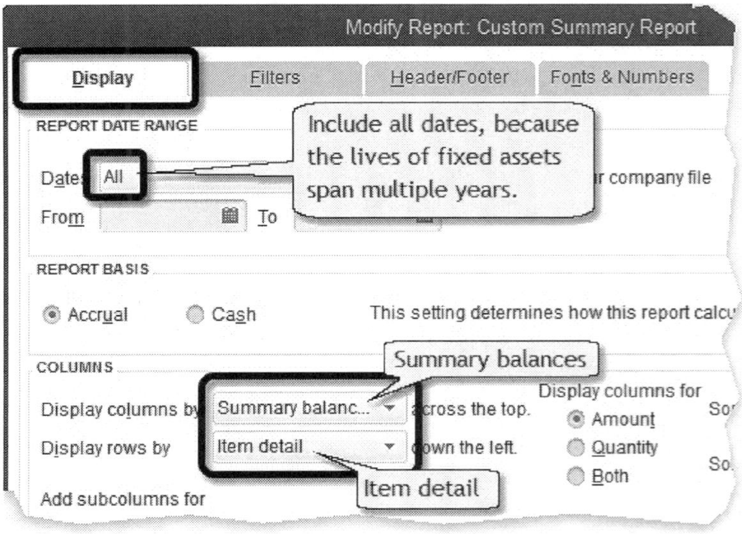

3. On the Filters tab, **set an Item filter by selecting the master parent Item**[55] you are using for fixed assets, such as the *Fx* Item described in *Organizing the Item List*[54] in Chapter 4.

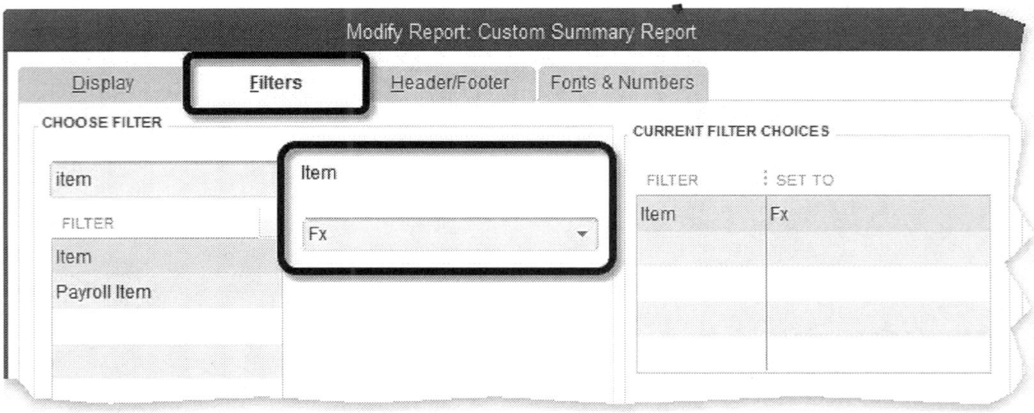

4. **Also set an Account filter, selecting the** *All balance sheet accounts* **option.**.

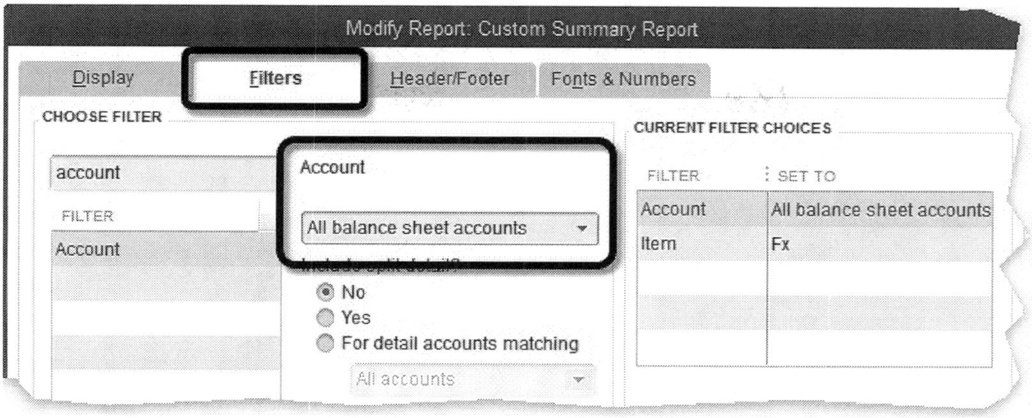

5. On the Header/Footer tab, **change the report title** to something like *Fixed Asset Book Values.*

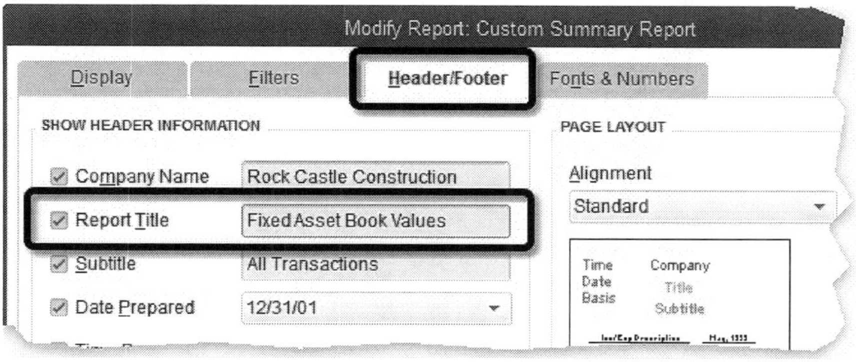

6. **Click the OK button** to close the Modify Report window and update the report.

The report will show the original basis and accumulated depreciation balances for each fixed asset, and will calculate the difference between those balances—which is the book value of each asset. The difference between and the book value of each asset.

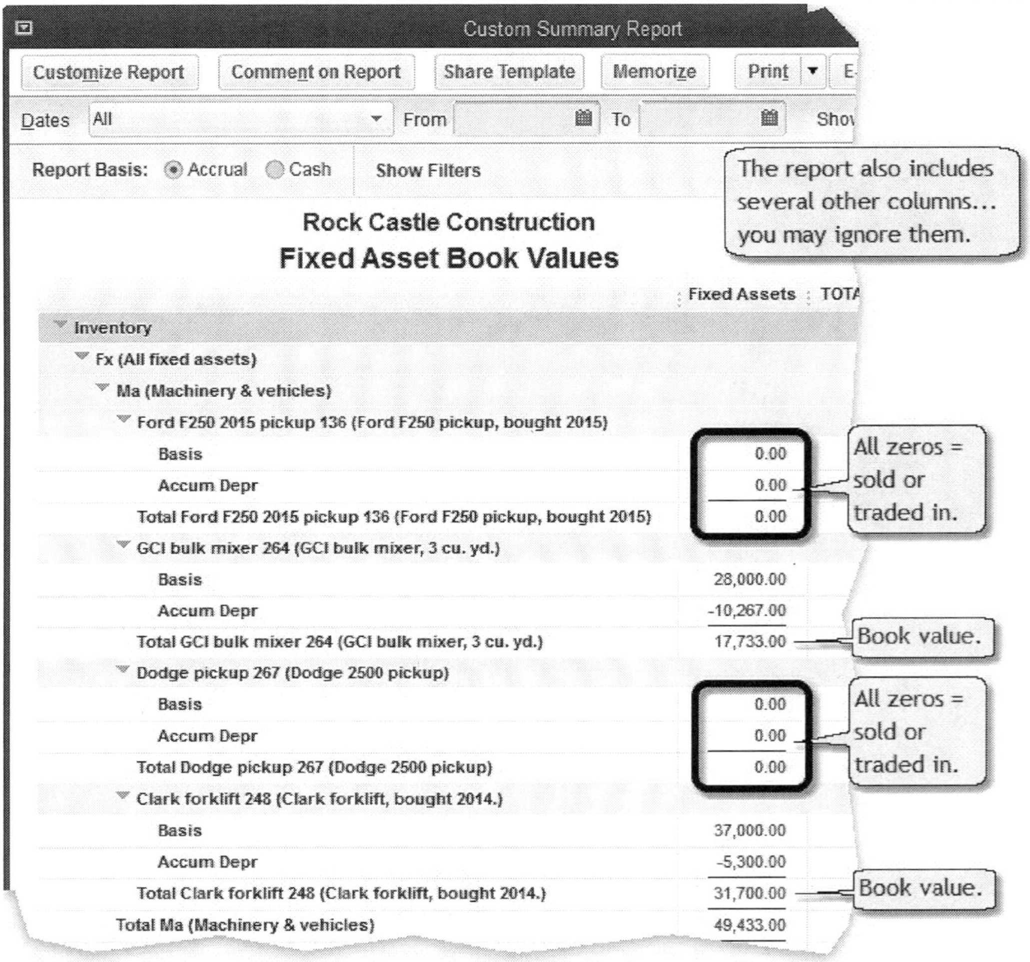

7. *Recommended:* **Memorize the report** so it can be recreated in the future with minimal effort.

To memorize a report...

Click the Memorize button in the upper part of the report window, then provide a name for the memorized report and click the OK button to save it.

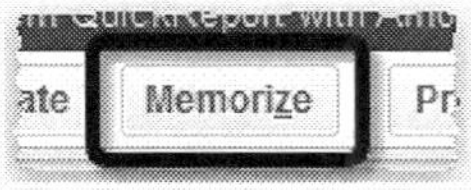

Whenever you want to recreate the report, select it from the Memorized Reports List (Reports > Memorized Report).

The above report example includes assets which have been sold. How do I remove sold assets from my reports?

You can retire old fixed asset Items by assigning them a different master parent Item, as described in *Retiring Items for Sold/Disposed of Fixed Assets* 121. Doing that will automatically exclude them from reports filtered for the master parent Item you use for assets still in your posession.

Some Reports WILL NOT Show What You Might Expect!

QuickBooks has many reports for getting information about Inventory Part Items. However, most of those reports assume certain account types are associated with Inventory Part Items; for instance, that an Item's *Asset account* field points to an asset account, and that its *COGS account* field points to a Cost of Goods Sold account. But S/S-style fixed asset Items 61 are set up differently, and that causes some Item reports to show results which *appear to be incorrect, even though they are not!*

To avoid confusion *only use the reports recommended in this book for getting various kinds of fixed asset information.* That will let you avoid reports which portray the information in a confusing or incorrect way.

Here are two reporting situations in which the reports *may not* show what you expect:

Inventory Valuation Detail
Inventory Valuation Summary

Inventory Valuation reports *should not be used* for S/S-style fixed asset Items.

The problem is that the inventory values in these reports are based on the Cost and Quantity On Hand which QuickBooks has calculated for Inventory Part Items. QuickBooks updates an Item's Cost each time it is used in a purchase transaction, so the Cost is really an average cost per unit for the Item, calculated by dividing the dollar amount of all purchases of the Item by the total quantity purchased. (Cost appears in the *Avg Cost* column of Inventory Valuation reports.)

QuickBooks recalculates an Item's Cost whenever the Item is used on a purchases form, such as the Checks form. The problem is that many S/S transactions *which are not really purchases*—depreciation expense 147 is an example—are entered on the Checks form. When that happens, QuickBooks includes the transaction in calculating the Item's Cost, even though depreciation expense and similar entries don't have any rational relationship to the Item's Quantity On Hand.

Consequently, the Item valuations appearing on Inventory Valuation reports are *almost never correct* for S/S-style fixed asset Items.

Item QuickReports for assets which have been sold

Item QuickReports are great for getting quick information about a fixed asset, but *after an asset has been sold, understanding the report becomes a bit tricky*.

After the sale of a fixed asset has been entered its Item QuickReport 211 will *imply* that balances for the asset's subitems have not been zeroed out *even though they have been.* (This is due to the way income accounts are used in setting up S/S-style Items.)

Reports for Income Tax Preparation

The reports you need for tax preparation depend on a lot of variables, such as whether your tax preparer directly accesses your QuickBooks company file to gather tax information or you provide him or her with printed reports, the report format your preparer wants for tax information, and so on.

This section shows how to prepare several kinds of reports your tax preparer may need for information about fixed asset purchases, sales, and trade-ins.

Fixed Asset Purchases & Trade-Ins Report

This report:

- Lists fixed assets acquired (purchased 89, or received in a swap 135) during the tax year, by showing their original basis as *positive* dollar amounts.
- Lists fixed assets traded-in 102 during the tax year, by showing their original basis as a *negative* dollar amounts.
- Shows the depreciation expense 156 amount entered during the year, for fixed assets which were neither sold nor traded in.
- Is normally prepared for the prior fiscal (tax) year, but may be prepared for any accounting period you want.

A fixed asset which was both purchased *and* resold during the same tax year will appear both in this report and in the sales report 222.

How to create the report

1. **Open a Purchases by Item Summary report** (Reports > Purchases > Purchases by Item Summary).
2. **Select** *Last fiscal year* **as the date range** for the report (assuming you are preparing taxes for the prior fiscal year).

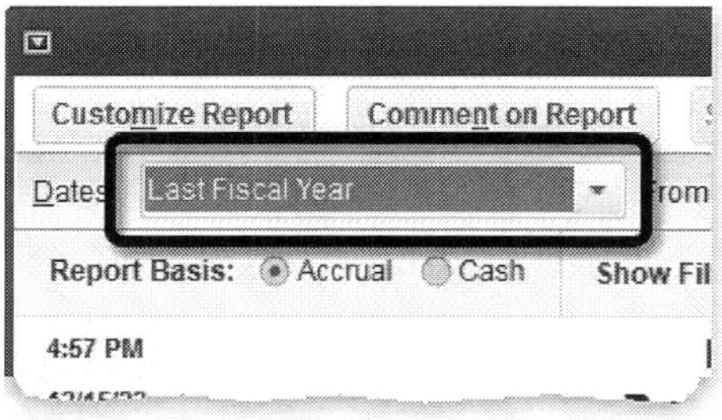

3. **Click the Customize Report button** at the top of the report window.

The Modify Report window will open.

4. On the Filters tab, **select *Item*** in the Filter panel, **then select the master parent Item** 55 **for fixed assets** from the dropdown list in the center of the window (such as the *Fx* Item described in *Organizing the Item List* 54, in Chapter 4).

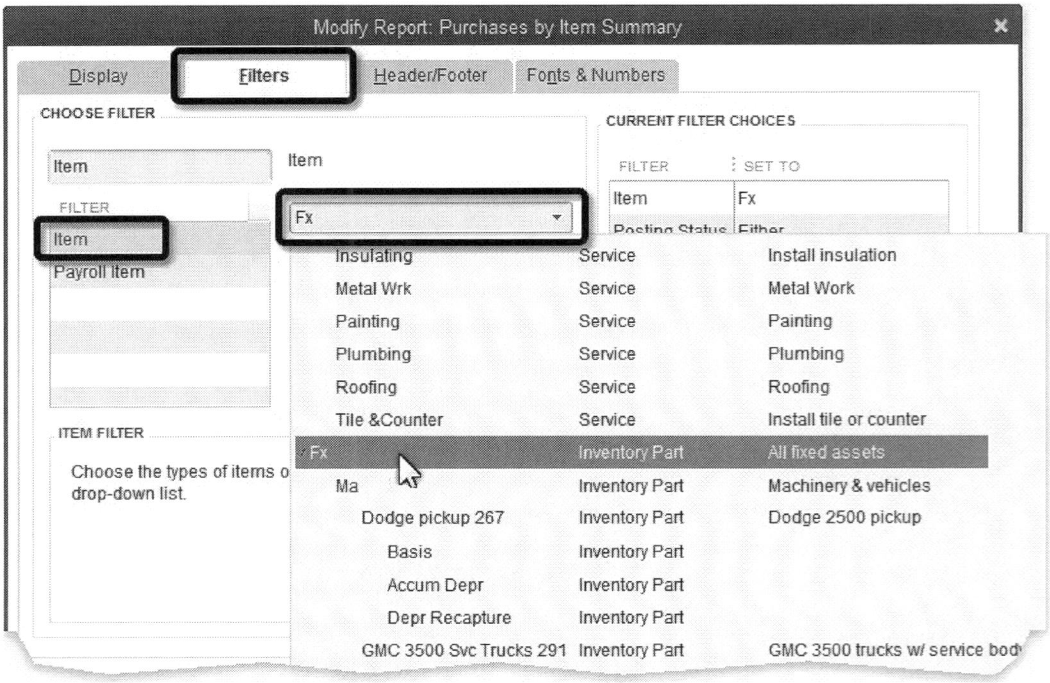

5. On the Header/Footer tab, **change the Report title** to something like *Fixed Asset Purchases & Trade-Ins.*

6. **Click the OK button** to close the Modify Report window and update the report.

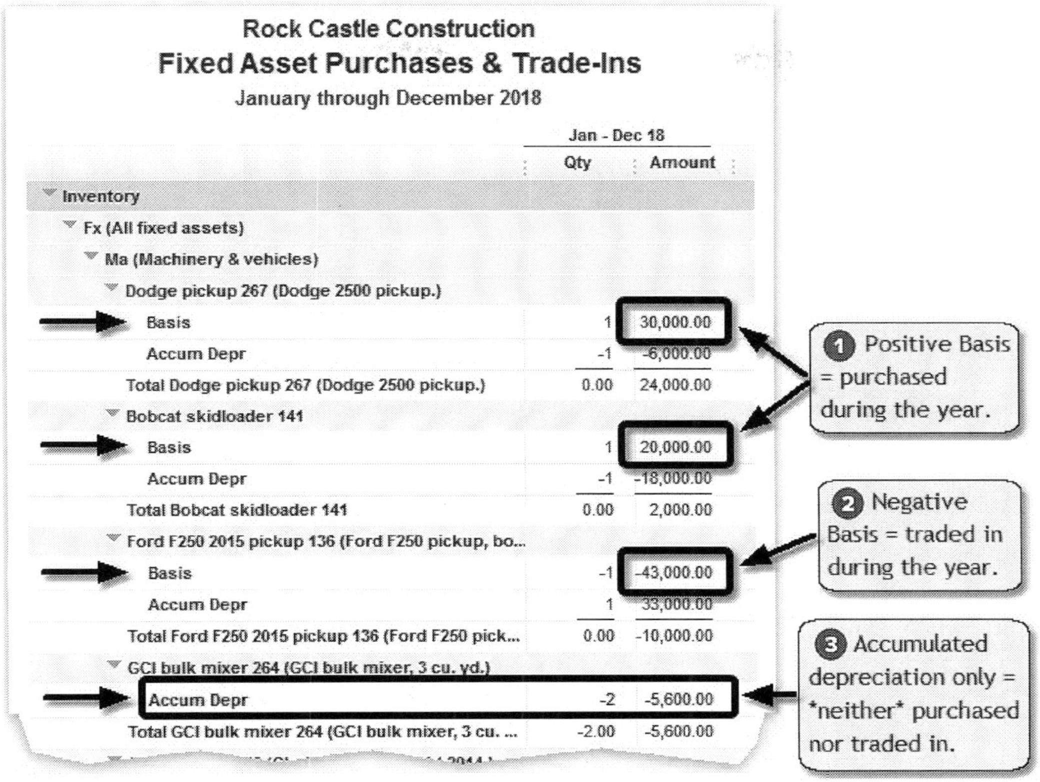

Rock Castle Construction

Fixed Asset Purchases & Trade-Ins

January through December 2018

	Jan - Dec 18 Qty	Amount
Inventory		
Fx (All fixed assets)		
Ma (Machinery & vehicles)		
Dodge pickup 267 (Dodge 2500 pickup.)		
Basis	1	30,000.00
Accum Depr	-1	-6,000.00
Total Dodge pickup 267 (Dodge 2500 pickup.)	0.00	24,000.00
Bobcat skidloader 141		
Basis	1	20,000.00
Accum Depr	-1	-18,000.00
Total Bobcat skidloader 141	0.00	2,000.00
Ford F250 2015 pickup 136 (Ford F250 pickup, bo...		
Basis	-1	-43,000.00
Accum Depr	1	33,000.00
Total Ford F250 2015 pickup 136 (Ford F250 pick...	0.00	-10,000.00
GCI bulk mixer 264 (GCI bulk mixer, 3 cu. yd.)		
Accum Depr	-2	-5,600.00
Total GCI bulk mixer 264 (GCI bulk mixer, 3 cu. ...	-2.00	-5,600.00

1 **A *positive* Amount on any fixed asset's Basis line** means the asset was purchased during the tax year (or other period covered by the report).

2 **A *negative* Amount on any fixed asset's Basis line** means the asset was traded in during the tax year (or other period covered by the report).

Is this also true for fixed asset groups? Yes, but sometimes only part of a fixed asset group may have been traded in. So for a fixed asset group, a negative Amount on the Basis line does not necessarily mean the entire group was traded in. To find out, drill down in the report by double-clicking the Basis line to see details of the trade-in transaction(s).

3 **Accum Depr.** Items which *only* have an Accum Depr line were neither purchased nor traded in during the tax year; only depreciation expense was entered for them.

7. *Recommended:* **Memorize the report** so it can be recreated in the future with minimal effort.

   This report is usually prepared the same way every year, with no need for any customization.

To memorize a report...

Click the Memorize button in the upper part of the report window, then provide a name for the memorized report and click the OK button to save it.

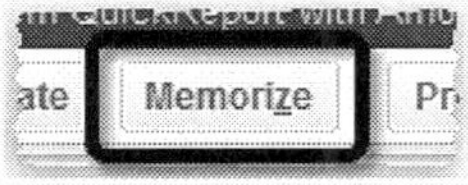

Whenever you want to recreate the report, select it from the Memorized Reports List (Reports > Memorized Report).

Using this report for gathering income tax information

The Fixed Asset Purchases & Trade-Ins report does not directly provide the fixed asset information you need for income tax preparation. Instead, it is a *starting place* for gathering that information. Things to know:

- One purpose of the report is to provide a **quick list of fixed assets purchased or traded in during the tax year.** (Why does the report show purchases and trade-ins? Because both are entered on purchase forms—Checks, Bills, and Credit Card Charges.)
- **If a trade-in was involved, the Basis line for the new asset does not show the cash amount paid** in addition to the trade-in. The reason is that an asset's Basis includes the cash amount paid *plus* the remaining book value of the trade-in, if any. To find out the cash amount paid, you must look up the source transaction (Check, etc.) where the purchase was entered.
- A second purpose of the report is to give you **easy access to source transactions** for fixed asset purchases and trade-ins. Drilling down on any Basis line in the report will lead to the transaction(s) related to the

Basis balance—the cash amount paid when the asset was purchased, what was traded in for it, and so on.

Drilling down means double-clicking a line in a report to open a window containing more detail—usually a specific transaction or list of transactions related to that line.

- There are several ways to **gather purchase information to take to your tax preparer,** but it's a good idea to avoid copying anything manually. The likelihood of making mistakes is high when financial amounts are copied by hand.

  One approach is to drill down to each of the purchase transactions in the report, then **print a paper copy or capture a screenshot of each one** and provide them to your tax preparer. (Captured screenshots can be assembled as a word processing document or in a PDF file.) These should provide the tax preparer with the information needed for proper tax treatment of most fixed asset purchases and trades. Here's a screenshot of a fixed asset purchase with a trade-in:

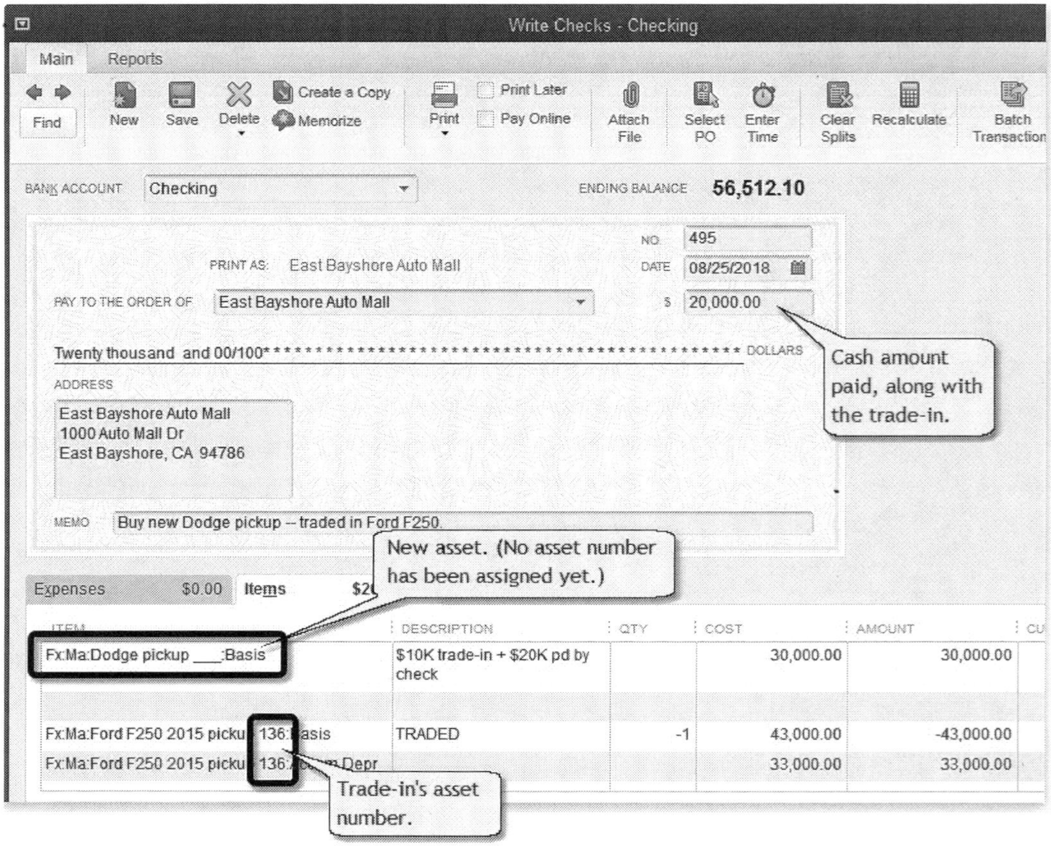

Your tax preparer will be able to use these easily, once you show him or her that Item names describe fixed assets, and that existing assets (such as the trade-in in the example above) have the preparer's asset number embedded in the Item name.

Fixed Asset Sales Report (with Gains and Losses)

This report:

- Lists all fixed assets sold outright (not traded in) during the tax year.
- Shows the amount of gain or loss on each sale, if any.
- Is normally prepared for the prior fiscal (tax) year, but may be prepared for any accounting period you want.

Any fixed assets purchased and then resold during the same year, will appear on this report *and* on the purchases report 222.

How to create the report

1. **Open a Custom Summary report** (Reports > Custom Reports > Summary).

   When the report window opens, the Modify Report window will also open. (If it fails to open automatically, click the Customize Report button in the upper part of the report window.)

2. In the Modify Report window, **select the Display tab options shown below**.

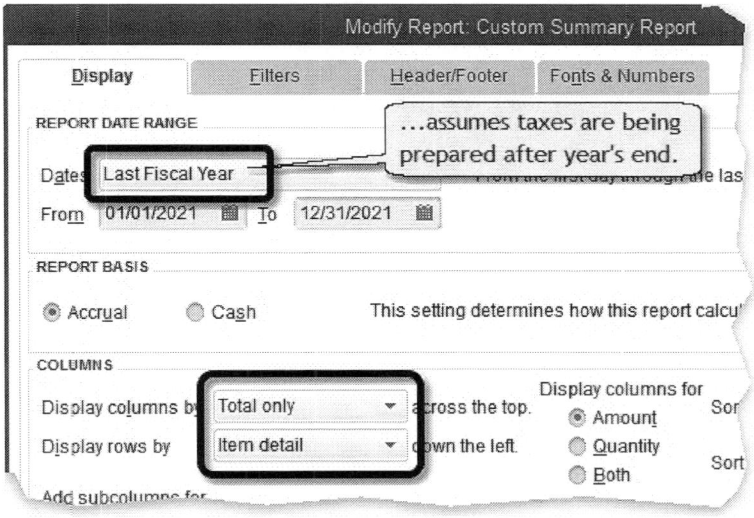

3. On the Filters tab, **set an Item filter for the master parent Item** 55 you use for fixed assets, **and an Account filter for the** *All income/expense accounts* **option:**

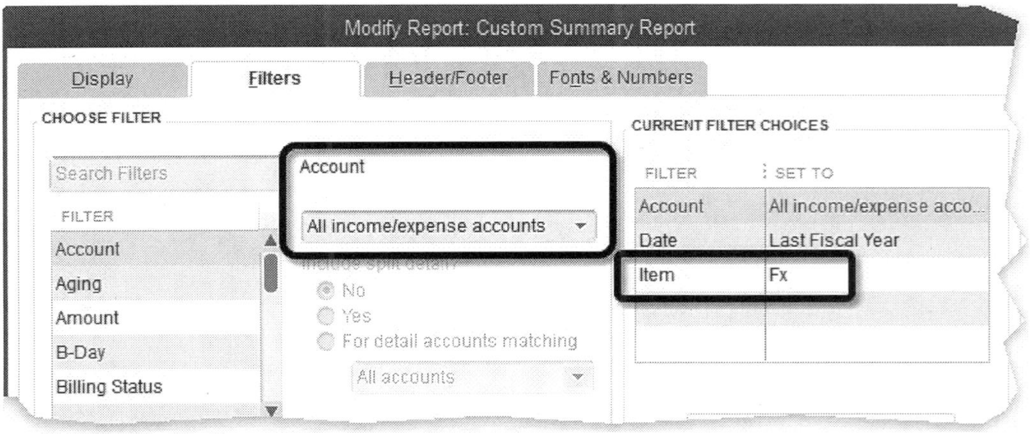

4. On the Header/Footer tab, **change the Report title** to something like *Outright Sales of Fixed Assets*. You may also change the report subtitle to make it clear that the report does not include trade-ins.

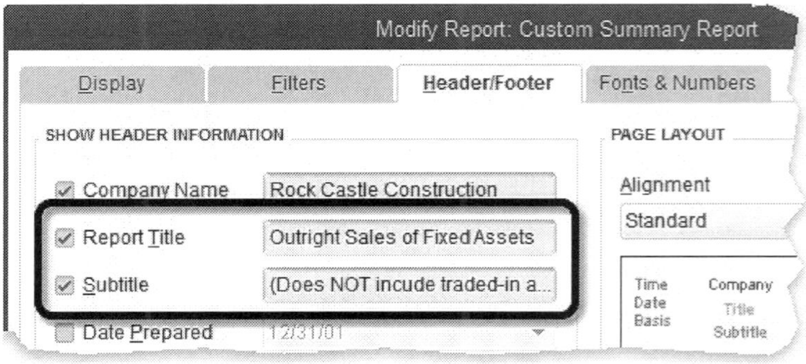

5. **Click the OK button** to close the Modify Report window and update the report.

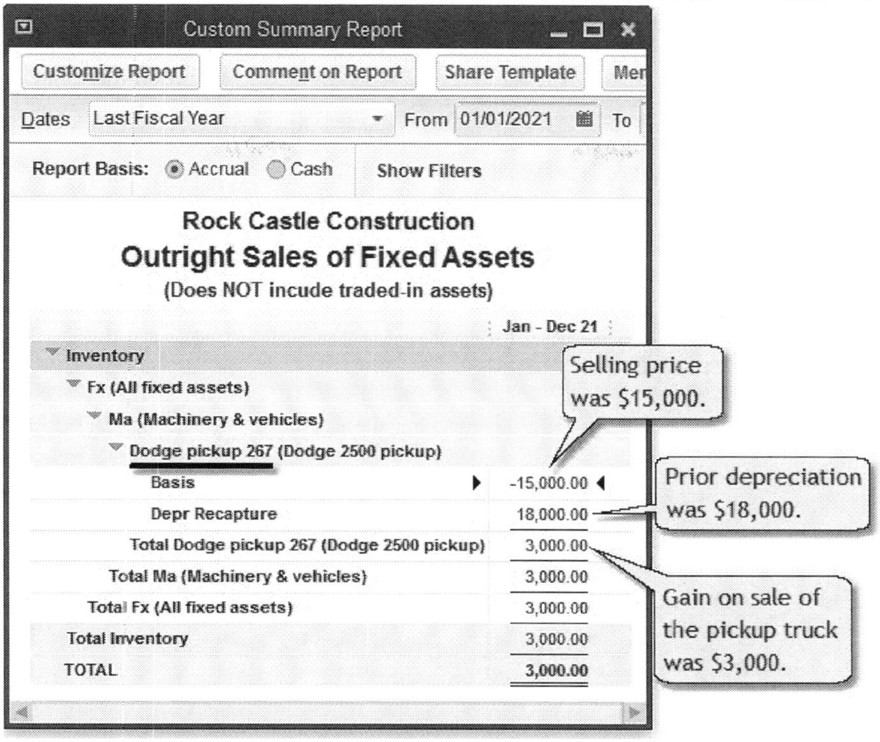

Why is there just one fixed asset in this report? Apparently, because that was the only fixed asset which the business sold during the year!

6. *Optional.* **Memorize the report** so it can be recreated in the future with minimal effort.

   This report is usually prepared the same way every year, with no changes to its customization options.

Tips for working with your tax preparer:

- **Prepare reports using the proper report basis: either** *Cash* **or** *Accrual,* to match how your taxes are filed.

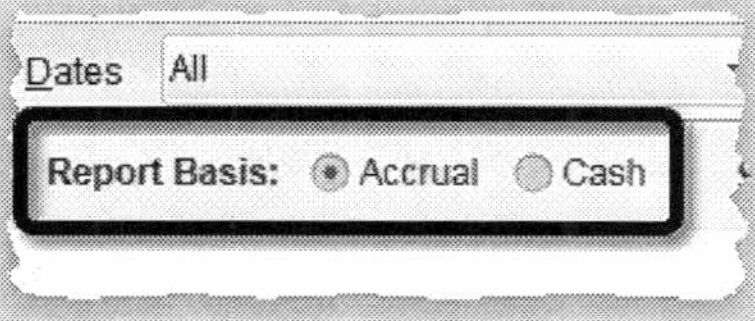

❖ **Include the tax preparer's asset numbers** [56] **in Item names or descriptions**, to avoid confusion about exactly which assets were sold, disposed of, or traded in.

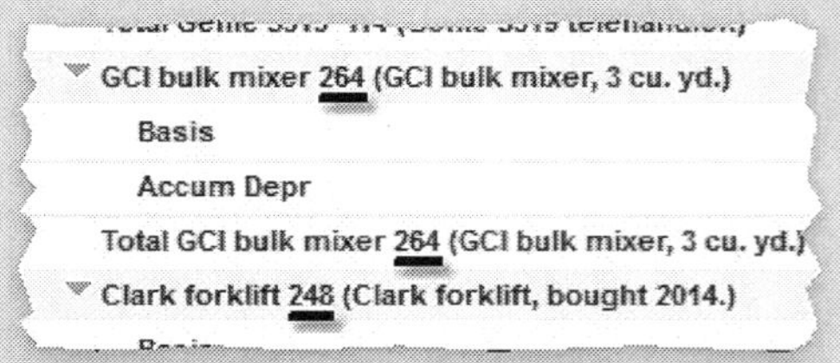

CHAPTER 11

An Even Simpler Method

About this chapter	Not everyone who uses QuickBooks needs or wants standards-based fixed asset accounting capabilities. If your needs are more basic, consider the simplified version of the S/S method [18] described in this chapter.

Does this Describe You?

- You use QuickBooks mostly as an income and expense ledger—to keep track of income and expenses for income tax compliance—but also partly because of its convenient features for things like managing payables (Bills) and receivables (Invoices), and keeping track of your checking account balance.
- You don't care much about keeping track of fixed asset book values and have no interest in entering depreciation expense. In fact, the only depreciation expense you care about may be the depreciation your income tax preparer calculates at tax time.
- You'd like to have *some* fixed asset information available in QuickBooks, and an easier way to provide information about purchases, sales, and trade-ins to your tax preparer at year's end.

If you feel you have a lot in common with these statements, then consider using the Even Simpler method described in this chapter.

Basics of the Even Simpler Method

> ### *Huh? Where did the name "Even Simpler" come from?*
>
> *Author's comment...* This name was chosen because it suggests an approach which is simpler and easier than the Simple/Smart method[18]. Even Simpler is not a name you will find in any accounting textbook; I simply needed a short name to distinguish this method from the Simple/Smart method.

- **Individual fixed assets are represented as Items,** the same as in the S/S method[18]. Using Items simplifies entering fixed asset transactions—purchases, sales, and trade-ins—and allow easier reporting at tax time.
- **Depreciation expense is not entered.** If you mostly use QuickBooks as an income and expense ledger you probably are not doing full accrual accounting, so there's little reason for entering depreciation expense. If you prepare balance sheet reports outside of QuickBooks—maybe in a spreadsheet—there is even less reason to enter depreciation expense: it won't be needed for updating fixed asset book values for balance sheet purposes. As for tax-based book values (remaining depreciable tax basis), you probably let your tax preparer maintain those along with doing depreciation calculations, and all of that happens outside of QuickBooks.
- **The list of fixed asset Items is structured differently than in the S/S method:** only one Item is needed for each fixed asset, and that Item is used directly in transactions. (No subitems are needed because you won't be tracking book values or accumulated depreciation—at least not in QuickBooks.)
- **Fixed asset Items are associated with different accounts** than in the S/S method.
- **Reports for income tax preparation** are also prepared differently than in the S/S method.

Item Types and Item Setup

Items

When setting up Items for the Even Simpler method, most of the principles discussed in *Organizing the Item List* 54 apply:

- **Use a master parent Item** 55 to make report filtering and transaction entry easier.
- **Group fixed assets into categories** such as machinery, buildings, and land by creating subitems of the master parent Item.
- **Set up a single Item to represent each fixed asset.** However, no subitems are needed because you won't be tracking depreciation expense or book values.

The fixed assets section of your Item List (Lists > Item List) might be structured like this:

Fx	*All fixed assets*
Ma	*Machinery*
Asset1	
Asset2	
Asset3	
Bl	*Buildings*
Asset4	
Asset5	
La	*Land*
Asset6	

Which Item type?

You could use Non-inventory Part Items. They support entering quantities in transactions; however, they do not make it possible to maintain an inventory, or count, of fixed assets, which may be important if you want to let some Items represent groups of like fixed assets 143 purchased at the same time, such as a fleet of vehicles, a herd of beef cows, or several units of the same model of construction machinery.

For this reason, the Inventory Part type may be the best choice—but set up differently than for the S/S method:

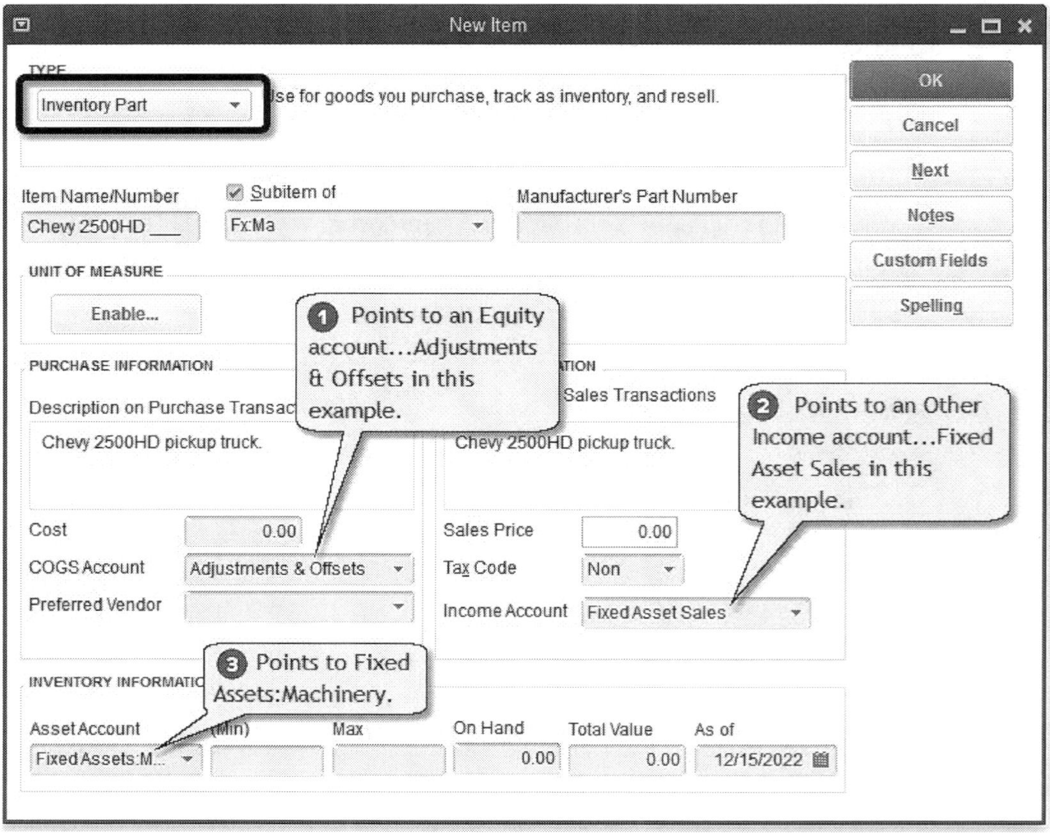

1 **COGS Account** points to an Equity account, one named Adjustments & Offsets in this example. This is so QuickBooks will discard the financial effects of the automatic COGS (Cost of Goods Sold) posting it makes when an Inventory Part Item is sold.

This would be improper for full accrual accounting. However, maintaining updated fixed asset balances is not a goal of the Even Simpler method.

2 **Income Account** points to an Other Income account set up specifically for recording fixed asset sales. Using an Other Income account will cause total fixed asset sales to appear below the Net Ordinary Income line on profit and loss reports.

If others outside of your business will view your profit and loss report, you may want to remove this account from the report by zeroing out its balance temporarily when the report is prepared.

For example, you could offset the balance to an Equity account such as the Adjustments & Offsets account mentioned above, then restore the balance after the report has been prepared.

3 **Asset Account** points to a Fixed Asset type account, Fixed Assets:Machinery in this example.

In the Even Simpler method depreciation expense is not entered, so the balance maintained in this account will not correctly represent fixed asset book values. If you use QuickBooks to prepare balance sheet reports, you will need to adjust the account's balance to assign a reasonable/relevant value to fixed assets, depending on the intended purpose of balance sheet.

Purchases, Trade-ins, Sales, and Disposals

Fixed Asset Purchases

Purchases are entered the same way as in the S/S method, except that there is no Basis subitem to use:

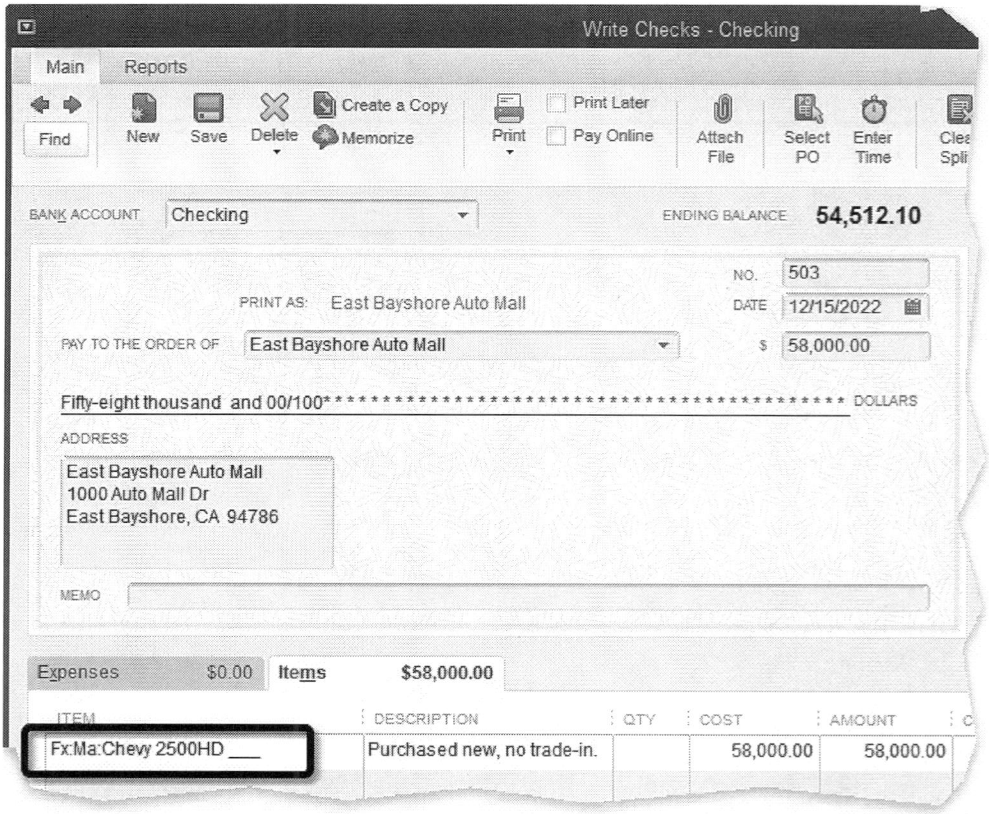

Fixed Asset Purchase with Trade-In

To enter a purchase with a trade-in:

1. **Enter the newly acquired asset,** valued at the cash price paid for it.
2. **Enter the traded-in's price as $0.**

   The main goal is to have adequate records for tax preparation. Your tax preparer needs to know the cash amount paid for the newly acquired fixed asset, and what old fixed asset was traded in. Other required information such as the trade-in's remaining depreciable value, will come from the tax preparer's fixed asset records.

   Here is an example:

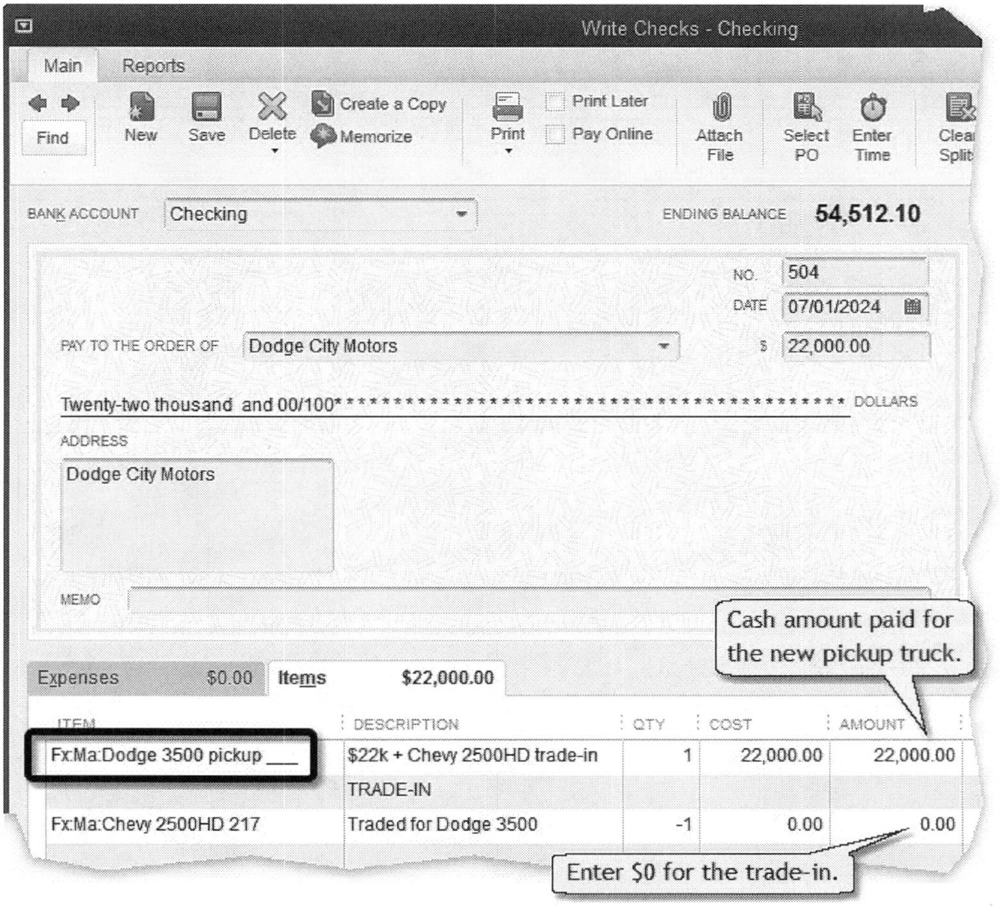

Fixed Asset Sales

Sales are entered in a straightforward way, as a single transaction. (Because you won't be entering depreciation expense in the Even Simpler method, no depreciation recapture[111] entry is needed when an asset is sold.)

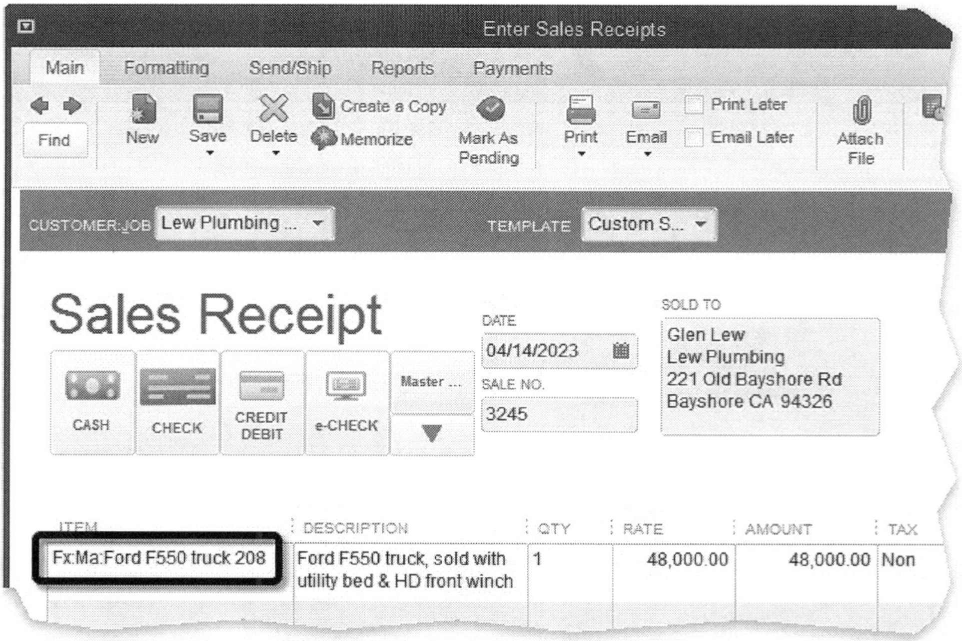

Fixed Asset Disposals

As for disposals (when a fixed asset is destroyed or salvaged, not sold) simply enter a "sale" of the asset for a $0 amount. That will cause the asset to appear in fixed asset sales reports, but at a sale price of $0.

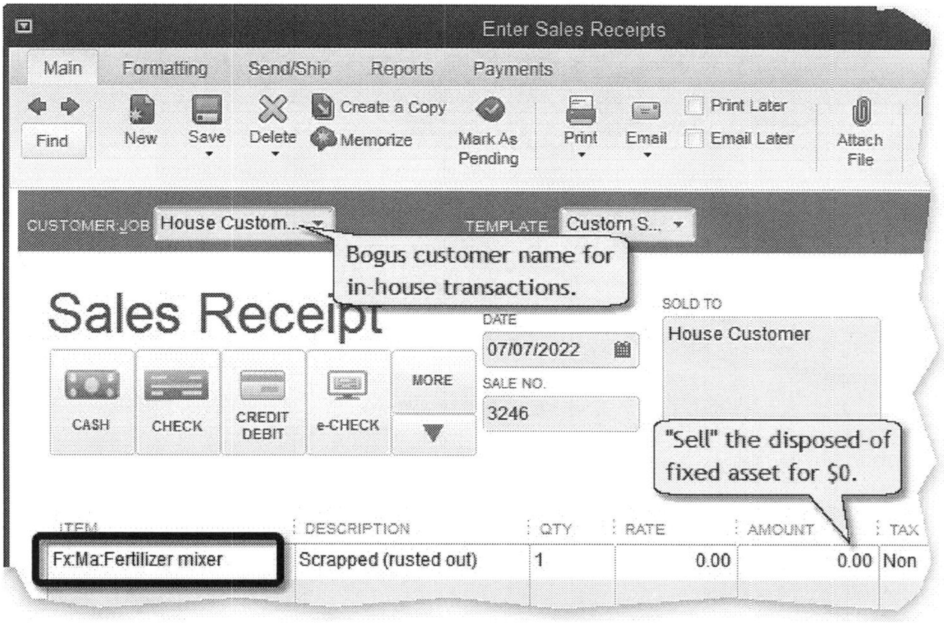

Reports and Income Taxes

Fixed Asset Purchases Report

You can get a list of asset purchases for the tax year using the Purchases by Item Detail report.

1. **Open a Purchases by Item Detail report** (Reports > Purchases > Purchases by Item Detail).

2. **Click the Customize Report button** at the top of the report window.

The Modify Report window will open.

3. In the Modify Report window, **select the Display tab option shown below**.

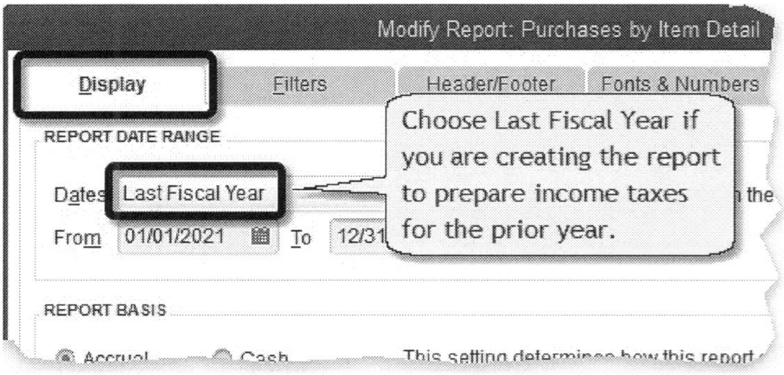

4. On the Filters tab, **set an Item filter by selecting the master parent Item** [55] you use for fixed assets, such as the *Fx* Item described in *Organizing the Item List* [54] in Chapter 4.

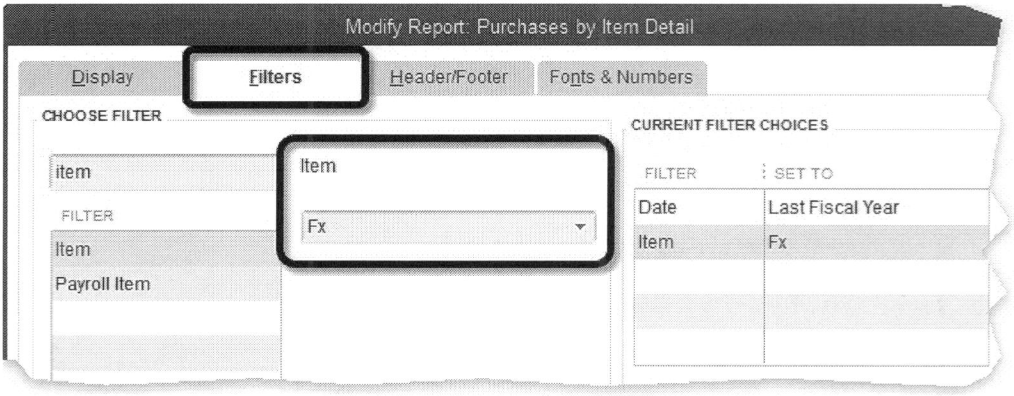

5. **Set an Amount filter to include only Amounts >= $0.01** so the report will *exclude* trade-ins (which are entered as $0 amounts).

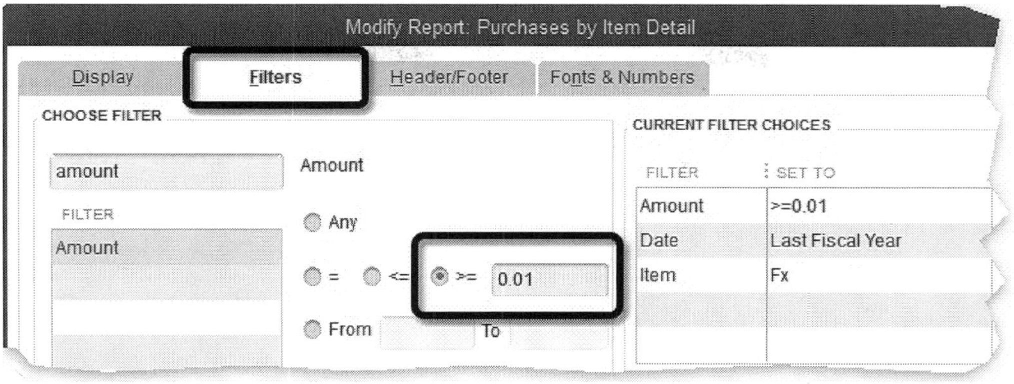

6. On the Header/Footer tab, **change the report title** to something like *Fixed Asset Purchases.*

7. **Click the OK button** to close the Modify Report window and update the report, which will list each fixed asset purchased during the tax year (or other date range you may have selected), along with the cash amount paid in each transaction. (Where a trade-in was involved, this will be the cash paid in addition to the traded-in asset.)

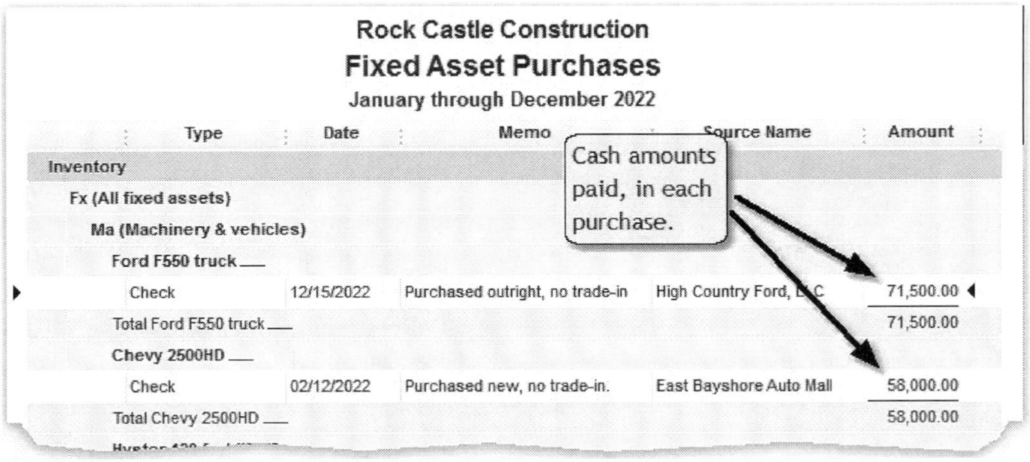
Rock Castle Construction
Fixed Asset Purchases
January through December 2022

Type	Date	Memo	Source Name	Amount
Inventory				
Fx (All fixed assets)				
Ma (Machinery & vehicles)				
Ford F550 truck				
Check	12/15/2022	Purchased outright, no trade-in	High Country Ford, LLC	71,500.00
Total Ford F550 truck				71,500.00
Chevy 2500HD				
Check	02/12/2022	Purchased new, no trade-in.	East Bayshore Auto Mall	58,000.00
Total Chevy 2500HD				58,000.00

8. You can **drill down on any transaction listed in the report** to see details about it, such as to find out what asset was traded in as part of a purchase.

   Drilling down means double-clicking a line in a report to open a window containing more detail—usually a specific transaction or list of transactions related to that line.

9. *Recommended.* **Memorize the report** so it can be recreated in the future with minimal effort.

To memorize a report...

Click the Memorize button in the upper part of the report window, then provide a name for the memorized report and click the OK button to save it.

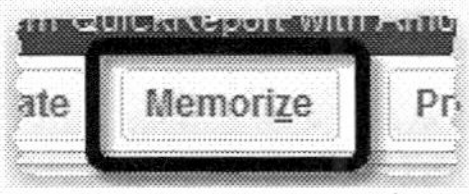

Whenever you want to recreate the report, select it from the Memorized Reports List (Reports > Memorized Report).

Fixed Asset Sales & Disposals Report

You can get a list of fixed asset sales for the tax year with the Sales by Item Detail report.

1. **Open a Sales by Item Detail report** (Reports > Sales > Sales by Item Detail).

2. **Click the Customize Report button** at the top of the report window.

The Modify Report window will open.

3. In the Modify Report window, **select the Display tab option shown below**.

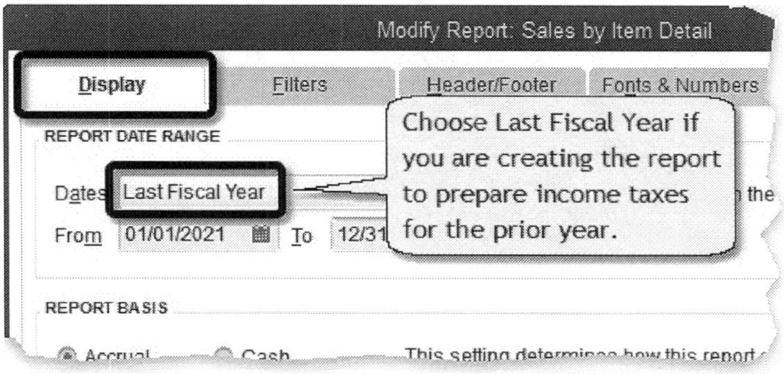

4. On the Filters tab, **set an Item filter by selecting the master parent Item** 55 you are using for fixed assets, such as the *Fx* Item described in *Organizing the Item List* 54 in Chapter 4.

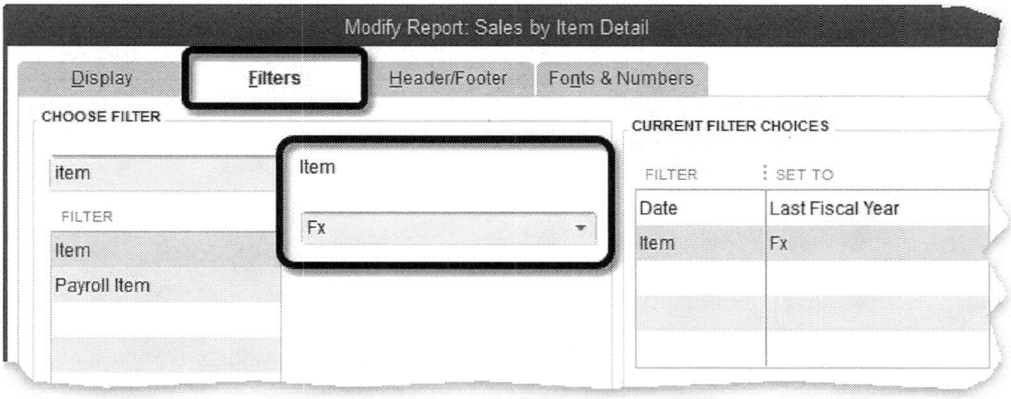

5. On the Header/Footer tab, **change the report title** to something like *Fixed Asset Sales & Disposals*.

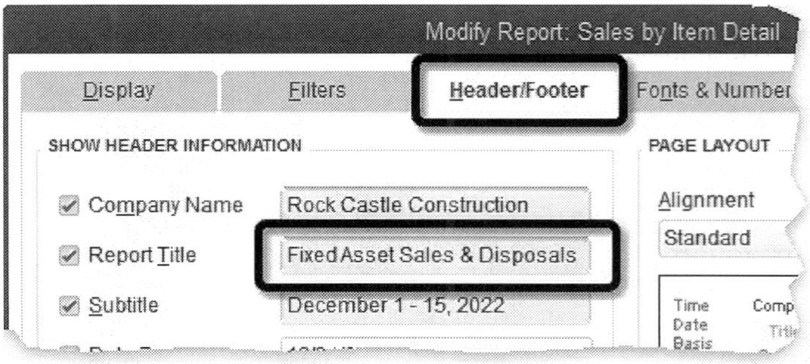

6. **Click the OK button** to close the Modify Report window and update the report, which will then list each fixed asset sold during the year (or other date range you may have selected) along with the amount received for each sale.

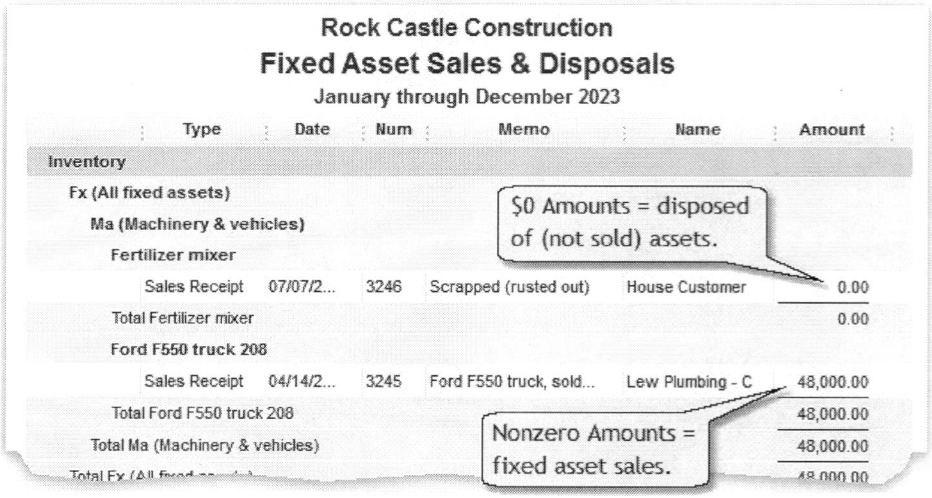

7. *Recommended.* **Memorize the report** so it can be recreated in the future with minimal effort.

To memorize a report...

Click the Memorize button in the upper part of the report window, then provide a name for the memorized report and click the OK button to save it.

Whenever you want to recreate the report, select it from the Memorized Reports List (Reports > Memorized Report).

Fixed Asset Trade-ins Report

Getting a list of fixed assets traded in during the tax year is very similar to getting a list of fixed asset purchases. You use the same report—Purchases by Item Detail—but with one change in the report filters.

1. **Open the Fixed Asset Purchases report** 241 (Reports > Purchases > Purchases by Item Detail).

   If you memorized the report, you can just select it from the memorized reports list (Reports > Memorized Reports).

2. **Customize the report** as described at the beginning of this section (if you didn't memorize the report).

3. **Click the Customize Report button** at the top of the report window.

   The Modify Report window will open.

4. In the Modify Report window, **change the Amount filter to include only Amounts <= $0.**

   This will limit the report to fixed asset trade-in transactions, because they are entered with $0 amounts.

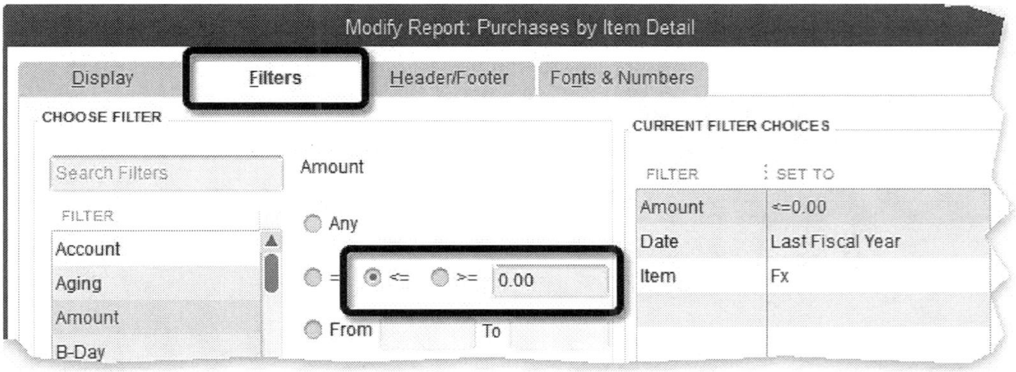

5. On the Header/Footer tab, **change the report title** to something like *Fixed Asset Trade-Ins.*

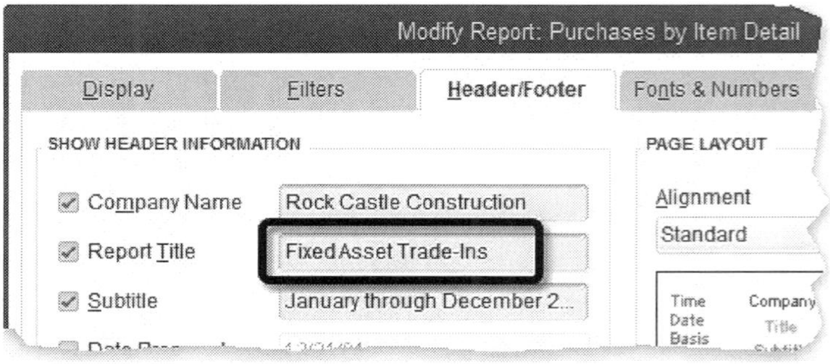

6. **Click the OK button** to close the Modify Report window and update the report, which will then list each fixed asset traded in during the tax year (or other date range you may have selected):

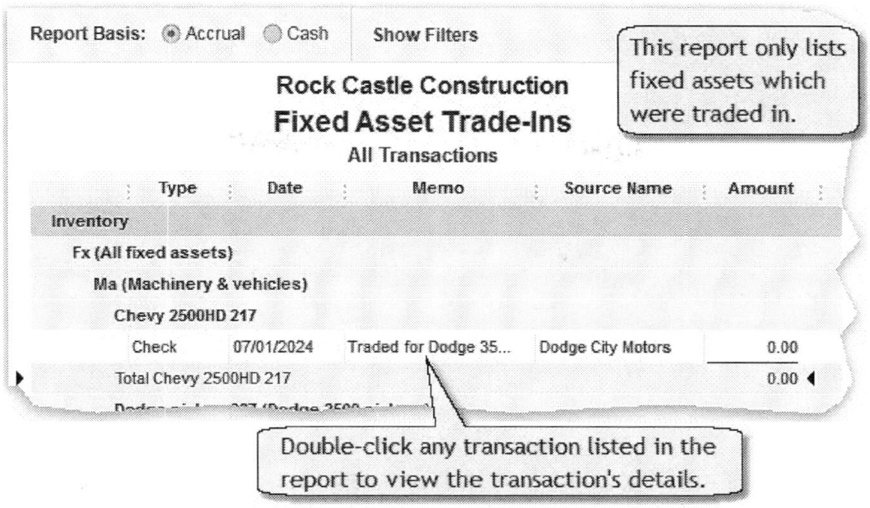

7. You can **drill down on any transaction listed in the report** to see details about it, such as to find out what new asset was acquired with the trade-in.

Drilling down means double-clicking a line in a report to open a window containing more detail—usually a specific transaction or list of transactions related to that line.

Here is the source transaction for the trade-in listed in the above report fragment, with the trade-in highlighted:

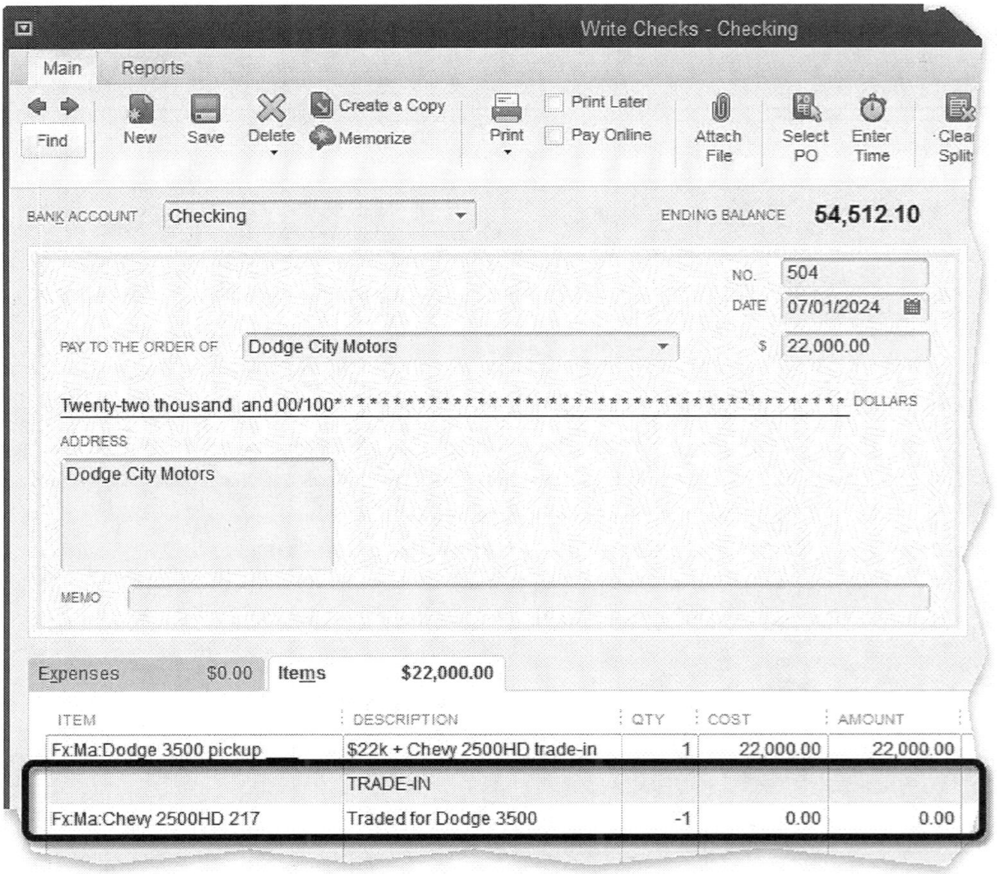

8. *Recommended.* **Memorize the report** so it can be recreated in the future with minimal effort.

   If you initially created this report by opening a memorized report, **be sure to use a different report name when memorizing this report.** If you don't use a different name you will overwrite (replace) the other report in the Memorized Reports list.

To memorize a report...

Click the Memorize button in the upper part of the report window, then provide a name for the memorized report and click the OK button to save it.

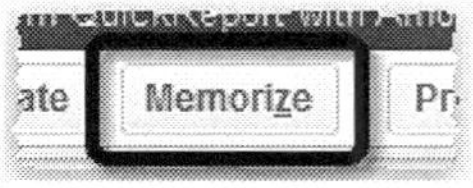

Whenever you want to recreate the report, select it from the Memorized Reports List (Reports > Memorized Report).

After Preparing Income Taxes

Retiring Old Fixed Asset Items

After preparing income taxes and printing or saving a copy of all desired reports for the year, fixed assets which were sold or disposed of during the year should be retired 121 so they won't appear in future fixed asset reports.

Don't retire fixed asset Items until after the year's taxes have been prepared, to assure that any fixed assets sold or disposed of during the year are included in tax reports.

Adding Asset Numbers to Item Names

After preparing taxes most preparers provide their clients with a fixed asset list which has an asset number assigned (by the preparer) to each fixed asset. For accurate communication about future fixed asset sales and trade-ins, it is a good idea to add the preparer's asset numbers to your fixed asset Item names or descriptions as described in *Basic Things to Know* 56 in Chapter 4

For the new fixed asset Item you create when an asset is purchased, it is a good idea to include some special characters in the Item name or description to serve as a "placeholder" for the asset number you will be adding later (after the number has been assigned by your tax preparer). Underscores "_" works well for this:

Once an asset number has been assigned, replace the underscores with the asset number:

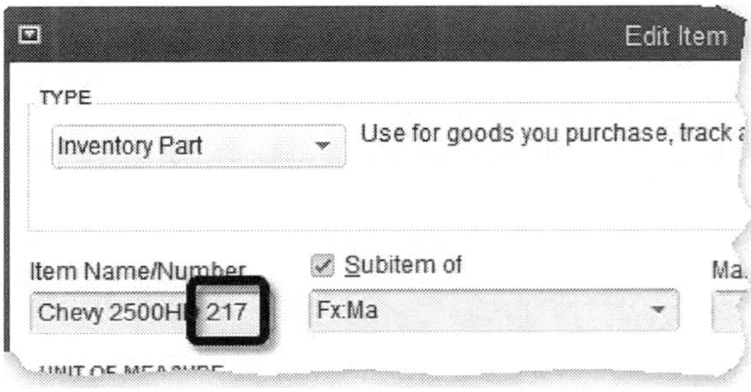

CHAPTER 12

Appendix

Other books and software products from Flagship Technologies, Inc...

The QuickBooks Farm Accounting Cookbook™, Volume I: QuickBooks Basics, Income & Expenses, and More...

The QuickBooks Farm Accounting Cookbook™, Volume I, by Mark Wilsdorf, is a 370-page book written for QuickBooks users in agriculture. This step-by-step guide and reference is written specifically for farmers and ranchers, and provides information about setting up QuickBooks for a farm business (Accounts, Classes, Lists, etc.) plus loads of transaction examples—all of them agricultural! It is called a "cookbook" because of its recipe-like approach to dealing with agricultural accounting topics and problems.

On the Web: www.goflagship.com/cbk.html

The QuickBooks Farm Accounting Cookbook™, Volume II: Raised Farm Production Inventories, Sales, and More...

The QuickBooks Farm Accounting Cookbook™, Volume II, by Mark Wilsdorf, is a 320-page book written for QuickBooks users in agriculture who need to work with **raised**—as opposed to resale—farm production. It reveals the benefits of keeping inventories in QuickBooks for at least some of the farm's production, and shows how to get raised production into QuickBooks simply and easily; track inventory quantities, storage locations, forward contracts and deliveries on contracts, grain inventories for multiple landlords; handle spoilage, thefts, livestock deaths, and other inventory losses; and much more.

On the Web: www.goflagship.com/cbk2.html

The QuickBooks Farm Accounting Cookbook™, Volume III: Farm Resale Items: Stocker and Feeder Livestock, Resale Produce, and More...

The QuickBooks Farm Accounting Cookbook™, Volume III, by Mark Wilsdorf, is a 250-page book focused on purchases, sales, and inventories of farm resale items such as resale livestock and produce. It shows how to set up and use QuickBooks for working with resale items. With the proper setup, QuickBooks will *automatically* keep track of the income tax information you need for resale Items—all you have to do is enter purchases and sales. At year's end you'll have totals for resale item sales and purchase costs ("Cost of items held for resale"), with no additional effort. The book has detailed examples of account and Item setup, purchases, sales, inventory adjustments (for things like spoilage and livestock death loss), inventory close-outs, detailed sales and purchases reports, and more.

On the Web: www.goflagship.com/cbk3.html

Online Banking, Transaction Downloading, and Online Bill Payment in QuickBooks

Online Banking, Transaction Downloading, and Online Bill Payment in QuickBooks, by Mark Wilsdorf, is a 105-page book about using online financial services in QuickBooks desktop editions. Written for people who use QuickBooks day-to-day in a small business, it guides readers through setting up and using online banking and other online financial services with step-by-step procedures and abundant screenshots.

On the Web: www.goflagship.com/onl.html

FormCalc SST
for QuickBooks

FormCalc SST is a QuickBooks add-on which gives you calculated columns, column totals and subtotals, statistical functions, text handling, IF logic, and a lot more on your QuickBooks forms: Invoices, Sales Receipts, Estimates, and others—any form where Items are used. It is the "newer, stronger, faster brother" of our older FormCalc product (described next, below).

FormCalc SST lets you set up calculations in its internal Excel-compatible spreadsheet, then applies your calculations "on the fly" to your QuickBooks forms. Our customers use it for calculating shipping weights on invoices, box and pallet counts, area calculations on customer orders (yards of fabric, board-feet of lumber, etc.), quantity totals for alcohol taxation recordkeeping requirements, and much more.

FormCalc SST works with nearly all Microsoft Windows versions of QuickBooks desktop editions (Pro, Premier, Enterprise), *including most older versions and most non-U.S. versions:* **US, UK, Canadian, and Australian.** FormCalc

SST also works in hosted QuickBooks environments, and in fact is certified to run on **Right Networks hosting,** a popular QuickBooks hosting service.

A **30-day free trial** is a free download from our Web site.

FormCalc SST on the Web: www.goflagship.com/sst.html

FormCalc™... for QuickBooks

FormCalc is a QuickBooks add-on which gives you calculated columns, column totals and subtotals, unique-item counts, and much more on your QuickBooks forms, such as Invoices, Sales Receipts, Estimates, and others —any form where Items are used.

FormCalc is an older product than FormCalc SST (described above). It does fewer calculations but is simple to set up for basic needs. Our customers use it for calculating shipping weights on invoices, box and pallet counts, area calculations, quantity totals on invoices and sales receipts, and more.

FormCalc works with nearly all Microsoft Windows versions of Quick-Books desktop editions (Pro, Premier, Enterprise), *including most older versions and most non-U.S. versions:* **US, UK, Canadian, and Australian.**

A **30-day free trial** is a free download from our Web site.

FormCalc on the Web: www.goflagship.com/fc.html

& Gold!

ManagePLUS™ for QuickBooks

ManagePLUS Gold for QuickBooks is a QuickBooks add-on program for gleaning management information from any set of QuickBooks accounting records, especially where the Classes feature of QuickBooks is used.

ManagePLUS Gold gives you reports with per-unit revenue and cost information...things like fuel and maintenance costs per mile driven by trucks in a fleet, materials costs per unit of production in a factory, herbicide and fertilizer cost per acre or per bushel of corn production, and so on. The expanded quantity handling and Class reporting it offers are not available in any other QuickBooks add-on.

ManagePLUS Gold's cost accounting and activity-based costing features give you an easy drag-and-drop way to allocate income and expenses to Classes identified as cost centers and profit centers of the business. It provides spreadsheet-based profit analysis reports for Classes, and can send allocation transactions directly to QuickBooks with a single mouse click.

ManagePLUS Gold works with these Microsoft Windows editions of QuickBooks:

U.S.: Pro, Premier, and Enterprise editions.
UK: Pro and Premier editions.
Canadian: Pro and Premier editions.

A **30-day free trial** is a free download from our Web site.

ManagePLUS Gold on the Web: www.goflagship.com/mp.html

ManagePLUS Gold is also listed on Intuit's QuickBooks desktop add-ons site: desktop.apps.com.

Catch Weights™ for QuickBooks

Catch Weights is an add-on for QuickBooks users in the meat, seafood, and food wholesaling industries. It allows entering a list of catch weights—multiple individual weights—for any line of a QuickBooks Invoice or Sales Receipt, then writes the total weight in the Quantity column and adds the list of individual weights to the Description column.

Catch Weights works with nearly all Microsoft Windows versions of QuickBooks desktop editions (Pro, Premier, Enterprise), *including most older versions and most non-U.S. versions:* **US, UK, Canadian, and Australian!**

A **30-day free trial** is a free download from our Web site.

Catch Weights on the Web: www.goflagship.com/cwts.html

Index

A

B

C

D

E

Made in United States
Orlando, FL
05 November 2026

90231093R00146